TACNA AND ARICA

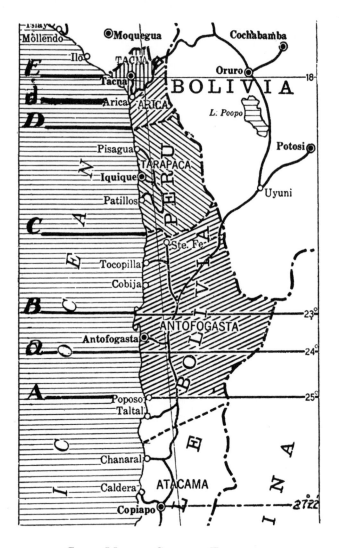

GUIDE MAP TO CHILEAN EXPANSION

A. Original Chile-Bolivian boundary; *B*. Claimed by Chile in 1842; *a*. Established by treaty in 1866, but in A-B nitrate revenues were divided equally; *C*. Original Peru-Bolivian boundary; *D*. Boundary of Chile as a result of the War of the Pacific, 1883, with D-E to be occupied by Chile ten years; *d*. Chile-Peruvian boundary by settlement of 1929.

Tacna and Arica

*An Account of the Chile-Peru Boundary
Dispute and of the Arbitrations
by the United States*

By

William Jefferson Dennis

Archon Books
1967

Library of Congress Catalog Card Number: 67-22302
Printed in the United States of America

CONTENTS

ILLUSTRATIONS

INTRODUCTION

THE Chile-Peru arbitration case, in which President Coolidge handed down his Opinion and Award on March 4, 1925, arose from a long-standing dispute usually called the "Tacna-Arica" question or the "Question of the Pacific."[1] It is sometimes referred to as a boundary dispute, but although the boundaries of Tacna-Arica were indirectly involved, they were incidental in the dispute.

The term Tacna-Arica results from the compounding of the names of two former Peruvian provinces, Tacna and Arica, which were a part of the territory captured from Peru by Chile in the War of the Pacific, 1879–84. This war was the result of a nitrate quarrel between Chile and Bolivia in which Peru entered as an ally of the latter. Chile, being victorious, forced Bolivia to sign the Pact of Truce of April 4, 1884, and obliged Peru to make the Treaty of Ancón, ratified March 28, 1884.[2] By the provisions of these treaties Chile retained Atacama, the coast province of Bolivia, for considerations to be arranged later, received from Peru the permanent cession of Tarapacá, the southern province of Peru, and was to occupy Tacna and Arica for ten years. At the end of the ten-year period a plebiscite was to decide the permanent ownership of the provinces, and the winning nation was to pay the loser ten million silver pesos.

The plebiscite clause, Article III of the treaty, provided that a plebiscite protocol stating details of the election would be drawn up and included in the treaty

Reference notes in this introduction will be included with those of chapter i on page 24.

as an integral part of it. But the protocol was not drawn up and the treaty was ratified without electoral provisions.

At the end of the ten-year period, March 28, 1894, the plebiscite was not held, and Chile remained in possession of Tacna-Arica. Each year of the overdue plebiscite added complications and engendered hard feeling until it became more than a mere question of qualifications of voters and manner of voting—if indeed those considerations had ever been the real issues of the question in its larger sense. The difficulties growing out of the unfulfilled plebiscite clause of the Treaty of Ancón constituted technically, then, the Tacna-Arica question. During Chilean occupation Chile designated the region simply "Tacna," but most writers use the compound form which will be used in this work.

The material resources of Tacna-Arica are not great. A casual traveler is inclined to think the region hardly worth a dispute. It lies down the coast 2,000 miles south of Panama, contains about 14,000 square miles, and has 39,359 estimated population.[3] Most of the region is arid desert rising quickly from the coast to the bleak Andes. About 130,000 acres are arable, some 30,000 being under irrigation. Grazing and the raising of vegetables and fruit are the principal occupations. Various minerals are found, but as yet in unimportant quantities except in the borax mines of Chilcaya so near the limits of Tarapacá that its exact geographical status was uncertain. On the north and south the disputed region is limited by the two old river beds or ravines called the river Sama and the river Camarones. These rise in the Andes and flow southwestwardly into the ocean at 17° 57' and 19° 11' south latitude, respectively.

These rivers flow through mountainous canyons in their upper courses with various channels. This fact raised the question which was the main channel and consequently the question which was the real boundary in the uplands of both sides of the region. It was a matter of secondary importance, although included in the Coolidge arbitration. When the armies of Chile evacuated Peru following the war, they remained in possession of three districts of Tarata among the upper channels of the Sama River.[4] On the southern, or Camarones, side there was the above-mentioned doubt about the jurisdiction of the Chilcaya mines. Naturally in settling the ownership of Tacna-Arica, its limits would not be left undefined, so the Coolidge Award provided for a special boundary commission independent of the plebiscite commission to fix these limits.

The importance of Tacna-Arica is strategic and, in the broad sense, historical. Arica is the natural outlet to the sea for Bolivia, and the only port of call for large steamship lines between Mollendo and Iquique. It is located at the terminus of the lowest and most direct route over the cordillera from the plateau of Bolivia. It should have been included in that republic when it was formed and its founders tried to do so. But as Tacna-Arica had long been a part of colonial Peru, Bolivia had to content herself with Atacama, her only maritime province, which afforded a poor and long outlet to the sea.* Besides the railroad leading up to Bolivia from Arica there is one connecting this port with Tacna, a city of 12,000 inhabitants and the pres-

* See map, frontispiece.

ent capital, situated about forty miles inland. There is at Arica commanding the port a Gibraltar-like promontory called the Morro of Arica. Near by is also a high rock island. Arica is very important geographically. The commerce clearing through it amounted to three to four million dollars annually.

Of greater importance in this question is the historical, and, strictly speaking, political, value of Tacna-Arica. It has been a veritable sentimental powder house ready to ignite with the least spark. In the War of the Pacific it was the strategic point. During, before, and after the war it was the lever of temptation by which Chile would break the *entente* which had existed between Bolivia and Peru since 1873. Near the city of Tacna the allies were decisively defeated and on the Morro of Arica the Peruvians made their last stand in their southern provinces. Peruvian school children recite the reply of Colonel Bolognesi when called upon to surrender the Morro in which he said he would fight to the last cartridge. Their histories tell how the Peruvian color sergeant, Manuel Ugarte, when the promontory was being carried by the Chilean arms, spurred his horse over the cliff into the sea rather than surrender the flag. While it may be said without detracting from the bravery of anybody, for every war has enough of valor as well as horror, that this beautiful story is largely mythical,[5] it was believed by practically all Peruvians, and a life-sized painting of Ugarte in his heroic plunge hangs in a museum at Lima.

In spite of the fact that the capture of this point was a horrible butchery, it was celebrated as a great feat in Chile and a monument bearing the inscription "Don't give up the Morro" (*No soltéis el Morro*) was erected at the base of the Morro by Chilean school children.

The revindication of Tacna-Arica meant to Peru morally what the reincorporation of Alsace-Lorraine meant to France. In brief, the award to either country of a permanent title to Tacna-Arica would have constituted a verdict of guilty or innocent in a tremendous moral question, the War of the Pacific. Commercially Tacna-Arica was a white elephant to Chile, yielding little revenue, costly to administer, and costly to defend. Likewise the region was scarcely worth to Peru the cost of the arbitration and the ten million pesos. But for Chile to have won permanent title to it would have given moral sanction to her conquest of Atacama and Tarapacá and to her long occupation of Tacna-Arica. It would have added moral victory to her undefeated military record and left her a clear title to the door to Bolivia.

For Peru to have won the region would have been to reunite her broken family of provinces, except for Tarapacá, and morally to convict the kidnaper. The great military and economic humiliation and the wounds of the War of the Pacific would have been measurably salved. Winning a moral victory in this case was more desirable to Peru than martial success. The fact that the question comprehended more than the manner of fulfilling the plebiscite clause of the treaty of peace was recognized in the supplementary act to the protocol of arbitration signed at Washington, which provided that in case the plebiscite could not be held the arbiter would help determine the disposition of the territory.[6]

The necessity of a thorough understanding in the United States of this, the most famous international question in South America, is quite apparent not only on its own rights and merits, but because of the very intimate and responsible connection of the American Government with the case. The complex Harding-Coolidge arbitration was really but the inheritance of an unfinished task which Secretaries Evarts, Blaine, and Frelinghuysen all attempted to perform. If General Pershing, as chairman of the Plebiscite Commission, found a solution to the problem difficult, and our ambassadors were embarrassed occasionally in these recent efforts at settling this question, it must be remembered that in an earlier phase of the case two American ministers, one to Peru and one to Chile, died while trying to secure peace and a third, finding his efforts disapproved, returned home and later committed suicide. The fact is that the United States, owing to the Monroe-Doctrine policy pursued then, prevented European intervention in this question forty years ago, and thereby indirectly allowed a treaty to be made at the close of the War of the Pacific which by its nature left a running sore on the side of South America.

The story of the Tacna-Arica dispute is the story of the expansion of Chile northward along the coast in quest of nitrates as rapidly and romantically as the expansion of the United States westward in quest of farms and gold. Apart from historical interest this story furnishes the political scientist interesting reflections upon the topics of the _uti possidetis_, the fluvial doctrine of dividing a desert in the middle, the question of outlets to the sea, the relations of intervention and mediation, and the Drago or Calvo Doctrine.

In telling this story, and especially in interpreting events, it will be difficult to avoid the appearance of prejudice, but it must be admitted that both nations could not have been in the right all the time; otherwise there would have been no question. Neither do the facts show, as has been claimed by some writers of Chile, Peru, and Bolivia, that the several failures of mediation by the United States were all due to stupidity or ill will. It has been untactful, even blunt,[7] but its greatest failure was due to the assassination of President Garfield.

Having lived a number of years in South America and knowing the splendid quality of friendliness so characteristic of Latin Americans, the writer sincerely rejoices in the final settlement of the Tacna-Arica question. The healing of all wounded sentiment as well as a better understanding of the good intentions of the United States in its mediation should now follow.

In connection with the economic motivation of this question, an introductory comment should also be made. Although the War of the Pacific was at first called the War of Ten Centavos because it started over a ten centavo duty on nitrates, the contest became a billion dollar struggle. Because of this powerful economic factor, too much Marxianism might be suspected in the treatment of the story. However, there is no exaggeration practiced in this connection and any reader knows that great interests of capital may or may not be wrongly employed. It will also be remembered that the nitrate war out of which the Tacna-Arica question grew had its beginning back in that wild period of American economic development which witnessed the Crédit Mobilier, boom towns, El Dorados, and wild railroad projects. Human nature is about the same in both Americas; it is only conditions that are different.

The purpose of this history, therefore, is a double one; first, to provide an English narrative of the highly dramatic events which produced the famous Tacna-

Arica dispute, and secondly, to interpret the attempted mediations of the United States which have been frequently misunderstood and which may illustrate the difficult rôle of a mediating government. It is intended however to be more than an English compilation, since much of the material is supplied from the sources and much of the interpretation differs from that of South American and European writers on this subject. It is also hoped that the relation of such a complex and dramatic international episode will be of interest and utility in connection with the further study of inter-American relations.

W. J. D.

Iowa City, Iowa,
January, 1931.

TACNA AND ARICA

CHAPTER I

THE BIRTH OF THE NATIONS

WHEN the South American republics secured their independence they took as their boundaries in most cases the Spanish colonial boundaries then in force. This principle, known in South American international law as the *uti possidetis* of 1810, was accepted by most of the countries and should have been a satisfactory method of territorial demarcation for the new republics.

In some cases the colonial boundaries had not been very well marked and the republics inherited questionable limits. Distances were so great and so much territory between colonies was uninhabited that an exact delineation of jurisdiction had not been made. When the Spanish Government made grants and decrees respecting land in America it was sometimes done without an exact knowledge of the latitude and longitude involved. Owing to a natural barrier, however, there should never have been any question of limits on the north of Chile. Before giving the boundaries of the countries concerned it will be well to notice briefly the way they were populated.

The three countries involved directly in the boundaries and nitrate question, viz., Chile, Peru, and Bolivia, and Argentina which was related indirectly at times to the question, were settled by two streams of immigration from Spain. These came from opposite directions; one, through Panama, Peru, Bolivia, and Chile to western and middle Argentina; the other came directly to Buenos Aires, up the La Plata and westward to middle

Argentina where it met the immigration stream from Panama and Peru.

Balboa had passed the Isthmus of Panama in 1513, while Solís discovered the Río de la Plata in 1515. Pizarro was at the island of Gallo on his way to conquer Peru in 1527 while Cabot was exploring the Paraná. Lima, Peru, was founded in 1535, the same year that Buenos Aires was founded. Pizarro had sent Valdivia from Peru to settle Chile in 1541, and expeditions from the latter had crossed over the Andes into Argentina and founded Córdoba in 1573, the same year that immigrants from Buenos Aires were settling Santa Fé. Settlements from these soon united the two streams on the plains of Argentina. The lines were thin at first and communication and territorial organization loose.

As political boundaries are often affected by geographic and climatic diversities, it is interesting to note the importance of these factors in the early settlement of Chile. Even in the time of the Incas, the Desert of Atacama, the Puna (plateau) of Atacama and the Puna of Jujuy formed natural barriers between the peoples of what are now Chile and Argentina on the south, and Bolivia and Peru on the north, and the great power of the Inca emperors was hardly sufficient to consolidate the peoples south of those barriers with their empire whose seat was at Cuzco.[8] This barrier was no less formidable to Almagro, the first Spaniard to reach Chile, than were the Araucanian Indians who inhabited the land beyond the desert.[9] Except for the river Loa, about 21½° south latitude, to the mouth of the Copiapó there is not a stream crossing this desert for six hundred miles. The *punas* or bleak plateaus above the desert are likewise forbidding. The streams starting in the towering Andes are soon lost in the burning sands and Atacama was for centuries a sort of no-man's land, to be avoided whenever possible. It will be seen that the territory between Chile and Bolivia and Peru was not of a character that would cause hairsplitting boundary demarcations when those republics were formed. The only possible use for such land would be for the seaports on its coast.

The first tillable land on the south margin of the desert was along the Copiapó River between twenty-seven and twenty-eight degrees south latitude. When Valdivia in 1540, following Almagro's unsuccessful expedition, was sent by Pizarro to Chile he called this valley the *"Valle de la posesión"* (the Valley of Possession), that is, where his possessions began, and from there he went farther and founded Santiago in 1541.

Of the numerous references to Copiapó during the colonial period as the northern boundary of Chile a few of the most representative will be given. The colony of Chile during the colonial period never actually embraced the Desert of Atacama, but since the claim was later put forth, a number of representative references to the northern limits of Chile will be cited. In the references to Copiapó that follow it will be remembered that there was a bay of Copiapó, as well as the city which is inland, the river, and the valley of Copiapó which refers to habitable land along that river and bay. All of these are between the twenty-seventh and twenty-eighth parallels, so they will be understood to refer to this region, the northern limits of Chile during the colonial period.

It will be remembered that in the early part of Spanish colonization in South America the political divisions consisted of a viceroyal province, a captaincy general and an *audiencia* (council). For nearly two centuries

Spain had two viceroyal provinces in America—New Spain (Mexico and Central America) and Peru. The viceroys at Lima, the capital of Peru, governed all of Spanish South America until in 1717 when the northern part comprising what are now Colombia, Ecuador, and Venezuela were formed into the viceroyalty of New Granada.[10] The viceroyalty of Peru then comprised the present countries of Peru, Bolivia, Chile, Uruguay, Paraguay, and Argentina. In 1776 what are now Argentina, Uruguay, Paraguay, and the southern districts of modern Bolivia were formed into the viceroyalty of La Plata. Modern Peru, Chile, and part of Bolivia remained all through the colonial period as the viceroyalty of Peru. What is modern Bolivia was called the Royal Council of Charcas (*Audiencia Real de Charcas*) and was governed by a royal council subject to the viceroy at Lima. The province of Chile was governed by a captain general under the viceroy at Lima. In the latter part of the colonial period, however, Chile was under the viceroy at Lima only in military matters, and enjoyed a large degree of colonial autonomy under the Spanish system. Instead of Charcas the term Alto Peru (Upper Peru) also was used much for what is now Bolivia until independence came and the name Bolivia was adopted in honor of General Simón Bolívar.

Some writers have stated that the boundary question between Chile and Peru dates from the original quarrel between Pizarro, the conqueror of the Incas, and his companion-at-arms Almagro. Then at least one Bolivian writer goes farther back and cites Garcilaso de la Vega* to show that the territory beyond the river Copiapó was under the Peruvian Inca Yupanqui.[11] Of

* *Comentarios Reales,* Parte I, Libro VII, cap. 18.

course, the citation of Indian limits to prove European or contemporaneous sovereignty is useless. Likewise the citing of the Almagro-Pizarro dispute could have no weight, for the history of the settlement of Chile begins with Valdivia.

Until 1776 the viceroys at Lima governed Charcas (Bolivia), Chile, and Buenos Aires, appointing governors and captains general when vacancies occurred until orders should arrive from Spain. The wheat and other grain from Chile went to Lima, metal from the great Potosí mines in Charcas went to Lima or Spain *via* Arica. The ecclesiastical government also radiated from Lima, the home of Santa Rosa, the patron saint of America and the Philippines. But the rise of Buenos Aires, the clash with the Portuguese, and the danger of commerce raiders caused the present countries of Argentina, Uruguay, and Paraguay to be separated from Peru, and the viceregal province of La Plata or Buenos Aires to be created.

With the creation of this new viceregal province in 1776 the consolidation and unification of Chile was hastened. The district of Cuyo east of the Andes which had been settled from Chile was placed with Buenos Aires as was Tucumán which had been settled from Peru. Two years later Chile was made independent of the Viceroy of Lima, except in military matters and concerning the islands of Chiloe, and so when she emerged as a nation at the opening of the following century her limits were clearly defined by natural boundaries, the Andes on the east and the Desert of Atacama on the north.

Charcas (Bolivia) was somewhat altered by the rise of Buenos Aires. The Audiencia of Charcas had been of great importance and wealth owing to its mines and to the number of its inhabitants, both Indian and European. Secure in its isolated location and strong in its wealth, it had even resisted the authority of the viceroy at Lima on one occasion. With the establishing of viceregal offices at Buenos Aires, Charcas lost more of its importance. While Tacna, Arica, and Tarapacá had long been assigned to the Audiencia of Peru, the port of Arica was still the principal outlet on the Pacific for Charcas, and should have been the seaport of modern Bolivia. This must be kept in mind, for the doctrine that Arica was the natural outlet for Bolivia later had an important bearing on Chilean-Bolivian diplomacy. Atacama still remained to Charcas as her coast although it was worthless land and had no good ports. Cobija had been established as a port and Mejillones was used somewhat for landing. There were a few districts above the desert in the large and practically unpopulated district of Atacama.

The name Atacama was originally applied to all the extensive desert extending from Copiapó northward. The people living in Chile when it became a nation, had no more idea as to the exact location of their northern boundary in that desert, than the people of the United States had of the western limits of the Louisiana Purchase. The first constitution of Chile gave as its northern limits merely "the Desert of Atacama," much as the early geographies of the United States gave "the Great American Desert" for its western limits.

The name Atacama in Charcas referred to that portion of the desert coast which lay within its colonial jurisdiction, to a district of the province of Potosí. Since the point of the exact division between Chile and Bolivia came to be the cause of the nitrate struggle which led to the war, it is important to settle it. What

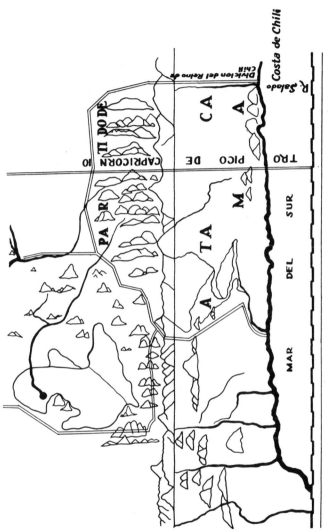

Colonial Map of *Partido de Atacama* in Potosí, Showing Northern
Boundary of Chile, 1787

was the colonial division? Did colonial divisions hold good for national divisions? These were the questions which arose not at first, but in 1842 when the value of nitrates discovered in those deserts became known. Shortly after the new viceroyalty of Buenos Aires was created, in 1787, the governor of Potosí had the inspector of the royal mint make a map of the province which indicates clearly the boundary at that date.

A section of this map is reproduced here (p. 6) from a photostatic copy of the original in the archives of the Indias in Seville in book manuscript entitled "Geographic, Historical and political description of the Imperial Town and Rich Mountain of Potosí; of the districts of Porco, Chayanta, Chichas or Tarija, Lipez and Atacama," showing the coast region east to the Andes and indicating the district of Atacama, or *Partido de Atacama*, as limiting Chile on the north. The dividing line is seen intersecting the Pacific Ocean, *Mar del Sur*, at the Río Salado. Although the boundaries around the province and between its six districts are drawn in colored lines, the maker of the map also notes, just south of the river and boundary line, "division of the kingdom of Chile (*Division del Reino de Chile*)." This boundary line, as indicated by the scale of latitude on the margin, is near parallel 26 and is given in the manuscript as 26° 15′.[12] This is extremely important because that is approximately the latitude given on modern maps for the Río Salado.

Thus as the period of independence approached at the opening of the nineteenth century, the actual dividing line between Chile and Charcas was the Copiapó region at the southern extremity of the Desert of Atacama and the legal colonial limits were at the Río Salado.

As previously stated, Chile at the close of its colonial period was practically independent of the viceroy at Lima. It had a rather compact basis for nationhood, being shut off on the east by the Andes and on the north by the Desert of Atacama. A map dated 1776 in the frontispiece of Abbé Molina's *Geographical, Natural and Civil History of Chile* shows the colony of Chile. The book, which is the only history of the country of that period, describes the province of Copiapó beginning: "This province is bounded on the North by the desarts of Peru, on the East by the Andes, on the South by Coquimbo, and on the West by the Pacifick Ocean."[13]

The map is worth special consideration because it shows no northern limits, although the map extends north to the Bahía de Nuestra Señora, at about a degree north of the Río Salado, or 24°, making the Río Salado at 25° (map opposite). Now the Río Salado is at 26° 20′. This shows an error in the latitude lines on Molina's map of 1° 20′, which would make the northernmost limits of his map approximately 25° 20′ which coincides with the Bahía de Nuestra Señora. That is to say, Molina showed the province of Copiapó, Chile's northernmost territory, as extending to this bay south of 25° south latitude, but gave that point as 24° on his map. This is to be remembered, for 24° actually passes a full degree north of the Bahía de Nuestra Señora. Twenty-five degrees is the farthest north that could be claimed of the desert by Molina's map, but 24° by latitude was later claimed by Chile.

Since Copiapó was on the margin of the desert, any nearby portion that was habitable would be under its sphere of influence, apart from other centers, and therefore would be considered as belonging to Chile.

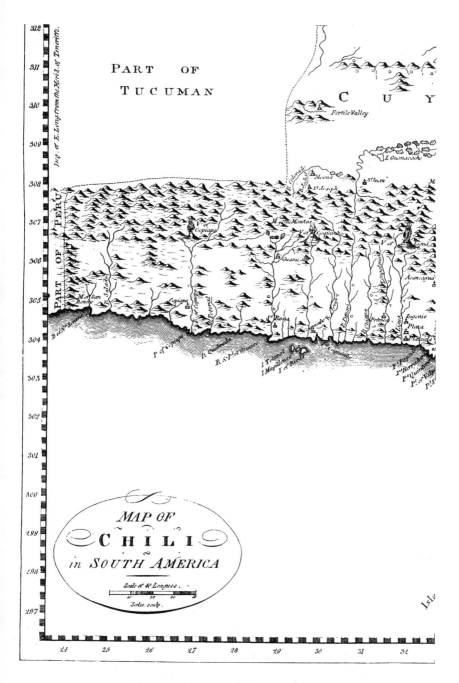

MAP OF CHILE BY MOLINA, 1776

So, in spite of the original royal grant to Valdivia, making Chilean limits at Copiapó and the Río Salado boundary of Charcas, Chilean influence began to expand northward. When, owing to fogs watering the slopes of the Bahía de Nuestra Señora, or Señora del Paposo, some vegetation was found, a small settlement of Chilean Indians who had at first come to fish in the bay was established there, and a Chilean judge administered whatever law they needed. In order to civilize these half-wild fishermen a royal order was issued in 1801 establishing a vice parish of Nuestra Señora del Paposo under the ecclesiastical authority of the presidency of Chile. Thus, at the close of the colonial period, a little group of fisherman-farmers, natural and actual dependents of Chile, legally under the Viceroy of Peru, dwelt at Paposo, about 25° south latitude— the advance guard of Chilean expansion into the Desert of Atacama.

As the struggle for independence in South America began in 1810 and the nations erected out of Spanish colonies generally took the colonial boundaries they had been given by Spain, the general demarcation of which had been internationally recognized by the Treaty of San Ildefonso, that principle of national demarcation came to be called the *uti possidetis* of 1810. The first uprisings were all suffocated by Spain, however, except in the United Provinces of La Plata, or strictly speaking Buenos Aires, and the doctrine was not immediately enunciated.

San Martín recognizing that all or none of South America would have to be independent led a liberating army over the Andes, thousands of feet higher than where Napoleon passed the Alps, and helped regain the independence of Chile and Peru. In describing the ex-

pedition an Argentine historian refers to the northern
limits of Chile, February 12, 1817, as follows: "On the
same day, the vanguard of another division commanded
by Captain Dávila occupied the City of Copiapó. Thus
all the north of Chile was reconquered on the same
day."[14]

While these colonies struggled for independence they
sent agents to other nations asking for recognition.
The United States then sent representatives to Argentina and Chile to report on these countries before
recognizing them as nations. Mr. Theodorick Bland
visited Argentina, crossed over to Chile in 1818 and
made his reports. Concerning the extent of Chile he
said:

> The long and mountainous territory of Chili com-
> mences on the Pacific at the mouth of the Rio Salado;
> thence ascending that river, and extending away from it
> toward Paquil by a line in a northeasterly direction, over
> a portion of the frightful desert of Atacama beyond the
> twenty-fourth degree of south latitude, until it intersects
> the great chain of the Andes. . . .[15]

He again refers to the boundary:

> The desert of Atacama may be said to commence in
> Chili, almost immediately after crossing the river Juncal,
> or Dry river as it is sometimes called; thence to the river
> Salado, the northern boundary of the state, is a distance
> of fifty miles; thence to the town of Atacama, in the vice-
> royalty of Peru, is a distance of nearly three hundred
> miles. . . .[16]

At another place in the report he gives the latitude
of Copiapó as 26° 1′, while it is actually 27° 22′.[17] This

indicates that Mr. Bland was using the latitudes employed on Molina's map which we have seen were 1° 20' in error, and when he says in the first citation that a line drawn northeast from a point up the Río Salado would intersect the Andes beyond latitude 24°, it should be latitude 25°. Places do not change latitude, however, and Mr. Bland states that the Río Salado was the northern boundary of Chile.

Mr. J. R. Poinsett, who was sent to Chile, reports copiously and makes the following references to the boundary: ". . . from the river Salado and the desert of Atacama to the straits of Magellan."[18] Again: "The country comprised between the 25th and 43d degrees of south latitude may be considered the length of the kingdom of Chili, it being unsettled and even unexplored farther south." Mr. Poinsett, also, evidently was using the Molina latitudes, for on the following page he said: "From the Salado to the Itata, that is, from 25 degrees to 36 degrees of south latitude, not a cloud, . . ."[19] It will be remembered that Molina gave Salado at 25° instead of 26° 20' as it should be. Mr. Poinsett said that most of the statistics in his report had been secured through the courtesy of the Chilean Secretary, Señor Irisarri, so it is evident that at the time the United States was asked to recognize Chilean independence the Río Salado was officially considered the northern boundary of that new nation.

In the proclamation of the independence of Chile dated January 1, 1818, and in the manifesto issued to foreign offices advising the world of the act no mention is made of national boundaries, so it would be assumed that the colonial boundaries were to be in force. In the various constitutions which were made before a permanent one was adopted in 1833, the northern limits were always described as "the Desert of Atacama."

The scene of nation making now shifts to Bolivia, which is to be Chile's neighbor on the north. San Martín resigned and retired from Peru in favor of Bolívar, who forced the royalists up over the Andes to a defeat at Junín in central Peru. Bolívar's right arm, General Sucre, after inflicting a decisive defeat at Ayacucho in southern Peru entered the old Audiencia of Charcas.

As Sucre was approaching La Paz he was met by a delegation asking for the national autonomy of Alto Peru (Upper Peru), formerly known as the Audiencia of Charcas, but at this time called the Audiencia of Chuquisaca. It was practically under Spanish military government, since the revolution had driven out the Viceroy of Buenos Aires in 1810. With the capitulation of La Serna following the Battle of Ayacucho, the last royal governor in South America was overcome and the question of self-government forced upon this region. Two days after arriving at La Paz, Sucre issued a decree, on February 9, 1825, recognizing the independence of Upper Peru and calling a constitutional convention to meet in Chuquisaca.[20]

Bolívar when he heard of this wrote to Sucre objecting and incidentally stating formally what came to be known as the *uti possidetis* of 1810:

Neither you, nor I, nor the congress of Peru, nor of Colombia, can break and violate the basis of public law which we have recognized in Spanish America. This basis is: that republican governments are being founded within the limits of the former viceroyalties, captaincy generals, or presidencies—for example, Chile. Upper Peru is a de-

pendency of the viceroyalty of Buenos Aires, just as Quito
is a contiguous dependency of Bogotá. Although Chile
was a dependency of Peru, yet it was in reality separated from Peru some time before the revolution began,
just as Guatemala was separated from New Spain.
Thus both of these presidencies might rightly become independent of their ancient viceroyalties; but neither Quito
nor Charcas [Bolivia] can rightly become independent
except by an agreement embodied in a treaty resulting
from a war between the parties, or resulting from the deliberations of a congress.[21]

On May 9 a delegation from the Congress of Buenos
Aires arrived with permission for national autonomy
in Charcas. With this recognition legal objection to
statehood ended, but Bolívar, who was then in Arequipa
in a triumphal tour over Peru, of which country he was
now dictator, evidently did not want to see a precedent
for the separation of Quito from Colombia, of which
country he was also president, and so he made a strenuous objection. He wrote to Sucre to dissolve the assembly and submit to the Congress of Peru.[22] It, however, decided to form a new government on its own
responsibility, and at the suggestion of Sucre decreed
that the new republic should be called Bolivia and Bolívar should be its father, protector, and first president.
Bolívar assented and on August 6 a formal declaration
of independence was made comprising the provinces of
La Paz, Charcas, Cochabamba, Potosí, and Santa
Cruz. Thus, the Desert of Atacama south to the Río
Salado as a district of Potosí became a part of the republic of Bolivia.

Sucre, to whom Bolívar after a few months delegated
his authority, was elected president and the capital was

renamed in his honor. In demarking the limits of Bolivia, Bolívar and Sucre tried to secure a good port.
They negotiated for Arica, offering to indemnify Peru,
and the proposition was at first well received, but later
rejected. This should be borne in mind in connection
with later diplomacy. Bolívar had arranged for duties
of 8 per cent at Cobija and sent a commission to investigate ports. From the reports of this commission
by Colonel O'Connor it would seem that Paposo at this
time was not inhabited. The handful of fishermen previously mentioned must have gone south for the season.
The report sheds some light on Bolivia's maritime
province:

> . . . we began the examining of all the ports men-
> tioned in my instructions, and we find that that of Cobija
> has the best depth for anchorage, and it is the most spa-
> cious port also; although water [fresh] is scarce it is
> possible to augment the quantity. I separated from the
> Comodor in the port of Loa, which is no more than a
> roadstead, and with the water of the River Loa so salty
> it can't be drunk. The port of Mejillones is beautiful but
> lacks water. That of Paposo has a river that enters it
> with fish, but the route from Paposo by land to Atacama
> [town] hasn't a. drop of water nor pasture, and for this
> reason is unusable.[23]

The same report discussed the colonial limits, saying:

> The limits then extended from the gorge of Santa Rosa
> [La Abra de Santa Rosa] on the north, the Morro of
> Sama on the coast, and from said Morro south to Hueso
> Parado which is within a few leagues of Copiapó, and in
> the uplands to the River of Quinca.

The same year it was decreed that Cobija should be the major port of Bolivia, and the name should be changed to La Mar in honor of one of Sucre's generals in the Battle of Ayacucho. The old name prevailed, however, and port facilities were developed at Cobija.

So at the opening of the period of republics in South America, we can say with respect to boundaries on the South Pacific that Chile extended to "the Desert of Atacama." We can define this point for Chile to be at the Río Salado, 26° 20′ south latitude. Then there was a sort of "no-man's land" to Paposo, about 25°, where at times there were Chilean fishermen. This was the limit of Chilean influence into the Desert of Atacama which for three centuries had been included in Charcas (Bolivia). Beginning at Paposo, by the principle of the *uti possidetis* and by organic acts of the Government of Bolivia, Bolivian territory extended northward to the river Loa, the boundary of Peru. This was known by nations recognizing Bolivian independence and not seriously questioned until nitrate mines were discovered in the Desert of Atacama. In this nation building the fatal error was the failure of Bolivia to secure Arica as her seaport. The shortest route from the populated parts of Bolivia, and the lowest pass over the mountains combined to make it the outlet intended by nature for the people of the Bolivian highlands. Efforts were made and a treaty drawn up, but as the including of Arica in Bolivia would have cut off Peru's southernmost province Tarapacá, Bolivia was born with an unnatural outlet to the sea.

Sucre, the first president of Bolivia, did all in his power for that country and he, as well as his successors, among other things looked after the maritime region Atacama. By a decree of 1825 Bolívar had made

Cobija the principal port.[24] Two years later Sucre decreed that all persons who should settle in the province of Atacama should enter duty free. In 1829 Andrés Santa Cruz, who followed Sucre as president, increased preferment to Cobija, began fortifying it, and built a road over the desert. The constitution promulgated by him in 1831 made a separate division of Atacama. Instead of including it in the Department of Potosí, as had been done under Spanish rule and in previous years, he called it the "Sea Coast Province."[25] This was in 1831 and Chile gave the name Atacama to a new province which she created around Copiapó in 1843. In a few years Santa Cruz was able to make to the Bolivian Congress the following report which shows much foresight:

The Provincia Litoral and Port of Cobija have made a rapid progress in every respect, in consequence of the Decree exempting them from the payment of duties, granted them by the Government, upon your authority. Their population and institutions have wonderfully increased; and by the impulse already given, we may indulge the hope that, before 10 years have elapsed, that province will become one of the richest of the Republic. The copper of its mines is one of its most valuable productions, and which, by the large returns it makes for the investment of capital, daily increases competition. The Government, which has always been convinced of the necessity of maintaining a secure means of communication with the exterior, has continually afforded Cobija the assistance to which it is so much entitled, and which may be considered as indispensable to our very independence.[26]

General Santa Cruz has been variously placed by

writers as a Gladstone, a Napoleon, a demigod, and a devil. Whatever else may be said about him he was capable and very versatile. He had had varied experience as an officer in the royal army, a captive in Argentina, a refugee in Brazil, and later as an officer under San Martín and Bolívar, campaigning in Bolivia, Peru, and Ecuador. He had acted as provisional president of Peru and from there had gone as Peruvian ambassador to Chile, from where he was called to the presidency of Bolivia on the departure of Sucre. Owing partly to his prestige and perhaps partly to former association with one of the parties, he was invited to intervene in a civil war in Peru. Victorious at arms and in Bolivian politics he tried his hand in international affairs.

Whether he was attempting to secure tranquillity in the two countries or to form a life position for himself in imitation of Bolívar is not known, but in 1836 he formed the Peru-Bolivia Confederation. There were three divisions: North Peru, South Peru, and Bolivia. Each was to have a president and Santa Cruz was to be president of the Confederation for a term of ten years. Santa Cruz was related to a strong Indian *cacique* near Cuzco and his idea might have been to establish a vital rule. San Martín had thought that the union of a British prince and an Inca princess would make the logical ruler for Peru. A few centuries before, Gonzalo Pizarro by an alliance with Inca royal blood had been able to defy the power of Spain, and had it not been for his personal loyalty to the monarch, would have established a line of Peruvian kings which might have changed the history of South America and the new world. As Santa Cruz was by birth a Peruvian and popular with the generation of liberators, the opposi-

tion in Peru might not have developed enough strength
to overthrow him; but Chile and the Argentine Republic opposed him and they prepared for war.

Before taking up the war against Santa Cruz a word
should be said about *émigrés*. When unsuccessful opponents of a president had to emigrate, they usually
fomented trouble against their homeland, especially
against the leader who had exiled them. Frequently the
country which had given them asylum did not observe
neutrality and even took an active part in the quarrel.
It will be remembered that in Latin American countries
personality has generally played an important rôle in
politics. Following a civil war in Chile ending in the
Battle of Lircai, the officers of the defeated party who
were not shot fled to Peru. The principal leader, General Freire, obtained ships in Peru in 1836 and in-
vaded Chile just before the elections. He was overcome, but his having fitted out ships in Peru was held
against her, and especially against Santa Cruz to whose
influence it was erroneously ascribed.[27] Besides this, he
was accused of placing tariff rates against Chilean
wheat. He also opened new seaports in the Confederation and so Portales, the power behind the presidency
in Chile, determined to overthrow him.

The next year an expedition was sent to southern
Peru, but was cut off from its base by Santa Cruz near
Arequipa. Instead of destroying it, as was expected, the
Protector accepted a truce, the Truce of Paucarpata,
which resulted in a peace signed by the Chilean plenipotentiary, who had accompanied the expedition. Chile
thus saved its army, but secured no vengeance against
Santa Cruz, who now appeared before the world as en-
lightened and magnanimous. Portales and Prieto disauthorized the peace and prepared a new expedition,

this time to be commanded by Gen. Manuel Búlnes who would link Chile and its destiny to the territory north of the historic Copiapó boundary. A European traveler who witnessed the embarking stated that some regiments were taken aboard unarmed and handcuffed by twos.[28] The returning veterans of the expedition were proud, however, for it was victorious in every way. This expedition was guided by the exiled Peruvian president, Gamarra, and a large band of *émigrés* from that country.[29] In the association of former President Gamarra of Peru and General Búlnes, who was soon elected president of Chile, is found the entry of Chile upon a career of nitrate expansion into the Desert of Atacama which finally extended to Tacna-Arica.

Returning to the limits of Chile and Bolivia, we find big new copper and silver mines discovered and old ones redeveloped in the early thirties. Copiapó experienced a boom and the whole province of Coquimbo took on new life. Yankee railroad builders constructed a line to Copiapó from the sea and built up for it a new port at Caldera. This port became a regular stop for vessels. William Wheelwright, a Yankee shipper and railroad builder who had had a line of sailing vessels from Valparaiso to Cobija since 1829, put on steamers and extended his line to Callao in 1840. This was the birth of the great Pacific Steam Navigation Company which later gave the English predominance on the west coast of South America. It is interesting to note that while the great railroad builders of Central and South America of the period from independence to the World War were Yankees such as Wheelright, Meiggs, and Keith, the capital employed was nearly all British.

During the mining boom around Copiapó, Chile's sphere of influence extended into the Desert of Ata-

cama almost to Paposo. Improvised ports or landing
places were found from time to time between parallels
27 and 25 as mines were discovered or abandoned. The
peak of the boom passed coincident with the discovery
of gold in California, and many adventurers left for
the new El Dorado, but northern Chile was conserving
much from these mining activities and the Copiapó
district was increasing in importance.

One great company of this period was an English
concern by name of "The Copiapó Mining Company,"
now "The Copper Mines of Copiapó, Ltd." It engaged
also in stock and alfalfa raising and general commerce,
and kept a record of its affairs. Copies of letters with
reports for a hundred years from its managers to the
London headquarters giving details of the business, reports of rains, cultivated lands, etc., were recently
found by Mr. Isaiah Bowman of the American Geographic Society.[30] Mr. Bowman, fearing that an earth-
quake might destroy them, took many pages of copy
and placed them in the archives of the Society at New
York. Of special interest for this study is a map of
about 1835 by Mr. Bingley showing the limits between
Chile and Bolivia at that time. Mr. Bingley was for
many years manager of the company, and judging from
his reports was careful and technical to a high degree.
Darwin, in the account of his expedition to South
America, spoke well of him, and the map should be considered as very important evidence in the case of this
boundary between Chile and Bolivia.

As seen by the copy (map opposite), Mr. Bingley's
map shows the boundary to be practically as described
by Poinsett. Many surveys were later made which corrected the error of Molina's map. The line according
to Bingley's map starts in at the lower part of the

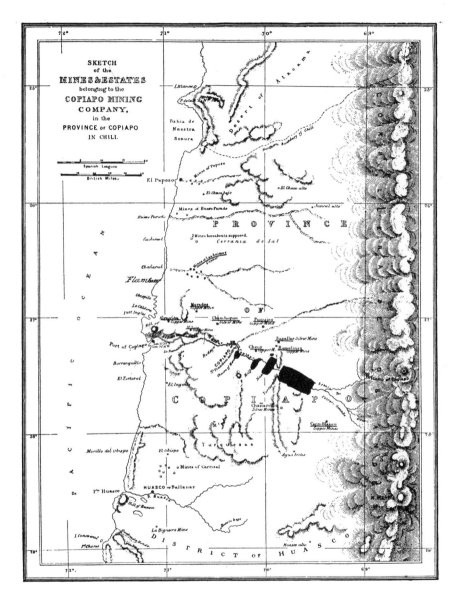

MAP OF COPIAPÓ REGION BY BINGLEY, 1835

From Desert Trails of Atacama, *by Isaiah Bowman, published by the American Geographical Society of New York.*

Bahía de Nuestra Señora, curves slightly southward, then northeastward intersecting parallel 25 at the sixty-ninth meridian on the slopes of the Andes, continuing at the same angle to their crest a short distance north of the parallel.

Of course, most of the territory shown in this map was and is desert, broken only by occasional fertile spots along a mountain stream on slopes of the Andes. It may be seen that north of the boundary line on the map occurs the name "Desert of Atacama." This is the desert correctly speaking, the land beyond the Copiapó zone of influence, the "Desert of Atacama" referred to in the constitutions and administrative acts of Chile. This was the boundary when Búlnes led the second expedition against Santa Cruz.

The success of the expedition silenced all opposition to the government in Chile, broke up the Peru-Bolivia Confederation where new national constitutions were adopted, and overthrew the power of Santa Cruz, who resigned when he saw his confederation melting away. Gamarra who was put in power in Lima by Búlnes' army inaugurated a nationalistic policy declaring a monopoly on guano (nitrate) sales and decreeing that all fishing should be done by Peruvians.

With the election of President Búlnes, Chile entered upon a new epoch of its development, for besides expanding northward it began to expand southward toward the Strait of Magellan. Coincident with this double movement is the beginning of her boundary questions with Bolivia on the north and Argentina on the south. Búlnes established a fort on the Strait and sent an exploring expedition north into the desert to look for nitrates. The result of this important expedition is best stated by the President himself in his message to Congress which follows:

Fellow citizens of the Senate and of the Chamber of Deputies. Being now recognized in Europe, the value of the substance called *huano*, which from time immemorial was used as fertilizer for the cultivation of the soil of the coast of Peru, I judged it necessary to send an exploring commission to examine the coast included between the Port of Coquimbo and the *morro* of Mejillones with the purpose of discovering if in the territory of the Republic there existed any *huano* fields whose product might afford a new source of revenue for the public treasury, and although the results of the expedition are not so much as had been thought, nevertheless from parallel 29° 35′ to 23° 6′ south latitude *huano* is found in sixteen places of the coast and near-by islands in more or less abundance, according to the nature of the localities in which those deposits existed.

Far from presuming after the examination made, that the *huano* fields of Chile have the importance attributed to those of Peru, I am inclined to believe that the benefits that may be derived will be small, but even so that would not excuse the leaving of its exploitation to foreign enterprise, depriving the national treasury of an income which without cost to the people would furnish funds for so many useful enterprises which need effective aid.[31]

Both chambers approved unanimously Búlnes' action and in October the project was promulgated as a law, Article 2 of which provided for the confiscation of cargoes of *huano*, or guano, if taken from that region without a Chilean license. Thus the nitrate conflict began.

President Búlnes thus placed the northern boundary

of Chile at parallel 23 without stating on what ground he based the decree. In making that claim to the desert coast beyond Bolivia's southern boundary it was necessary to reject the doctrine of the *uti possidetis*. Before taking up the reaction of Bolivia to the Búlnes' decree and the explanation of the "substance huano" which was the admitted cause of Chilean expansion northward, the story of the birth of the nations will be closed with a quotation of the view of Gonzalo Búlnes, principal historian of Chile and descendant of President Búlnes, on the beginnings of the Tacna-Arica question and his view of the *uti possidetis* theory of boundaries:

The new Republics adopted as a common principle of demarcation the administrative limits which they had at the time of separation from Spain. This was called the *uti possidetis* of 1810, a principle suggested to a great extent to prevent European nations getting a foothold in America on the ground, or pretext, that there existed in America unoccupied lands between that could be occupied by them on the grounds of *res nullius*.

The *uti possidetis* of 1810 was the legal principle of territorial demarcation of the American countries among themselves.

The administration of Búlnes deserves the credit of having established the limits of the Republic on the north and on the south, getting ahead of the rest in America, and thus with the rare foresight of the Chilean race, providing a territory adequate for its desires for work and expansion.

In the space of one year, between 1842 and 1843 he fixed the northern limits of the country at Mejillones and the southern at the Strait of Magellan founding a colony which was then called Fort Bulnes, now Punta Arenas.

That of the Strait has no bearing on this work. It is necessary to refer only to the northern possession, Mejillones, for having been the beginning point of the fierce and prolonged struggle which I purpose to treat.[32]

REFERENCES

1. *The Opinion and Award of the Arbitrator,* Government Printing Office, Washington, D. C.

2. The date used in this work for the Treaty of Ancón is the date of signing, October 20, 1883; the plebiscite was to be held ten years hence from ratification, March, 1884.

3. Rand McNally, *Commercial Atlas of America,* 56th ed., p. 604.

4. Taratá was returned to Peru by the Coolidge award. See *Opinion and Award,* p. 60, also *infra,* p. 208.

5. Sir Clement R. Markham, *The War between Peru and Chile,* p. 207.

6. See text of Protocol of Submission, *Tacna-Arica Arbitration, The Case of the Republic of Chile,* pp. 3-5.

7. William Howard Taft, *The Independent,* LXXVI (December 18, 1913), 543.

8. T. A. Joyce, *South American Archaeology,* p. 216.

9. W. H. Prescott, *The Conquest of Peru,* II, 80.

10. José Comancho, *Historia de Bolivia,* p. 56.

11. D. S. Bustamonte, *Bolivia su estructura y sus derechos en el Pacífico,* p. 90.

12. *Revista de Archivos Bibliotecas Y Muséos,* II, 587.

13. Abbé Don J. Ignatius Molina, *The Geographical, Natural and Civil History of Chili,* I, Supplement, 251.

14. Bartolomé Mitre, *Historia de San Martín,* quoted in Supple, *Spanish Reader of South American History,* p. 132.

15. Theodorick Bland, *American State Papers,* IV, 295.

16. *Ibid.,* p. 298.

17. The present location by latitude of these places is based on a table in *Chile, A Handbook,* p. 23, ed. John Barrett, International Bureau of American Republics.

18. J. R. Poinsett, *American State Papers,* IV, 332.

19. *Ibid.,* p. 333.

20. Comancho, *op. cit.,* p. 126.

21. Vicente Lecuna, *Papeles de Bolivar,* I, 89.

22. Comancho, *op. cit.,* p. 126.

23. Prescott, *El problema continental*, p. 19.

24. *Ibid.*, p. 20.

25. Constitution of Bolivia of 1831, Title I, Chap. 2.

26. *British State Papers*, XXIII, 160.

27. Oscar de Santa-Cruz, *El General Andrés de Santa-Cruz*, pp. 118–119.

28. J. J. von Tschudi, *Travels in Peru*, I, 20.

29. Charles Wilkes, *Narrative of the United States Exploring Expedition*, I, 225.

30. Isaiah Bowman, *Desert Trails of Atacama*, p. 180. Map p. 177.

31. Gonzalo Búlnes, *Guerra del Pacífico*, I, 13.

32. *Ibid.*, p. 12. Note: In a pamphlet entitled *The Question between Chile and Bolivia*, issued in 1879 by official or semiofficial Chilean agencies, there is a statement that the king of Spain sent an expedition of two boats commanded by captains Malaspina and Bustamonte to fix a boundary between Chile and Charcas [Bolivia] and that the line was fixed at parallel 22. It also states that these captains made a map showing such a division and presented it to the king. However, the writer was unable to find record of such a map or boundary and considers the evidence conclusive placing the line between Paposo and Copiapó as set forth in the preceding chapter.

CHAPTER II

NATIONS PLUS NITRATES

NOW what was this "substance called huano" which had occasioned the expansion message of President Búlnes and what was its effect on the nations claiming the desert coast containing it?

Travelers down the west coast of South America even today notice two phenomena: hundreds of miles of bleak coast and hundreds of millions of sea gulls—desert and sea gulls. Through the swarms of birds may be seen from time to time an island or mainland cliff whitened with the deposit of these fish-eating birds. Centuries before the coming of the Spaniards, the Incas used the deposit or *huanu* to raise corn, potatoes, and other crops. The Quechuan (Inca) word was *pishu huanu*, meaning bird dung.[1] This was shortened to *huanu* and spelled *huano* in Chile but *guano* in Peru and Bolivia and in English-speaking countries. The Incas had prohibited the killing of the birds and had used comparatively little of the deposits of centuries which the absolutely dry climate had preserved. In some cases capes and islands were raised thereby fifty feet above their original elevation. Since loading was a simple process and freight rates on sailing vessels cheap, it can easily be seen that fabulous wealth existed there, for the product often sold at $80 a ton. All the wealth of Pizarro and Cortez and their followers is a small item compared to what this desert has yielded.

Aside from this guano there was found on the mainland in the heart of the Desert of Atacama some fields of *caliche* in which there were deposits of saltpeter.

Early Spanish priests had made gunpowder from this to celebrate church festivals, and native fireworks employing it are found in Bolivia today. During the colonial period agriculture was allowed to decline in Peru and Bolivia in favor of mining, and the use of guano was very inconsiderable. It was shown to Humboldt when he visited South America in 1804 and he took samples back to Europe. He perhaps delayed its exploitation, however, by a mistaken idea of its nature and value. Later when one or another enterprising exporter wanted to ship the fertilizer to Europe where it was so much needed, it sufficed to quote Humboldt to discourage the movement. However, the idea of its utility persisted especially among European miners and British and Yankee exporters and whalers who had come to the silver and copper regions near the desert. In spite of the fact that the first shipload sent to London was dumped into the Thames, the material came to be valued in Europe in the thirties and forties.

A French scientist, Alexandre Cochet, experimented with it in a small laboratory which he set up in Peru's part of the desert. He was encouraged by Gamarra, who aspired to control the gunpowder supply, secure new revenues, and otherwise improve his country. Cochet learned that nitrate of soda could be had cheaply and in unlimited quantities from the deposits of *caliche* as well as of guano, and he believed that billions of dollars' worth of fertilizer were to be had from the desert as well as from islands of that rainless region.* He went to Lima in 1840 to get the Government to exploit the material. Being uncommercial, it is not probable that he was attracted by the possibility of

* From this point on the term "nitrates" refers to both guano and saltpeter, unless otherwise specified.

becoming very wealthy from a share of the proceeds, but others did have that idea. When Cochet came to Lima the few shipments of guano that had been made had been surrounded by some mystery and it was not known exactly whether it was a big paying venture or a big hoax. Both were claimed. At any rate Cochet brought the guano business into the open after coming to Lima.

Concerning that Frenchman, a Peruvian congressional committee later appointed to pass on his claims said in part:

This person came to Peru in 1826, as a scientific traveler, with the intention of returning to his country at the close of his explorations. He brought letters of recommendation to the government of that epoch, and invited by it and pressed by Generalissimo Gamarra, who knew his merits, to fix his residence in Peru, he has, to the present time, remained in the land of his adopted country, relying on the distinguished protection which the government tendered to him, as appears from the documents in his possession. From that time he devoted himself to travel over and survey of the whole territory of the republic. . . . There he observed, speculated, and made interesting discoveries in the vegetable, animal, and mineral kingdoms. He extracted quinine and balsams. . . . He traveled over a greater part of the Cordilleras, so rich in varied and valuable minerals, which he has examined and utilized; and also over the sea-coast and plains of Peru, where he discovered untold riches, especially in the saltpeter deposits of Tarapacá, where he converted the nitrate of soda into nitrate of potash. This discovery, and the information of the method of utilization, up to that time unknown, even in the country, would be a source of immense wealth for the nation, affording at the same time a livelihood for many poor families, and facilitating the manufacture of gunpowder, which, becoming an article of exportation, would give a supremacy over the contiguous states of this continent, and even of Europe, and would bring very large sums into the nation's treasury.[2]

The committee was somewhat in error regarding his discovery of the method of transmuting nitrate of soda into nitrate of potash. He never claimed that; he said he made it practicable and commercially profitable. This committee which was reporting secured a vote to give the scientist a reward of 6,000 pesos ($3,000), which he declined. He went back to France and died in poverty in a Bordeaux hospital.[3]

Cochet had interested another Frenchman, Allier, who was disloyal to him. With a Peruvian named Quiroz they secured a contract from the government of Gamarra for all the guano they could export for a term of years, forming a sort of monopoly in partnership with the Government. Their contract named the deposits on the Chincha Islands only. Cochet was left out of the firm name in the contract and was overlooked in dividing the first proceeds. Allier falsely told him that Quiroz had left him out, having secured the contract without the former's consent. Cochet said they could get around that for there were great deposits on the mainland also. Allier then got the contract changed to include the mainland and a longer term of years, still omitting Cochet. When the scientist discovered the deception he went before the Council of State and exposed the fraud and the contract was shortened in 1841.

Some cargoes had been shipped, and from $90 to $120 a ton was realized as they were sold for ammonia.

That price could not prevail for fertilizer and the fertilizer value still was not known well in Europe. There were confusing rumors and conflicting statements about the business. The Government had chemists in London working on the analysis of guano and nitrates, but general commerce was not yet engaged in the industry.

For some reason, either for a desire to vindicate his scientific arguments for a cheap fertilizer, or despairing of ever getting returns for himself and the Government for his discoveries, Cochet, in Lima in 1841, published his ideas and formulas for fertilizing.[4] It created a sensation. The Government canceled its contract with Allier and Quiroz, and independent firms were soon bidding for guano contracts. So many contracts were received that the Government suddenly received $600,-000 a few days after the Battle of Ingavi in 1842, when money was so much needed.

From here on, contracts and countercontracts were made and annulled in Peru and suits, diplomatic claims, and even the War of the Pacific evidenced the pungent smell of fertilizer. It can now be understood what President Búlnes had in mind in his "huano" message to the Chilean Congress in 1842 and in inferring that 23° south latitude was the northern boundary of the nation. This is not an attempt to make a case against anyone, but a recital of historical sequences. Cochet was sponsored by Gamarra. Gamarra as an *émigré* to Chile guided Búlnes' army back to Lima to free it from the domination of Santa Cruz. Captain Wilkes, a Yankee observer in Valparaiso, remarked on the strangeness of the fact that nobody seemed to know where the money for the Búlnes expedition was coming from and that there was plenty for provisioning it well. He said it was suggested that the church had furnished the money,

but that would hardly seem plausible. Gamarra doubt-
lessly received money from the sale of guano, as early
as 1838, in sufficient quantity to arm the expedition.
He set up his government in Lima under the protection
of Búlnes and Búlnes in his message to Congress mentioned the example of Peru in obtaining money from
guano. Búlnes by decree placed the northern boundary
of Chile at the 23° parallel, and Peru paid from the
sale of guano a share of the South American Revolu-
tionary War loan secured in London by Chile. Thus, it
is seen the thread of nitrates is clearly woven in the international politics of the west coast of South America
in 1842.

President Búlnes' decree making the 23° parallel the
northern boundary was protested by Bolivia. A special
mission was sent to treat with Chile. There was not so
much public clamor about it as might be supposed, owing to civil war in Bolivia. The boundary affair was
also overshadowed by another international matter.
Bolivia was still under Chile's aegis with respect to
Santa Cruz. The former protector was a dangerous
émigré in Ecuador; and Bolivia, Chile, and Peru were
arranging a treaty providing for a trip to Europe with
a life pension for him. Nevertheless, Bolivia's boundary
commissioner, Casimiro Olañeta, presented a protest at
Santiago in January, 1843.[5] The Chilean Chancellor
replied that he would have to make a careful study of
the question in order to make recommendations to his
Congress. He later reported to Congress that he would
have to study the archives for documents relating to the
northern boundary. President Manuel Montt in his
message to Congress stated that he had secured a professor to explore and make maps of the region. It would

be interesting to know when he discovered the error of
1° 20′ in latitude.*

On being pressed for a reply, the Chilean Minister
gave an answer in which he advocated the doctrine that
a desert was like a river between two countries, belonging half to one and half to the other country on its
shores. He suggested that the Desert of Atacama be
divided equally. The answers to exchanges were slow
and the growth of the nitrate business fast.

In 1843 as many as fifty vessels were reported loading guano at a single island off the Peruvian coast.
Prospectors of all nationalities were searching the
mainland capes and fortunes were made quickly. There
were two bases for the industry. One group of shippers
outfitted from Valparaiso and the other from Callao.
Between these a center was developing in Tarapacá,
that part of the desert north of the river Loa, at the
Peruvian port of Iquique.

Besides sending the commissioner to Chile, the Bolivian Government in 1842 ordered the Prefect of
Cobija to exert vigilance to prevent smuggling of
guano along the coast between the river Loa and Paposo "which comprise the littoral of the Republic."
Had Bolivia confined her efforts to the defense of that
coast it is probable that she would have been unmo-
lested north of Paposo, but when the question was
raised her commissioners at times claimed to parallel
26° and even to Copiapó, near parallel 27°, the old
Inca boundary. Since Chilean interests had penetrated
beyond Copiapó, and Bolivia had not claimed the desert
between Paposo and that point before, her claim was
debatable, for it laid open to question her real boundary at Paposo. And while the debate progressed the im-

* *Supra*, pp. 8, 11.

portance of the debated ground grew, especially the part near Mejillones, close to the 23° parallel.

In 1846 a Chilean war vessel landed some men on Angamos near Mejillones. Chilean writers refer to this as an act of peaceful occupation and Bolivian writers say that Chile under date of July 3 disavowed the act. A year later another vessel, the bark *Martina*, backed by the Chilean Government, landed at Mejillones to work guano. Bolivian authorities from Cobija ordered it to put to sea or comply with Bolivian regulations. The Chilean Minister reported the affair as follows: "The bark *Martina* was exploiting guano in the territory of the Republic of Chile and so those on board legally resisted the requirements placed on them by the authorities of Cobija."[6] Bolivian representatives protested again. The same year a Chilean war vessel stopped and set free some laborers who had been imprisoned by Bolivian officers and built a little fort near Mejillones, hoisting upon it the Chilean flag. Bolivia in the meantime had bought an armed brig, the *Sucre*, which in turn appeared and destroyed the fort. The fact was that this did not call forth protest from Chile and was not much commented upon. The nitrate business was as yet an infant industry in Chile and created little interest outside of Valparaiso.

For ten years now Bolivia was left in undisputed control of her littoral to Paposo, granting concessions to a polyglot mining population that was drifting into the desert, composed in a large measure of English capitalists and Chilean laborers, although Yankee ships outnumbered the rest as carriers for the business. The business must have been considerable, for England, the United States, France, and other countries maintained consuls at Cobija and Mejillones. Besides issuing licenses to shippers and otherwise exercising jurisdiction, Bolivia had an international sanction to her sovereignty at Mejillones. Early in the contest the Bolivian Consul in London brought suit against a Chilean vessel, the *Lucow*, for smuggling guano without license and received judgment from a British court.

While interests centering at Valparaiso were penetrating north into the Bolivian littoral, Peru's bird guano deposits on the islands and headlands were bringing in immense returns and affecting the internal, if not the international, politics of the country. A British officer reported seeing the following vessels loading around a single island at the same time: forty English, forty-four Yankee, five French, two Dutch, one Italian, one Belgian, one Norwegian, one Swedish, one Russian, one Armenian, and three Peruvian. These had gross capacity of 97,104 tons.[7] Between 1850 and 1872 ten million tons were shipped from one group of islands, netting twenty to thirty million dollars annually.[8]

In addition to the ancient deposits of bird guano, mention has been made of deposits of *caliche* on the mainland in the Desert of Atacama. These extend from approximately the southern boundary of Arica through the Peruvian province of Tarapacá and the Bolivian littoral of Atacama almost to the boundary of Chile at Paposo, or from latitude 19° 20′ to 25° 12′. The deposits paralleled the shore but lay back over a low coast range or series of dunes and sand hills. This interesting nonmetallic mineral is not yet fully understood, and has been found in commercial quantity only in this region unless recent discoveries in Texas and Africa prove of value. The question later arose as to whether it was a mineral or not. There has been much scientific discussion as to whether this nitrate-producing mineral comes from ancient guano deposits which once lined the waters of basins inclosed by the coast range and the Andes, from filtration from the soil of the Andean slopes above, or from the nitrification of decomposing seaweeds.[9] The rock is broken up by tremendous charges of explosives and with it and its by-products the Desert of Atacama soon surpassed in output of wealth the royal mines of Potosí towering above it in the Bolivian Andes.

It is not surprising that an industry with the promise of this should have sought secure conditions under which to develop and that Chile should have given its official protection to it. No less a country than Great Britain with many sources of revenue for its treasury and industries for its people was sorely tempted to take the guano islands of Lobos from Peru. It is an interesting moral study to read the diplomatic correspondence and see how tempting to Liverpool shippers was the new enterprise of shipping the valuable guano.[10] In 1845 a Liverpool firm wrote to Viscount Sandon for information as to whether the British flag could be hoisted over the Lobos Islands. Again in 1851 the Foreign Office was besieged with correspondence telling of the wealth on these barren islands and advancing the argument that they did not belong to Peru because they were uninhabited. The *London Times* told the story of how a Yankee whaler, Captain Morrell, had published a book in 1832 entitled *Four Voyages* and how it had aroused the interest of one T. W. Buller, an Englishman, who realized the possibilities of commercializing the guano islands described in it.[11] Buller left nothing undone to get the British Government to take possession of the islands or at least break the

Peruvian monopoly of the shipping of guano. The chairman of the Liverpool Shipowners' Association took up with the Foreign Office the question of what instructions were issued to British warships regarding the interests of British subjects in that region. He was told that the instructions to captains were to protect legal commerce, but said nothing specifically about guano. Then ensued correspondence with the Peruvian consul, who produced old Spanish maps to show that the Lobos Islands had been a part of colonial Peru and that they were not inhabited because people would frighten away the birds. Thus, while Chile and Bolivia were citing old maps and decrees to sustain claims to the Desert of Atacama, Peru was doing the same thing in London to hold its guano islands. Verily, guano was scented afar. The British Government did everything to learn if Peru had a title to the islands and, when convinced, advised its commercial interests to that effect. The moral fiber of the British Foreign Office was probably never better tested than in the fifties over the Lobos Islands' ownership, and it can be said to her credit that England refused to take advantage of the situation. She could have made out as good a case as Napoleon III did in Mexico, or Spain in the Chincha Islands.

With this great treasure under the sands of her desert littoral, Bolivia remained indifferent, apparently more interested in the struggles of her "barracks presidents" while the followers of President Búlnes in Chile, Manuel Montt and José Pérez, encouraged the development of the industry. There was a striking difference between the manner of development of the nitrate industries in Chile and Bolivia as compared with Peru. In Peru where the industry began with the shipment of

guano the Government owned most of the deposits. It
borrowed great sums of money for internal improvements and for maintaining an immense state pay roll;
it gave the lenders permission to ship a certain amount
of guano and deduct payment. This was virtually a
government monopoly and the fabulous sums received
led to great extravagance. The *caliche* or saltpeter deposits of Peru, which were found in the department
of Tarapacá, were developed by private capital and
merely yielded a duty to the Government on the amount
shipped. This latter method was followed almost completely in Chile. It was largely due to the fact that
comparatively small deposits of guano proper were
found in the part of the desert claimed by Chile.

While in Peru the concession holders largely employed foreign workmen, mostly Chinese coolies, to help
the boat crews load the guano, in Chile and Bolivia the
Chilean *rotos* did most of the work. These latter were a
hardy laboring class of native-born Indian and low-
class Chilean stock who had been used in railroad building and day labor in general. In Peru the Indian element was strictly agricultural and it was necessary even
to import *rotos* to help build railroads and public
works. The guano shippers used mostly Chinese, who
were virtually slaves and often threw themselves from
the islands into the sea rather than work in the ill-
smelling guano.

In Chile and Bolivia while most of the capital invested, especially in the saltpeter works, was British,
there were many Chilean stockholders. A stock company system of development of the saltpeter industry
in the Atacama Desert sprang up, radiating from
Valparaiso. It can readily be seen that the industry
centering at Valparaiso would interweave Chilean na-

tional interests with those of a great industry. Supplied with British capital and tutelage, a tutelage at the hands of the commercial master of the world, the enterprising Chilean people lent themselves readily to the rapid development of a lucrative industry. Peru, with much of the capital and all of the labor furnished by foreigners, received as her tribute from the great new bonanza merely gold; true, she received much gold, but it was also the root of much national evil. Wealth is more than gold, as Peru had yet to learn.

Bolivia's part in the matter was largely that of granting concessions to Valparaiso companies for some money consideration. A French traveler at this period said that in a group of twenty nitrate workers in Atacama there were seventeen Chileans, one Englishman, one Peruvian, and a Bolivian colonel.[12] He said that the Englishman managed, the Chileans did the manual labor, and the colonel did the governing. He failed to say what the Peruvian did, but he was usually a laborer or trader.

By the middle of the century nitrate and copper mining, coupled with the guano shipping, had given to the desert coast considerable international importance. Besides maintaining consuls at the ports, some nations, especially England and the United States, kept several warships in the Pacific. An additional observer of the coast was Lieut. J. M. Gilliss, who conducted a naval astronomical expedition to South America during the years 1847–52. He made a map of the guano coast which is here reproduced, and in his reports makes the following statement about the boundary between Chile and Peru at that time:

Elsewhere it has been said that Chile claims to the 24th

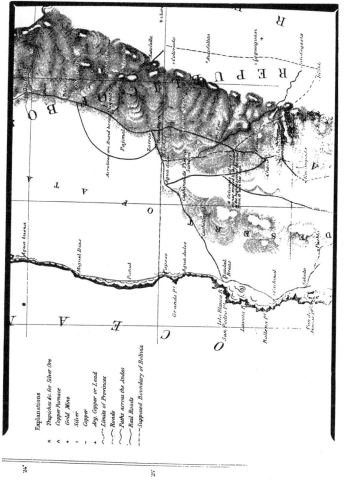

MAP OF BOLIVIA-CHILEAN COAST BY LIEUTENANT GILLISS, 1847

parallel of latitude. In the instructions from Captain Fitzroy, R.N., to one of his officers about to leave on detached duty, he says: "Remember that Paposo is the northernmost inhabited place over which the government of Chile has authority;" and by the observations of that officer Paposo was found to be in latitude 25° 2′ 30″. Native writers of geography, speaking of the boundaries, say, "On the north by the desert of Atacama,"—a broad tract several degrees in width so that where Bolivia begins and Chile terminates is yet to be decided. I have copied a boundary line, as far as it is laid down, from a MS. map in my possession, compiled from data furnished by Don Bartolomé Navarete.[13]

An additional and final reference will be given now to show that the legal boundary of Chile as late as 1850 was known academically to be at Paposo. W. F. Ballaert made the following statement to a geographical society in London in an address which he read on a survey of southern Peru and the land route to Chile:

. . . I came to *Hueso Parado*, which is the old acknowledged boundary between Peru and Chile: but since guano has been exported from the coast, the Chileans appear to think that the boundary of their country is farther north than Paposo. The frontier line is at 25° 23′ S., which, about 1½ miles from the shore, is marked by a whale's jaw placed upright in the sand, and it is the general opinion that it had been placed there by the old Spanish boundary commissioners. Herrera places the boundary in 26° S.[14]

The Spanish words *Hueso Parado* mean standing bone. It will be recalled that Colonel O'Connor, at the time of the founding of Bolivia, reported that its coast extended to *Hueso Parado*.*

After the Búlnes message and proclamation claiming 23° as the northern limits, until 1857 Chile had not maintained the claim by official acts of possession. She carried on a desultory diplomatic debate with Bolivia when the latter pressed the question. She had even remained passive when Chilean guano operators and captains of frigates occasionally came into conflict with local Bolivian authorities from Cobija and Mejillones. However, in 1857, while the factions of José M. Linares and Jorge Córdoba were fighting in Bolivia, Chile landed some soldiers from her recently acquired steam corvette *Esmeralda,* took possession of Mejillones and ordered operators to quit work or get Chilean licenses. The Bolivian factions ceased fighting and sent an agent to Chile who demanded the disoccupation of Mejillones as a *sine qua non* of discussions, which Chile refused. A second agent offered to divide the disputed territory. Thus far the matter in Chile had not occupied the Government at Santiago very seriously, being largely of interest to shippers of Valparaiso, but in 1863 the President's message included the following remarks:

I have hopes of the renewal, within a short time, of the negotiations formerly initiated for the arrangement of a Treaty of Limits with the neighbouring Republic of Bolivia. That Government has lately accredited a Diplomatic Agent for the purpose, to whom it has been made known that we are ready to commence the discussion.

The importance which that part of our territory has lately acquired will not influence the Government or the

* See *supra*, p. 14.

people of Chile to swerve from the rules of justice which
have always governed us in international questions, and
which must also guide us in the decision of that pending
with Bolivia.

Although the recent protests of the Bolivian Government are not consonant with the friendly and fraternal
sentiments which it professes, I trust that a calm examination of the titles adduced by both parties may lead to a
solution that shall put an end to the present dispute.[15]

The matter dragged, with Bolivia nominally in possession of most of the territory. Chile retained Mejillones until 1863, when the Bolivian Congress gave its
president discretionary powers to declare war. The
crisis of 1863 was acute. Peru offered to mediate, but
the Chilean Chancellor refused, saying that the situation was "entirely exceptional." The following year the
United States offered mediation, which was refused and
war seemed imminent, but a new international complication averted it. The danger of Spanish revindication
caused the republics to patch up their quarrel and
unite with Ecuador and Peru in the American Union in
a short but victorious war against Spain.

The war with Spain corresponded in a way to our
second war with Great Britain. Spain had delayed
recognizing the independence of Peru and there were
troublesome property and damage claims. In 1863 relations were strained by a clash between Spaniards and
Peruvians on a *hacienda*, or ranch, at Talambo. Shortly
afterward a Spanish fleet under Admiral Pinzón, which
had been designated in Spain as a "Scientific Expedition," anchored at Callao, Peru, where an envoy, Sala-
zar y Mazarredo, disembarked and tried to arrange an
adjustment with Peru. Terms were not agreed upon

and the Spanish fleet seized the Chincha Islands, the
center of Peru's guano industry. The following January (1865) a preliminary treaty was signed with President Pezet of Peru by which Peruvian independence
was to be recognized and Peru was to pay heavy claims
and expenses of occupation. The Spanish occupation of
the Chinchas alarmed Chile, Bolivia, and Ecuador, and
Pinzón's fleet was soon engaged in a quarrel with Valparaiso which resulted in an ultimatum from the Spanish admiral. The Peruvian people declared Pezet's
terms humiliating and they, headed by Colonel Prado,
rose up against his administration. They secured the
forming of the American Union, repudiated the agreement with Spain, and together with the allies declared
war on Spain in January, 1866.[16] Valparaiso and
Callao were bombarded by the Spanish fleet. The former was unfortified and suffered $12,000,000 damages
but the latter heroically repulsed the attack; a small
naval combat took place along the coast of Chile and
the United States finally offered mediation which resulted in an armistice in 1871. Later the three countries
signed treaties separately with Spain. This war deferred the Chile-Bolivia question temporarily and
greatly affected affairs in the three republics because a
veritable "entangling alliance" was formed between
Chile and Bolivia.

We have seen the effect of nitrates upon nations from
1842 to 1866.[17] Chile had decreed her boundary to
parallel 23° and was occupying Mejillones at the time
of the American Union in 1866, when she made the first
treaty with Bolivia in connection with the nitrate coast
of Atacama.

REFERENCES

1. J. J. von Tschudi, *Travels in Peru,* I, 168 n.; R. E. Coker, *National Geographic Magazine,* June, 1920.
2. *Senate Documents,* Forty-seventh Congress, first session, Docs. 71–88, p. 665.
3. F. B. D'Avricourt, *Les chemins de fer du Pérou,* p. 166.
4. *El Comercio* (Lima), October 2, 1841.
5. D. S. Bustamonte, *Bolivia su estructura y sus derechos en el Pacífico,* p. 116.
6. Gonzalo Búlnes, *Guerra del Pacífico,* I, 15.
7. *British State Papers* (1854), XLV, 1249.
8. *National Geographic Magazine,* XXXVII, 543.
9. Geo. P. Merrill, *The Non-Metallic Minerals,* p. 319.
10. *British State Papers,* XLV, 1246.
11. *London Times,* April 17, 1852.
12. Diego Barros Arana, *Histoire de la guerre du Pacifique,* I, 38.
13. Lieut. J. M. Gilliss, *U. S. Naval Astronomical Expedition,* I, 44.
14. W. F. Ballaert, "Observations on the Geography of Southern Peru," *The Journal of the Royal Geographical Society,* XXI (1851), 127.
15. *British State Papers,* LIV, 991.
16. Teresa G. de Fanning, *Historia del Peru,* p. 131.
17. Chas. A. McQueen, *Peruvian Public Finance,* pp. 5, 6 (Department of Commerce Trade Promotion Series, No. 30).

CHAPTER III

CHILE-BOLIVIAN ENTANGLING ALLIANCES

BESIDES temporarily halting the Chile-Bolivian crisis the second war with Spain had other important results. Of course it ended the idea of Spanish revindication and Peru was definitely recognized. The importance of sea power and coast protection was now apparent to statesmen of Peru and Chile. Peru, who was involved first, ordered built in England two ships embodying improvements made in naval construction in the United States' Civil War. They were iron ships and one, the *Huascar*, had a turret similar to that of the *Monitor*. The President of Chile also ordered two smaller ships and made plans for fortifying Valparaiso. Bolivia was a little late in getting into the armament game and thereby lost her nitrate desert.

In the mutual danger, and inspired by a common cause, there was much talk of Spanish-American fraternity by the members of the American Union. The city of Valparaiso, bombarded by the Spanish fleet, rejoiced so over the repulse of the fleet by the fortress of Callao that it voted a gold sword to President Prado who had led the Peruvian resistance. President Melgarejo of Bolivia was especially friendly to these felicitations and fraternizations. He was the worst of Bolivia's "barracks presidents," and is generally execrated even by Bolivian histories. With the mutual congratulations on the victory over Spain, Melgarejo received high honors from Chile, including an honorary degree from the University.[1] It is difficult to understand how this happened, for at that time the University of Chile was in the flower of its culture under the leadership of the illustrious Andrés Bello, and included on its faculty eminent scholars of South America and Europe. Nevertheless, the degree of *Vocal honoris causi* was conceded to this man who according to reliable historians killed with his own hands an opposing candidate.[2] He was also made honorary brigadier general in the Chilean army.

Bolivia was in the darkest period of its history. From the fall of Santa Cruz that country had a series of tragi-comedy governments under Belzu, Velasco, Melgarejo, and Daza with a few bright spots in Linares and Ballivián. From 1825 to 1898, the beginning of modern Bolivia, there were some sixty revolutions and six presidents were assassinated. Melgarejo was the climax of these tyrants, with Daza a close second—the two presidents who figure largely in the nitrate entanglements with Chile.

It is doubtful whether he had much to do with the drafting of the treaty which was soon made with Chile, known as the mutual benefits arrangement, but of course it would have been impossible to have made it unless he had been willing. There were seven main provisions to this treaty.[3] Parallel 24° was adopted as the international boundary of the territory, which should be permanently marked by experts to the eastern limits of Chile. Chile and Bolivia would share equally all customs duties on guano and minerals in the region between parallels 23° and 25°. Bolivia would instal a customhouse at Mejillones which would be the only one to receive duties on guano and metals in the zone mentioned. Chile would have the privilege of naming accountants to inspect this customhouse. All other ex-

ports from the zone would be duty free, as also would
be the natural products of Chile imported into Mejillones. The two governments would form the same sys-
tems of licensing and selling guano in their part of the
zone. Chile and Bolivia agreed to give preference to
each other in the case of sale of material in the zone.
The owners of Bolivian licenses whose work had been
interrupted by Chile when she occupied Mejillones
were to be paid from a fund of eighty thousand pesos
to be derived from 10 per cent of the duties of the
Mejillones customhouse.*

As can be seen this treaty divided the sovereignty of
the Desert of Atacama at parallel 24°; i.e., it established that as the nominal boundary, but by the joint
benefits clause it entangled the sovereign rights of each
country's part of the desert with provisions for rights
of control which ordinarily belong to sovereignty.
When this later led to trouble Bolivian writers complained that the treaty was not equitable and had been
secured unfairly. There is an important and apparently reliable account of how the Treaty of 1866 was
made which will be quoted here for two reasons. Bolivian writers have generally blamed President Melgarejo for the treaty and this account sheds light on
that point. In the second place the account shows that
at this early stage of the Tacna-Arica question, it was
recognized that Arica was the logical port for Bolivia,
and Bolivia was urged to take it from Peru. This
Arica-for-Bolivia doctrine runs from this point all
through the Tacna-Arica history. Recently, when the
Coolidge plebiscite attempts failed, and it was proposed
that Arica be sold to Bolivia, it was asserted in the

* Text of Treaty, Appendix II.

Chilean press that Secretary Kellogg originated the proposition and he was sharply criticized for it. The following account by Mariano D. Muñoz, former Secretary of State of Bolivia, plainly shows where the Arica-for-Bolivia doctrine entered the Tacna-Arica question:

It was in the course of these conferences that I heard the Chilean Plenipotentiary make the propositions to which you refer in the letter to which I now answer, and to the effect that "Bolivia should agree to renounce all her rights to the disputed zone, from 25° south latitude to the River Loa, or at least to and including Mejillones, with the precise promise that Chile would aid Bolivia, in the most efficacious manner, to acquire by armed occupation the Peruvian littoral as far as the Morro de Sama [this includes Tacna-Arica], as compensation for the cession of the Bolivian littoral to Chile; the reason adduced being that the only natural outlet of Bolivia to the Pacific was through the port of Arica."

This proposition was repeatedly made by Señor Vergara Albano, I may say, from the first to the last conference which we held, and he did not fail to reiterate it to President Melgarejo, whose warlike spirit and tendencies he tried to flatter, insinuating the idea of his carrying out a glorious campaign which his predecessors had not been able to undertake. [This reference is to the previously mentioned attempts to secure Arica as an outlet for Bolivia.] With tenacious perseverance Señor Vergara Albano was seconded in his efforts by his secretary, Señor Carlos Walker Martinez, who had gained the intimate sympathy of Melgarejo, and from whom he obtained the brevet of major in the Bolivian army, offering himself as his aid-de-camp in the future campaign against Peru, to which they were both urging him. In the files of the army register of that date the entry of this commission is undoubtedly to be found.

The loyal and firm refusal with which both Melgarejo and myself met these insinuations did not suffice to make the Chilean Government desist . . . because, when I was at Santiago on a special mission, a few days before the final termination of the boundary treaty, which was signed at that city on the 10th of August, 1866, between the Plenipotentiaries, Alvaro Covarrubias on the part of Chile, and J. M. Muñoz Cavrera on the part of Bolivia, Señor Covarrubias strenuously insisted upon the demarcation and exchange of littorals which Señor Vergara Albano had proposed to me; and it was not solely Covarrubias, the Minister of Foreign Affairs of Chile, who insinuated the same idea to Muñoz Cavrera and myself, but also many other notable persons of that city, who, although using other arguments, strove to persuade us that Chile was advocating in favor of Bolivia, and that she only had in view the equilibrium of the nations of the Pacific and the desire of rectifying the boundaries of the three countries in the most natural manner.

Vergara Albano, Covarrubias and Walker Martinez, and many others to whom I refer are still living; let them give me the lie if they refuse to lend their homage to the truth of this statement.[4]

Melgarejo either had queer notions of nationality or else little faith in the loyalty of his own soldiers, for the Chilean Minister at La Paz wrote to the President of Chile in 1866 that the Bolivian President wanted a garrison of fifty Chilean soldiers sent to Cobija to be under the orders of the prefect of the department. President Pérez of Chile took to the idea readily and offered at once to send the men. Melgarejo decided he wanted one hundred instead of fifty and they were about to be sent when the Bolivian Minister in Santiago held up the procedure on the ground that the barracks at Cobija were not ready.

The Treaty of 1866 was not long in force before questions arose over the carrying out of its terms and by 1872 a revision was necessary. Before taking up this revision, known as the Lindsay-Corral Agreement, attention should be turned to the development of the nitrate business.

In 1866 two Chilean *cateadores* or frontiersmen discovered nitrate deposits at Carmen Alto. These men, Ossa and Puelma, came to the coast and marked the cliffs, so that they were picked up by Chilean ships and taken to Santiago.[5] A concession was secured through the same officials that Bolivia had sent to Chile to make the Treaty of 1866. The place where they marked the cliff came to be Antofagasta and their company was the beginning of the great *Compañía de Salitres de Antofagasta* or The Antofagasta Nitrate Company, which later was the cause of war. It became a monopoly, or rather a consolidation of Ossa y Puelma, *Compañía Explotadora del Desierto de Atacama*, and Melbourne, Clark & Company.[6] In addition the company expected to engage in agriculture, and its concession included besides five square leagues of nitrate lands, four of agricultural lands.

The work of the nitrate company went on very rapidly and the ingress of Chilean laborers and the consequent activity began to arouse alarm in Bolivia. Chilean interests at Mejillones where the first clash had occurred in 1857 were steadily growing as were those at other lesser centers. In 1871 Chile ordered built in

England two new cruisers, which fact did not tend to calm Bolivia's fears.

By 1872 this alarm had increased and the United States Minister in La Paz, L. Markbreit, made the following observations:

Since the conclusion of this treaty [Treaty of 1866] it has been found that the guano deposits at Mejillones are of considerable value, and about two years ago the wonderfully rich silver mines of Caracoles were discovered by a Chilean, Diaz Gana. It is now feared by the Bolivian government that Chile may attempt to possess herself of these mines, as well as of the guano deposits of Mejillones, availing herself of the first opportunity, with that purpose, which may offer. It is claimed that Chile is greedily awaiting for some excuse however trivial, to take this course. Mejillones is situated between the twenty-third and twenty-fourth parallel of latitude. I have had several unofficial conversations with the President and minister of foreign affairs upon this subject, and have found that their only hope seems to be, should such an emergency arise, to secure the intervention of the United States. Of course I have been careful not to commit in the slightest manner our government nor myself.

The guano-deposits at Mejillones are variously estimated at between four and ten million tons, while the mines of Caracoles, situated about one hundred and twenty miles from the bay of Mejillones are said to contain immense riches. The capital invested in the latter place, chiefly by Chilians, amounts at the present time to about $14,000,000. The population consists of about five thousand souls; while two years ago all that region did not contain a solitary inhabitant. A commission is now in session in this city [La Paz], which has before it twenty-eight propositions made to the Bolivian government for the construction of a railway from the coast to the mines. Most of the propositions ask no guarantee from the government, but seek simply to obtain the right to construct the road.

This morning a battalion of infantry left this city for Caracoles, with the avowed purpose of maintaining order among the miners, but the real object evidently is to be, at least in some measure, prepared to meet any hostile movement on the part of Chile.

Whether the alarm felt by the Bolivian people relative to what they believe to be the attitude of that republic is well founded, the near future will show.[7]

Other deposits had been discovered in 1870 and the discoverers wished to work them, but Melbourne, Clark & Company, by their contract, had exclusive privileges. President Melgarejo of Bolivia was overthrown at this time and most of his contracts declared null and void. The discovery of the great silver mines near Caracoles raised a question about the dividing line, which by the terms of the Treaty of 1866 was the twenty-fourth parallel, "from the Pacific coast to the eastern boundaries of Chile." This did not state explicitly that the boundary was to coincide with the parallel; it was to begin on the parallel at least. Bolivia claimed that Caracoles was north of the twenty-third parallel and not within the joint-benefits zone, while Chile said the dividing line ran north of the silver-mining center. The question also arose as to whether the by-products of nitrates such as borax, iodine, and sulphur were minerals or metals and came under the joint-benefits provision. From these developments since 1866 it can be seen that a revision of the treaty was necessary.

There were several distinct movements between 1866 and 1879, the date when war came, all intermingled and difficult to separate or analyze. All were caused by the great industry, nitrate, and the consequent expansion of Chile, the country that offered the best opportunity to investors and promoters. While most of Bolivia did not see beyond the Andes, some of her statesmen like Bustillo and Ballivián saw the trend of things and tried to control the situation for the good of the nation. They advocated firm action and military preparedness. Parallel to this group was a Peruvian group who looked with apprehension at Chilean nitrate expansion, both as competition to the Peruvian guano industry and as national rivalry. From 1873 to 1879 these two groups were influenced by each other and a Bolivia-Peru-Argentine alliance was agitated.

The events of 1871–72 and 1873 are also difficult to chronicle with respect to their sequence and bearing upon each other. Friction in the dual administration of the nitrate customs increased. Bolivians soon claimed that the Treaty of 1866 was leonine, impossible, and was illegal because Melgarejo was a self-appointed dictator. Chileans said that the treaty was a liberal concession on her part, a free gift of half the benefits from parallel 23° to 25° when she might have had them all. Búlnes, often quoted in this work as the leading Chilean historian, says the treaty was "conditional."

Melgarejo was overthrown in November, 1870. In the chaos in Bolivia there arose a problem of *émigrés*, which greatly affected the dispute. When Melgarejo was overthrown Col. Agustín Morales became president and Rafael Bustillo, who had been minister of state in the administration before Melgarejo's and was expatriated by that chief, was now named, 1871, envoy to

Chile, where he had spent his banishment. During his ministry in 1863 Bolivia had protested the seizure by Chile of guano boats with Bolivian licenses, and during his banishment later in Chile he had observed with jealous eye the power of the nitrate industry, so that he was not a calm and tactful envoy to be sent to Chile in time of trouble such as was brewing in 1871.

That year two Bolivian *émigrés* of Melgarejo's *régime*, now in turn exiled, General Quevedo and former Minister Muñoz, fitted out in Valparaiso an expedition to seize the nitrate littoral of Bolivia, ostensibly in the name of a new Bolivian government which they were to head. They let, in advance, nitrate concessions, and shares in a stock company were sold publicly in Valparaiso and Santiago. Bustillo was at the time trying to secure the revision of the joint-benefits treaty which he saw was involving the sovereignty of his country. He reported that President Errázuriz belonged to the group in Chile who respected the rights of Bolivia, but that other influential men in the Government were bent on expansion at any price. Bustillo was obsessed with the idea of protecting the rights of his country and settling definitely the boundary trouble with Chile before that country penetrated all of the desert. General Quevedo armed a few men, and, evading the Valparaiso authorities who had been requested to stop him, got his men embarked on a boat, the *Maria Louisa*, under the flag of Guatemala. A few days later Quevedo and Muñoz got away on another bark, the *Paquete de los Vilos*.[8] The port authorities had inspected the vessel and had reported to the Peruvian consul, who was also acting Bolivian consul in Valparaiso, that they had found nothing belligerent on the boat, but would detain it if the consul so requested. The consul would not take the responsibility and the boat sailed. Up the coast Quevedo went through the maneuver of overpowering the officers and then landed at Antofagasta, where no resistance was offered to him.

Bustillo protested, denounced it all as a frame-up and alleged that all responsibility for the filibusters would be laid to the Government of Chile. His note was so bitter and insinuating that he was asked to explain. He returned the communication unanswered, whereupon he was given his passports and the Bolivian Government was notified that he was *persona non grata*. A company of soldiers from the Bolivian garrison at Mejillones came down to Antofagasta, whereupon Quevedo took to his boat and went up to Tocopilla. He went to land with his small band and was received by a volley of shots. Taking to the sea again, he had some trouble in getting away and was taken on board the Chilean warship *Esmeralda* and held on the ground of breaking neutrality.

Chilean writers admit the foregoing account of the Quevedo affair in so far as what took place is concerned, but deny that the Chilean Government approved or sponsored the expedition. Bolivian writers assert the contrary, and even quote Muñoz as later publishing an account of the expedition, in which he said that its failure was due to the fact that Chile had placed as a condition of its aid the cession of a part of the Bolivian littoral, in exchange for which Chile was to aid Bolivia in acquiring Iquique and Arica.[9] Be that as it may, the Quevedo-Muñoz affair added fuel to the strained relations between Bolivia and Chile and did more than anything else to call the attention of Peru and Argentina to the expansion of Chile.

The Government of Peru became especially apprehensive and made a naval demonstration off the Bay of Mejillones. A note was sent saying that "Peru would not look with indifference upon the occupation of Bolivian territory by foreign forces." This and the Argentine reaction will be considered later in connection with the "secret treaty of 1873."

The next official action between Chile and Bolivia was an attempt at modifying the Treaty of 1866 known as the Lindsay-Corral Agreement, which was made in 1872.[10] The new proposal was fundamentally as bad as the one of 1866, for it maintained the joint-benefits arrangement. However, it smoothed out some of the sore places and served as a *modus vivendi*. The accounting system was adjusted; borax, sulphates, and other by-products were defined as "minerals"; and the conflicting clause about Mejillones being the only customhouse was corrected. It was approved by Chile, but the Bolivian assembly of May, 1873, postponed action on it until the next session.

When Melgarejo was overthrown in Bolivia and civil government restored, his contracts were annulled, so Melbourne, Clark & Company made a new contract under the name of *Compañía de Salitres y Ferrocarril de Antofagasta*. The same assembly, October, 1872, also asked for a defensive alliance with Peru as a result of the Quevedo-Muñoz affair. The new contract with the Antofagasta company had one clause, Article IV, which provided that there would be no further taxes or duties on its products for a period of fifteen years from the date January 1, 1874. The breaking of this agreement with the company later was the occasion of the Chilean military occupation of Antofagasta, and of war.

In 1873 Adolfo Ballivián, son of General Ballivián

of Ingavi fame, became President of Bolivia and events led up to an alliance with Peru which had been requested by the assembly of 1872. Ballivián had during Melgarejo's *régime* been banished to Tacna and Valparaiso, where he married a Chilean woman. The new administration in Bolivia sent him to London on a financial mission, from where in 1872 he wrote a letter which showed his appreciation of the international situation of Bolivia and his reasons for trying to secure warships. He said:

I am convinced of the urgency of this necessity by the reflection that to the end of the world, right will never be anything without the aid of might [*fuerza*]. In all international disputes it is always the case that, having a mine, makes it necessary to protect and work it if it is to be of any advantage. The nation to whom there is opened by chance at the edge of the sea the wide door of an incalculable amount of riches and future fortune, should either close it or guard it well against the envy and rapacity of violence. He who cares for coasts, ports, and railways should not neglect the responsibilities which they entail.[11]

On his return to Bolivia when called to the presidency, Ballivián stopped in Lima and interviewed President Pardo and doubtless the question of an alliance was taken up there, and the so-called "secret treaty of 1873" with Peru was the result.

While the Lindsay-Corral Agreement might serve as a makeshift, leading men in Bolivia, Chile, and Peru saw that a conflict over the wealth of the desert was probable. In Chile, President Errázuriz ordered two warships of the armored-cruiser type built in England. Bolivian and Peruvian writers say that was a part of the Chilean nitrate politics of forcible expansion. Chilean writers attribute it to a measure of national precaution suggested by Argentine boundary trouble, by the Peruvian naval demonstration at Mejillones the previous year, and by the belief that Peruvian intervention might be expected in Chilean affairs. Bolivia, as stated, sought an alliance with Peru. Chilean writers ascribe the act of the Bolivian assembly asking for such an alliance to a burst of friendly feeling over the Peruvian naval gesture at Mejillones. It will be remembered that Peru, owing to her victory of May 2, 1865, over the Spanish fleet that attacked Callao, and to the new ships which she ordered during the war with Spain, now had naval preponderance in the Pacific.

A vicious circle was started. Bolivia feared Chilean expansion at Antofagasta, Mejillones, and Caracoles. Peru, and especially her minister, Riva Agüero, feared that the failure of Bolivia to stop that expansion would result in Chilean preponderance, and Chile feared Peruvian interference with her expansion into the desert. The situation was intensified by the diplomatic maneuvers of Chile and Peru. Nothing is long secret in diplomacy. Peruvian statesmen soon knew about it when Chile proposed to Bolivia the cession of the Desert of Atacama for aid in securing Arica as the latter's natural port. Chile quickly knew what was transpiring when Bolivia asked for an alliance with Peru and knew when the latter tried to include Argentina in the alliance. It was somewhat like the military time-table that threw Europe into war in 1914, only it was slower in getting under way. If the statesmen of Bolivia, Peru, and Chile had frankly called a conference, seeing there was a dangerous situation, and met it in an open way, trouble could have been avoided. But arbitration commissions

were not yet popular. Chile had an advantage in having
continuity of government during this period. She had
three presidents who ruled ten years each, while Bolivia
and Peru had frequent changes. The civil administration of Ballivián in Bolivia has been mentioned as starting in 1873, but Ballivián died the following year and
an old councilor of state, Tomás Frías, who was beset
by militarists, was elected by the assembly. Before elections could be held a general of the Melgarejo type,
Hilarión Daza, proclaimed himself dictator.

Bolivia was now in a sad plight. The civilist movement was crushed and the administration failed to
grasp the complex state of affairs in the coast province
of Atacama. The assembly had sought an alliance with
Peru and that country was trying to form a triple
alliance, with Argentina included, to guarantee the
neutrality of each country against invasion. Bolivia
was between two fires. On the one hand Peru was urging that she demand a revision of the mutual benefits
arrangement that was compromising her sovereignty in
Atacama, and on the other side representatives of Chile
were urging a strict compliance with all its provisions.
Bolivia failed to secure a revision which would clearly
demark the sovereignty of each country and was
obliged to continue the entangling arrangement until
it led to war.

The question of causes of war is always a momentous
one and is usually intricate. In South America volumes
have been written about the causes of the War of the
Pacific; French, Italian, and British writers have written their histories of the war with more or less partiality. The query might well arise as to why the War
of the Pacific should be delved into in considering the
Tacna-Arica question of today. Would it not be suffi-

cient to begin with the peace treaty which provided the
plebiscite clause for Tacna-Arica? That is precisely
what President Coolidge attempted to do in arbitrating
the case and it was the principal cause of the failure of
the plebiscite feature of the award. It would be just as
easy to understand the difficulty of Reconstruction in
Georgia without taking into account the slavery question, Sherman's march to the sea, as well as the hated
"carpetbag" rule before the reconstruction work could
really begin, as to understand the Tacna-Arica question without following the War of the Pacific, out of
which the question grew.

From the foregoing some erroneous conclusions
might be drawn regarding economics and nationalism
in the abstract. The experiences of Chile, Bolivia, and
Peru with the nitrate struggle might lead to an obvious,
but not necessarily correct, conclusion that the War of
the Pacific could be chalked up against political nationalism. Especially is there a tendency at the present
time to see nothing but the evils that occur, which may
be chargeable to governments or groups inspired by
national consciousness, particularly where economic
factors have a part. In view of this tendency attention
should be called to some other considerations in connection with this great nitrates struggle, because the true
historical development of actual movements is the first
duty of the chronicler.

In the first place, the presence of so much wealth in
the unsettled and unpoliced Desert of Atacama demanded for its proper development a strong social control. Historically it was the lack of strong national
solidarity that permitted the forays of *émigrés* and
revolutionists. The fitting out of the Freire expedition
(mentioned on page 18) cannot be charged to Peru,

nor even to the action of its rulers. Neither Santa Cruz nor Orbegosa, the two men most responsible for national acts of Peru, were in Lima when the expedition sailed and Freire advised Orbegosa of his sailing only on the date of his departure when it would have been too late to stop him. It was rather lack of national consciousness than anything else that allowed the public sale of stocks in Valparaiso in the filibustering Muñoz-Quevedo expedition to the nitrate fields of Atacama. In fact Chile was the only one of the three nations involved which had any great degree of national hegemony, and the only one that had any expression at all of that which would register through a representative body to the extent of causing or hindering national aggression. Economically there was no national policy at this time and it was the unnational nature of nitrate exploitation that is striking in the case of the War of the Pacific, the many contributing causes of which will be taken up in the next chapter.

REFERENCES

1. D. S. Bustamonte, *Bolivia, su estructura y sus derechos en el Pacífico,* p. 130.
2. W. S. Robertson, *History of the Latin-American Nations,* p. 322.
3. Prescott, *El problema continental,* pp. 258–264. For an English version in abridged form see Appendix, p. 291.
4. V. M. Maurtua, *The Question of the Pacific,* pp. 20–22.
5. Gonzalo Búlnes, *Guerra del Pacífico,* I, 43.
6. *Ibid.,* p. 47.
7. *U. S. Foreign Relations for 1872,* p. 64.
8. Búlnes, *op. cit.,* I, 32.
9. Bustamonte, *op. cit.,* p. 136.
10. Prescott, *op. cit.,* pp. 266–270. Also abridged English text in William Jefferson Dennis, *Documentary History of the Tacna-Arica Dispute,* p. 53 ("University of Iowa Studies in the Social Sciences").
11. Alberto Gutiérrez, *La guerra de 1879,* p. 53.

CHAPTER IV

WHO STARTED THE WAR OF THE PACIFIC?

ONE of the strange things about wars is that after they are over and the damage done people begin to wonder seriously how they happened. Partisan nationalists, of course, accept none of the blame for their own countries, nor attribute it to other causes than a Machiavellian policy of the government of the late enemy. Historians are then inclined after a war to lean too far the other way and find out within a few years after peace is declared that the *populacho*, from its lack of correct information and its susceptibility to mob psychology, was needlessly carried away by an incompetent administration and that the enemy was withal very much in the right. In the case of the War of the Pacific there were individual leaders as eager to precipitate Chile into a war of expansion as were some of the leaders of western expansion in the United States. There were also men high in office, financially interested in Chilean expansion, there were war-mad mobs, and there were pacifists. It is doubtful, however, if there was ever another struggle where more factors so conspired to bring about war, where conditions were so conducive to the test of Mars.

A Chilean historian writing a year after the outbreak of hostilities declared that the conflict had been inevitable from the beginning of Chilean mining activities in the Desert of Atacama. He said:

From the time the creeping rails and the exploitation of nitrate beds attracted to that republic like a human ava-

lanche an active, vigorous and intelligent race which was
to be confronted with another, indolent, luxurious and demoralized by the climate and idleness—from the moment
mines were found at Antofagasta and Caracoles war was
inevitable.[1]

The average Chilean will tell you that the war was
caused by the "secret treaty," which they attribute to
Peruvian initiative and jealousy of Chile. On account
of this it will be necessary to examine the antecedents
of this famous treaty. Peru's interest in Chile's pene-
tration into the Bolivian littoral dates from the Quevedo-Muñoz affair, and she was in a receptive mood
when the Bolivian assembly in 1872 asked for a defensive alliance. The proposal was favorably received
by President Manuel Pardo and the cabinet, November
17, 1872, and by February 6, 1873, a treaty was
signed.

These events were taking place while the Lindsay-
Corral Protocol was being prepared, and it was signed
in December, 1872, and approved by Chile in January,
1873. Peru's minister in Bolivia, Riva Agüero, urged
Bolivia not to approve the protocol, which in no way
settled the dual sovereignty question, and to demand an
immediate revision of the Treaty of 1866. The "secret
treaty" contained a kind of compulsory arbitration
clause, and Riva Agüero, who became Peruvian Minister of Foreign Affairs, evidently hoped to break up the
dual arrangement in Atacama before Chile's two new
ships should be completed. Then he believed it would be
too late for the allies to force an arbitration upon Chile.
Ballivián had returned from Europe in March and had
become the President of Bolivia where he lent his influence to bring about a revision of the Treaty of 1866.

The efforts of these two men would have been even greater had they known that during 1873 President Errázuriz of Chile was cabling to England for speed in finishing the two warships. The Bolivian assembly refused to ratify the Lindsay-Corral Protocol. A new minister from Chile, Walker Martínez, sought to make another one, always keeping the entangling mutual benefits arrangement as a main feature of the treaty, and he was not aware of the Bolivia-Peru alliance. This Treaty of 1873 is not novel, Bolivia and Ecuador having had a very similar one in 1842, but the fact that it was secret was used extensively for war propaganda in 1879.[2] In 1864 the Chilean Minister to Ecuador had tried to secure a treaty of alliance against Peru which was not completed owing to the success in forming the American Union.[3]

In 1872, that climactic year in the Tacna-Arica question, Chile sent a commissioner to Buenos Aires with a note asserting her claim to the disputed Patagonia region as far as the Río Santa Cruz. Argentina was facing a possible conflict with Brazil and the Peruvian chancellor, Riva Agüero, took occasion to resort to that European diplomacy known as the balance of power. He purposed to get Argentina to join with Bolivia and Peru in a triple defensive alliance. On May 20, 1873, he wrote the Peruvian Minister in Buenos Aires, Manuel Irigoyen, the following instructions:

You are doubtless aware that for some time back grave questions have arisen between Chile, on the one hand, and the Argentine Confederacy and Bolivia on the other, relative to the delimitation of boundaries between the former and the latter republics.

Bolivia, which, unaided, would not have the necessary

strength to resist the pressure which Chile might bring to bear upon her, and alive to the convenience of strengthening the bonds which bind her to us, solicited through the intermediary of her Plenipotentiary, and in agreement with a Legislative Resolution, copy of which I enclose, the moral and effective support which were necessary to enable her to discuss and uphold her rights, dispassionately and in complete security. The Government of Peru could not remain indifferent to the legitimate appeal of her neighbor and signed with her the Defensive Treaty of Alliance, copy of which is enclosed, and which, already approved by the National Congress, will very shortly be submitted to the Bolivian Assembly and exchanged by both Governments.

An examination of this Agreement will bring the conviction that it has been prudently drawn up so as to prevent any cause for disagreements thus avoiding every excuse for war. Arbitration is therein stipulated as the sole just and reasonable means which must be adopted for deciding boundary disputes.

As it has been agreed, according to Article 9 of the Treaty, to solicit the adherence of other Governments, you will endeavor to secure that of the Argentine Republic, which, at this present time, would not seem arduous in view of the difficulties which have been encountered until now and which have stood in the way of and prevented a decision on her boundary line with Chile.

It is as much in the interest of the Argentine Republic as to Bolivia's, and indeed of that of all American countries whose boundaries have not yet been defined, to become members of the Defensive Alliance; especially at this moment when the Patagonia boundary question threatens to enter upon an aggressive phase, which we must all endeavor to prevent, confining it to that of discussion and of arbitration.

This is, therefore, the principal purpose of your Mission, and to which you will devote your best endeavor. With the strengthening of the Alliance, by the entry of other Republics, wars for territorial expansion will become impossible in America, because the exaggerated ambitions of any one of these Republics would have to be restrained when confronted by the firm and unyielding attitude of the Allies.[4]

The proposition of Riva Agüero for a triple alliance was at first well received in Argentina. President Domingo Sarmiento recommended it to his Congress which passed it except for a financial provision to make it effective. Then it was delayed by the ministry in a long correspondence over details of *casus foederis*, application to Brazilian frontiers, and similar matters. In the meantime Riva Agüero was urging Bolivia to break definitely the entangling mutual benefits arrangement and the Chilean Minister, Walker Martínez, was insisting on a new agreement for the nitrate interests, embodying the joint administration of the littoral. Riva Agüero said in his instructions to his envoy in La Paz that he wished only that an unambiguous definite settlement be reached before Chile's two new warships should be finished.

By January, 1874, Chile had learned of the "secret treaty" and then played a cautious hand. President Errázuriz cabled for night shifts and shortened the time in which one of the ships of war was to be delivered.[5] Walker Martínez and the Chilean Minister in Buenos Aires were advised by the Chilean Chancellor, Adolfo Ibáñez, to take no important steps for the time being. Gonzalo Búlnes, the eminent Chilean historian, says that one must read between the lines of Ibáñez' instructions and see that the time referred to was the time necessary for the new warship to leave England. The situation was finely balanced. During the summer President Ballivián died and the Government of Bolivia was intrusted to the old Bolivian statesman Tomás Frías who wished to settle the question pacifically and so rather favored the Walker Martínez proposals. Soon after this, news from Europe changed the whole diplomatic board.

One of the new ships, the *Cochrane*, named after the famous British-Chilean admiral, had put to sea with her interior finishing incomplete, but armed. Riva Agüero now instructed his minister in La Paz to advise Bolivia to accept the Walker Martínez proposals. He said that Chile was now ready to impose whatever conditions she wished on Bolivia regarding the littoral, and to refuse to accept the treaty would result in new complications, since "the Chilean navy is now reinforced by a new vessel which has just come off the ways in England and at this date is sailing toward the Pacific." The proposals were embodied in the Martínez-Baptista agreement, or Treaty of Sucre, which was so hastily drawn up that Article VII threatened the validity of the original Treaty of 1866. Therefore a supplementary treaty was drawn up early in 1875 and ratified in July as an integral part of the treaty of 1874.[6]

Argentina remained out of the Bolivia-Peru alliance in 1875 but still had the Patagonia question pending. The great Antofagasta Nitrate and Railroad Company, employing practically all Chilean labor and owned by Englishmen and Chileans—many of high official rank—formed a natural channel for Chilean expansion into the Bolivian littoral, that was not appreciated or properly policed by that nation.[7] Annexationist societies called *carbineros* were formed there by Chileans and all conditions existed for the formal taking of the region when the occasion should arise.

The war, growing out of nitrate high finance, came, although it is probable that few people in either country involved saw the many factors that were moving in these nations like small pawns for a play of nitrates. Both Chile and Peru were racing toward national bankruptcy. By the time war began each had a large annual deficit and neither was paying interest on its debt. Our minister in Chile predicted there would be no war between Chile and Argentina in 1878 over Patagonia because neither country had the funds.

For several decades the financial system of Peru had been such as to create a false economic basis for public revenues. The immense guano deposits were the property of the Government which usually arranged a sales contract or contracts with a large firm, usually European, for hundreds of tons of guano. There was some expense for inspectors and agents abroad; there were large commissions paid the contracting firms, and the handling and other losses were extravagant, but nevertheless the proceeds were great. In order to show shipments, the sums received, the nature and extent of agencies abroad, and the amounts expended, a table showing guano operations in Europe for 1870 is included in the Appendix.[8]

England and France were the principal users, the former receiving in one year 170 cargoes of 254,442 tons and the latter 150 cargoes of 150,160 tons. Consignments were made to six other countries and the fertilizer was a staple article in European agriculture.

England did not use all of this great consignment in one year. She was the greatest consignee, using a large quantity herself and reshipping a great deal. Often the deposits were overstocked, there were waste and loss from dampness and other causes so the result was a comparatively small net income. Often advances at high interest rates were made to the Government against the deposits on hand or to be received. But so certain was the demand and so good the price that loans for millions could be secured easily. This led not only to careless budgeting but to mortgaging the future of the nation's resources to an industry that brought only capital and not wealth into Peru. It also led to strife over the management[9] and placing of the loans and a tendency to increase government pensioners.

Practically none of this great tonnage was carried in Peruvian ships, no technical training was developed by the shipping, and no industrial independence or hardihood resulted. Even the report of the *fiscal* given above was printed in Paris. On the other hand the citizenry was spoiled for paying taxes in support of the Government.

Peru was soon to finish its orgy of extravagance with guano money, this great wealth which was owned by the Government. By 1875 there were signs of a failing supply of the commodity and returns from it were diminished by competition of nitrate of soda works then developing in Tarapacá on an even larger scale than in the Antofagasta region. At the instance of bankers who had seen the government returns from the guano monopoly, the Government of Peru decreed the monopoly of the immense Tarapacá nitrate mines, December 14, 1875. Capitalists then formed the Peruvian Nitrate Corporation for the purpose of monopolizing the nitrate shipping business, with the Government as a silent partner. In anticipation of this, operators exported 322,745 tons that year, which reduced the price of guano so that a special session of Congress was called in June the following year. After bitter debate the measure passed, the banks took possession, and limited the output to 2,000,000 quintals, or about 20,000 tons.

At first thirty-six operating companies conformed while fourteen, mostly representing foreign operators, refused. After attempting to prorate the output to these same companies, allowing the corporation to act merely as a sales company, the Government decreed the forced sale of all the mines to be paid for with government certificates. The corporation was to receive 5 per cent for commission, pay 60 per cent of the proceeds to certificate holders and 40 per cent to the Peruvian Government. The dispossessed owners formed local organizations of certificate holders in Chile, England, France, Germany, and other countries, all bent on getting back their mines, for they did not believe that with the competition in Bolivia of the Antofagasta and other companies, the Peruvian Corporation would ever pay them all, even though satisfactory price terms could be agreed upon. These certificate holders were not agreed as to what they should do, but they formed a powerful group determined to have Tarapacá taken out of the Peruvian monopoly.

The occasion for war soon arose. Article IV of the Martínez-Baptista Treaty regarding the Antofagasta Nitrate and Railroad Company provided that no additional duties were to be levied on it for twenty years. In 1878 the city council of Antofagasta consisting of five nationalities, none of which were Bolivians, asked the Bolivian national Government to put a tax of ten centavos on the company to help defray expenses of light and police.[10] The Bolivian Government authorized this tax of ten centavos a quintal on exports instead of the taxes then paid. It was a different kind of tax whether or not a net increase.

This measure was passed in February. The Chilean Minister in La Paz, Pedro Videla, objected and the Bolivian ministry agreed to defer the matter until a satisfactory agreement could be made. July 2 Videla asked to have the matter put in writing. The assembly was considering the revision of features of the contract with the company and naturally capital wanted stability of conditions, so Videla reported matters to his Government. His note of July 2 remained unanswered for three months and there did not seem to be anything serious in the situation. However, on November 8 Chile sent a note which was a virtual threat to abrogate the Treaty of 1866 and reclaim all the desert to parallel 23° if the tax law were put into effect. Hilarión Daza was now President of Bolivia. Being a dictator from the barracks he was angered by the Chilean note and had his ministers reply that the company had recourse to the Bolivian courts in their grievance, and that it was not a diplomatic case. Here he made a grave blunder for on December 12 Chile had again adjusted her quarrel with Argentina. Chile replied that the collection of the tax would result in the revindication of the coast to parallel 23°. Daza stubbornly promulgated the tax law with orders to collect back tax to February 14, 1878. He was sorely vexed with the concession hunters from the coast and especially disliked the English.

Accordingly on January 6 the Bolivian prefect of Antofagasta, Colonel Zarata, ordered the payment of

the tax and the jailing of the English manager, Mr.
Hicks. On December 27 the Minister of Bolivia started
a note to Chile offering to arbitrate the question on the
basis of the tax being paid meanwhile. On January 3
Chile started a note to Bolivia offering to arbitrate on
the basis of the tax not being collected meanwhile.
About this time one of President Daza's ministers remembered and told him of the "secret treaty" with
Peru, and coincidentally a prominent Chilean capitalist and former consul to Bolivia, Lorenzo Claro, suggested to Daza that he remove the cause of trouble by
canceling the concession of the Antofagasta Company.
Daza consulted his ministry which also seems to have
had the cupidity to think that would be a good solution.[11]

On February 1 Daza started his cancellation decree to Antofagasta and a letter telling the prefect
about his finding the treaty of alliance with Peru. The
letter was intercepted by Chilean army officers and sent
to the President of Chile with the statement that it
might be valuable to prove Peruvian complicity. On
February 8 Videla learned of the cancellation order
and gave Bolivia an ultimatum of forty-eight hours to
withdraw it or Chile would revindicate the coast to
parallel 23°. Two weeks later the Chilean Minister of
Interior, who had not had time to know of the cancellation order, wrote the President and ministers of foreign
affairs and of war that Chile should occupy Antofagasta and prevent the collection of the tax, and that an
envoy should be sent to Ecuador to work for an alliance in case Peru should aid Bolivia. The initiative for
other important moves in this question will be seen to
come from the Minister of Public Works.

News of the cancellation order reached Santiago

February 11 and orders were sent to Videla to retire.
This he had already done announcing Chile's purpose
to revindicate the coast to parallel 23°. February 14
the Chilean fleet which had been previously assembled
at Caldera, then the end of the telegraph line from
Santiago, was at anchor in Antofagasta Bay. Troops
were landed which occupied the plaza without resistance on the part of the small Bolivian garrison while
the city was dressed out in Chilean flags. Chilean
troops soon occupied the littoral to parallel 23° and the
meager Bolivian garrisons fell back to Cobija and
Tocopilla. Daza received the news during the annual
carnival, February 20, and not wanting to disturb the
celebration withheld the notice and published his proclamations February 25 and 27. His proclamations defending Antofagasta and giving amnesty to political
enemies were dated February 20, letters of marque were
issued on the twenty-sixth, and the general war manifesto February 27, 1879.[12]

While the War of the Pacific technically began with
the proclamation of President Daza, the real contest
did not begin with that date. Although Chile occupied
all of Atacama to parallel 23° and prepared to take
the rest of Bolivia's coast province which would be to
the river Loa, she did not declare war for over a
month. Many people in Chile including the President
hardly expected Bolivia to resist. Bolivia had little national solidarity and no army worth mentioning. Daza
had a special guard of four hundred trusted followers
whom he had armed with Winchesters and he kept
whatever other scattered companies there were in the
army armed with old muskets. He was taking no
chances with the ambitions of some other colonel who
might proclaim himself president. Bolivia did however

rely much on help from Peru and perhaps on Argentina as a sentence in Daza's proclamation indicates. It said: "So cynical a calculation of the rights of humanity imposes on all the States of the American continent a sacred duty of eminent justification and of foresight which sooner or later they will have to fulfill." While it was known in Chile that Peru was unprepared for war the President expressed some apprehension as to the attitude of that potentially powerful neighbor in the matter of Chile's revindication of Atacama.

With all conditions favorable for the annexation of the region now penetrated by the nitrate industry it is not probable that the President, nor at that time the Congress, of Chile would have gone to war over a ten centavo tax had there not been powerful interests which forced the issue. It is true that expansionists were in the ascendancy in the cabinet, the nation was practically bankrupt, yet, with its new ships, the *Cochrane* and the *Blanco Encalada*, it was potentially able to defy all of South America. With great wealth near by being developed largely by the enterprise of her own citizens, while its nominal owners were indifferent to the magnitude of the industry, Chile was subjected to very great temptation. But, there must always be master minds who direct the other factors in great moves. In this instance the master minds are found in the dispossessed European and Chilean nitrate mine owners of Tarapacá who were forced to accept certificates from the Peruvian Government for their holdings when Peru made a monopoly of the nitrate industry in 1875. If anything else were lacking to bring on the war it was these certificate holders. Many of the dispossessed saltpeter operators transferred their activi-

ties to Tocopilla, Bolivia, from Tarapacá, Peru. The
Peruvian monopoly attempted to control this center
by securing a concession from the Bolivian Government
through great importers like Henry Meiggs, but it
was only partially successful. Saltpeter was found at
Taltal, and Chile offered these operators free lands and
concessions if they would transfer their activities to
Valparaiso, Chile.

The attempted Peruvian monopoly was unsuccessful
and the certificate holders never ceased trying to regain their former holdings. They lobbied in Santiago
for a war that would put the entire nitrate coast under
the Chilean flag. It is getting ahead of the story
chronologically, but pertinent here, to note that when
James G. Blaine was before the congressional committee named to investigate his attempts while Secretary
of State to mediate in the War of the Pacific, he said
that it was not a war by Chile against Bolivia and
Peru. He stated emphatically that it was a war of British capitalists against Peru and said that some time
before the war their agents prevented Peru from
buying armaments in England.[13] He shared the current
anti-British sentiment of his generation however and
attributed British nationality to the certificate holders
who were of all nationalities and in part were non-
national. Another important testimony relevant at this
point is that of Charles R. Flint, an international
broker of armaments and munitions of New York. The
monopoly which Chilean writers later blamed on President Pardo was really, according to Mr. Flint, con-
ceived by a group of international and non-national
bankers and financiers. The Government of Peru was
merely to receive certain proceeds after the Spanish
custom of *estancos* or state monopoly taxes on certain

commodities like salt, tobacco, and matches. It was to
have been a world monopoly which would have yielded
enormous returns. Flint bluntly says:

> My firm were the agents of this monopoly in the United
> States, and we secured the European agency for Baring
> Brothers. The result of this organization was detrimental
> to the nitrate producers and merchants of Chile, a fact
> which led up to a war of conquest, by which Chile annexed
> all of the Peruvian nitrate territory.
>
> That war took me into what was, perhaps, an abso-
> lutely unique avenue of business: the supplying of muni-
> tions to belligerents—which I will describe later.[14]

Since this matter of who started the war is so important as an object lesson on how little the average
citizen, or even the average congress of a nation, may
have to do with bringing on a war, another count should
be given against the creditors of Peru.

Besides the production of nitrates from *caliche* in
Tarapacá, the monopolization of which has just been
recorded, there were extensive shippers of bird guano
from the promontories and nearby islands of the
coast. The guano deposits of Peru were mortgaged
highly, that is, large sums of money had been advanced against further shipments. Then when the nitrates from *caliche* were monopolized the Government
of Peru had also regulated the output of both so that
the two products would not come into competition
against each other. The guano creditors of Peru then
added their efforts to those of the certificate holders of
caliche mines to put the whole nitrate coast under the
Chilean flag which they believed would allow capital
to exploit the industry unhampered by state fiscal control. When the war was in progress and Chilean forces

had occupied Tarapacá, the Minister of Public Works of Chile, Augusto Matte, wrote to the general commanding the region regarding the activities of nitrate exploiters. The communication sheds light on the expected source of war funds:

Recently I have sent a note to Mr. Proctor advising him that in view of the uniformity of opinion which exists among the creditors of Peru, the government of Chile was willing to permit the exportation of guano, which as you know is mortgaged to them, under a Chilean duty of 30 chelines a ton. The creditors have recently held a meeting approving of this and clamoring [*piden a grito herido*] for the annexing of Tarapacá by Chile. And the truth is, my friend, that these gentlemen, the creditors, have been a powerful lever in Europe to prevent the Peruvians from securing war elements and to create for us a beneficent atmosphere in the opinion of those peoples. . . .

But what bothers me is the question of nitrates. By dispatches and other means of communication I see that the nitrate works of Tarapacá, either through fear of the reprisals of Peru, or because they haven't yet got together the necessary elements for exploiting on a vast scale, be it an attempt by resistance to lower the duty or not I don't know, but I say, I see that they have paralyzed the exportation.

Be that as it may, I believe that so far as we are concerned, they cannot or should not impose other considerations on us than those of providing us with all the funds for carrying on the war. We cannot wrap ourselves up in spider webs when we have in our hands a purpose to which is united the fate of Chile. Therefore if anyone or anything gets in our road we ought to override it with cold firmness. The war may last who knows how long and it is consequently necessary to levy on the enemy's territory as far as possible.[15]

Having now examined the economic motivation of the war it will be necessary to return to political events following the occupation of Antofagasta and the consequent war proclamation of President Daza of Bolivia. The revindication of the Desert of Atacama, now taking the name of Antofagasta, was very popular in Valparaiso and other shipping centers of Chile. Although military forces did not immediately occupy the region beyond parallel 23°, all preparations were made for doing so as soon as Chile should formally declare war against Bolivia. The remnants of Bolivian garrisons retreated to Calama near the foothills and little was feared from Bolivia in a military way. What gave concern to Chilean officials was the question of Peruvian neutrality.

President Pinto did not expect Peru to lend military aid to Bolivia. He knew of the state of near bankruptcy and confusion of Peru following the Piérola revolution, and was well informed of the unpreparedness of her warships which were then in drydock. The Peruvian press sympathized with Bolivia and the Chilean Minister in Lima sent alarming reports to President Pinto over the anti-Chilean feeling. This minister, Joaquín Godoi, was the most zealous member of the Chilean war party in fanning the flame of war—even suggesting to the President what steps should next be taken.

Peru was called upon by the Bolivian Minister to comply with the alliance of 1873 and come to the defense of her ally. Wholly unprepared, Peru did not want war at least until she could prepare, and sent a well-trained diplomat, Antonio Lavalle, to Chile to offer mediation. Godoi assured Pinto that this move was to gain time, that Peru was an ally of Bolivia, and urged his Government to demand a declaration of neutrality at once. The Chilean public did not know about the "secret treaty" of 1873 between Bolivia and Peru, but the fact was known in official circles. Lavalle's mission was therefore practically impossible. The public in Chile sensed interference in their annexation or revindication plans and resented it. The following hand-bill called a mass meeting for the day Lavalle landed in Valparaiso:

On Tuesday next, according to trustworthy information, an emissary from Peru is to arrive; he comes, according to some, to interpose his officious mediation in our quarrel with Bolivia; and, according to others, with the intention of demanding a strict account from our Government for the *"revindicacion"* of our northern territory.

Chile on putting her foot upon the desert has said, as MacMahon did at Malakoff: *J'y suis et J'y reste.* There is no reason for the mission of the Peruvian Envoy.

This is what our country should be made to know, with undeniable force and by means of public and solemn unmistakable acts.

Diplomacy has its uses, its hypocrisies, its circumlocutions, and its reticence; but the people know nothing about it, nor do they have any use for it; the people only listen to and understand the manly and honest language of truth.

And the people of Chile wish to have it understood by the Peruvian Plenipotentiary that, no matter if he comes as an officious mediator or as an examining judge, his

mission is vain and hateful; and in like manner they wish
that the Government of Chile shall know that the gates of
the Moneda [the Executive Mansion] are to be closed
against him who should wish to enter them clothed in the
very thin disguise of a fallacious diplomacy.

It is for this purpose that the inhabitants of Valparaiso are hereby asked to meet on Tuesday next, the 4th
instant, at eight o'clock in the evening, at the Plaza de la
Intendencia, that they may give form and expression to
these views, and so as to adopt, in the presence of the
Peruvian Envoy, the dignified attitude which becomes the
sons of Caupolican and Lautaro.

Therefore, get thee to the Plaza de la Intendencia, noble
people of Valparaiso, March 4th, 1879.[16]

The people got to the plaza all right, but ignobly
yielded to the mob spirit of the handbill. They stoned
the Peruvian Consulate and tore off its insignia before
being quelled by police.

On March 14 Bolivia announced through the Lima
representatives of foreign powers that a state of war
existed with Chile. The Chilean Minister in Lima,
Godoi, advised President Pinto that this move was to
prevent Chile from securing armaments abroad, that
Peru was arming, and that she should be required to
declare her neutrality at once. Meanwhile Lavalle was
attempting to mediate for Peru at Santiago and seemed
to be making progress toward a settlement with President Pinto. On March 21 Godoi, who had been trying
to get definite information as to the provisions of the
"secret treaty," had an interview with President Mariano Prado and learned the position of Peru. He telegraphed the news to his Government together with instructions how it should proceed. He said:

Last night President explained to me treaty of alliance with Bolivia, convoke Congress for decision, and request an explanation of Lavalle to our government. Lavalle is evasive to gain time. Warlike preparations and public excitement continue. I think I should insist on a declaration of neutrality immediately and not receiving it should ask for my passports.

Confronted with this message Lavalle, who either did not know the nature of the alliance with Bolivia or was concealing it, stated that if Prado said so it must be true.

On March 24 President Pinto wrote a member of the cabinet that he believed Peru was "bluffing" and that he did not think Prado or many people in Peru wanted war. He was right. Few people in Peru wanted war for the country was not solidified after the Piérola civil wars. But they were bound by a treaty between Bolivia and their Government, although it was made when both countries were under different administrations. The following day Lavalle wrote his Government that Pinto had told him that Godoi was excitable and influenced by visionaries, that allowance should be made for his temperament. However, military time-tables had started and when they start all the peace ships and conferences in the world can hardly stop them.

The Chilean Government instructed Godoi to demand of Peru the abrogation of the alliance and a declaration of neutrality, and if that was refused to demand his passports. On March 28 the Chilean Council of State planned an expedition against Callao, Peru, which was known to be unprepared, named a civilian, Rafael Sotomayor, as General Secretary and Assessor of the fleet—a sort of envoy of the Government—and asked Congress to declare war.

Even after the meeting of the Council of State, March 28, 1879, which planned the expedition against Callao, efforts were made to secure peace. A proposal was made by a Chilean jurist providing that each country should cease war preparations, and that the tax of ten centavos should be suspended pending the deliberations of a congress of plenipotentiaries to be called at Lima. Lavalle agreed, but the Chilean war ministry refused. As late as April 2, the United States Minister at Santiago, Thomas Osborn, wrote to Washington that Lavalle was still in Chile and peace was still possible. But he did not know that military time-tables had started.

The assessor of the fleet, Sotomayor, was due to arrive on April 1 at Antofagasta where the fleet was stationed. Congress was to give authority for war April 2, as it did, but withheld the declaration a few days. The Chilean ministry wanted the fleet to strike quickly at Callao while the Peruvian fleet was unprepared. One of the iron ships of the latter had its boilers out and the other was being overhauled in docks. The Chilean fleet was advised April 2 of the war authority granted by Congress and ordered to sail in war order, *procedan como en campaña*, meaning to Callao. April 3 Lavalle and Godoi were to receive their passports which would give two more days before war should be formally declared. Here a strange thing happened to the military time-table. On April 3 Sotomayor cabled to Chile: "President—Fleet is going to Iquique[17] not to Callao. Iquique 4,000 men 300 cavalry. Sail tonight." Superior orders apparently were given at nitrate centers.

On April 5, the anniversary of the Battle of Maipo, Chile declared war on both Bolivia and Peru. The same day the Chilean fleet anchored at Iquique and an officer notified the commandant and foreign consulates that the port was under blockade. Seven days after the proclamations of war a circular was issued to foreign chancelleries stating the position of Chile in the struggle. It is interesting to note that on the same date, April 5, the Government had published in the *Official Gazette* a long and thorough description of the desert not only to parallel 23°, but to the river Loa or the Peruvian boundary, written in the glowing style of a descriptive prospectus of a stock company's mine. Each of the three belligerents issued circulars to foreign chancelleries in which, as is usual, the enemy was held wholly responsible for the war.[18]

REFERENCES

1. Vicuña Mackenna, *Historia de la Campaña de Tarapacá*, p. 32.
2. *British State Papers*, XXXI, 1046.
3. Prescott, *El problema continental*, pp. 271–275; and Gonzalo Búlnes, *Guerra del Pacífico*, I, 65–68. [Text of Bolivia-Peru Treaty of Alliance or "secret treaty," included in Appendix, *infra*, III.]
4. Manuel Irigoyen, *La adhesión de la República Argentina al tratado de alianza defensiva Perú-Boliviano de 1873*, pp. 7–9.
5. Búlnes, *op. cit.*, I, 86.
6. Prescott, *op. cit.*, pp. 276–280. [Martínez-Baptista Agreement.] Also William Jefferson Dennis, *Documentary History of the Tacna-Arica Dispute*, pp. 62, 63.
7. Diego Barros Arana, *Histoire de la guerre du Pacifique*, I, 14.
8. *Oficio Dirigido al Sr. Ministro de Hacienda y Commercio*, 1870, p. 95. [Table.] Also, Chas. A. McQueen, *Peruvian Public Finance*, pp. 8, 9.
9. Búlnes, *op. cit.*, II, 107. *Infra*, p. 103. [Note: The Piérola revolution is a good example, see p. 85.]
10. J. Perkin Shanks, "The Chile-Peru Dispute," *The Forum*, May, 1923.
11. Alberto Gutiérrez, *La guerra de 1879*, pp. 109, 110.
12. *Senate Executive Documents*, Forty-seventh Congress, first session, Doc. 79, p. 201.

13. James G. Blaine, Testimony, *House Reports,* Forty-seventh Congress, first session, VI, 217.

14. Charles R. Flint, *Memories of an Active Life,* p. 66. Courtesy of the publishers, G. P. Putnam's Sons.

[Note: The ramifications of the guano industry during the period from 1870 to 1885 are vividly illustrated by a guano scrapbook which was made in 1876 by pasting clippings on the subject in a diary. These clippings were only from England, France, and Peru, although typical of every other nation of Europe, and all dealt with a proposed new guano contract between President-elect Prado of Peru and Messrs. Raphael, Candamo, and Heeren. The new contract called for a first payment annually to Peru of 700,000 pounds sterling before any could be set aside for service and payment on loans. The meetings of bondholders' committees created a lively repercussion in the press. The scrapbook, which is in the possession of the author, has clippings from the following papers: *London Times,* April 10, 17, May 1, June 9, 18, and 19, 1876; *Daily Telegraph,* April 17, May 1, June 9, 14, 15, 17, 19, and 24, 1876; *Le Soir,* February 10, April 13, 14, 20, May 2, June 9, 10, 11, 13, 15, 16, 17, and 19, 1876; *Messager de Paris,* April 12, 21, June 13, 15, 17, 18, and 19, 1876. On these approximate dates there are articles from *Revue Parisienne, Bulletin Financier, Le Figaro, La Liberté, The World,* and *La France.*]

15. Búlnes, *op. cit.,* II, 107.

16. V. M. Maurtua, *The Question of the Pacific,* pp. 51, 52.

17. Iquique was the capital and chief port of Tarapacá the great Peruvian nitrate region, the base of operations of the Peruvian Nitrate Company.

18. *British State Papers 1879–80,* pp. 926–933 [Bolivian War Circular]; *United States Foreign Relations for 1879,* pp. 168–172 [Chilean War Circular]; *Senate Documents,* Forty-seventh Congress, first session, Vol. IV, Doc. 79, pp. 229–236 [Peruvian Counter Manifesto]; abridged English versions occur in Dennis, *op. cit.,* pp. 70–76, 83–92, and 94–101.

CHAPTER V

THE WAR AND ITS OBJECTIVES

THERE are many features of the War of the Pacific which are unique and interesting in themselves. It was a war of contrasts. In it the sling shots of the sons of the Incas were mixed with splendid German field artillery fresh from the factory of the Krupps. Turreted cruisers with nine-inch armor steamed alongside old wooden ships. Some wounded were carried to hospitals under the Red Cross flag, used for the first time in this war, and some were knifed on the field. Some troops in the desert campaign drank water supplied by tank trains and some, the stoical Indians from the Andes, went without it for days immune to thirst from the chewing of coca leaves. And like all wars there was enough heroism to please the most romantic and enough barbarism to make people claiming any standing in the scale of civilization blush with shame. In this chapter the war will not be treated as war *per se*, but as a struggle with its objectives.

When President Daza of Bolivia sent an envoy to Peru to request aid according to the terms of the alliance of 1873, the latter country was unable to give effective aid. She was, as has been pointed out, practically bankrupt, great loans had been contracted against the declining deposits of guano, the monopolization of the nitrate works of Tarapacá had not helped matters, and twenty million *soles* of paper money had been issued.

Nicolás Piérola had headed a revolution against President Mariano Prado, and seized the best ship of the Peruvian navy, the *Huascar*, which the President had to proclaim a pirate ship. When Piérola interfered with some British passenger ships in order to get news and supplies, the commander of two British warships, Admiral de Horsey, attempted to take the *Huascar* as a pirate ship. Piérola resisted and the *Huascar* fought de Horsey's ships to a draw.[1] Although Piérola had little following and he surrendered the *Huascar* to the rest of the Peruvian fleet, the incident weakened the prestige of Prado's government, and it is related to show the state of unreadiness for war in Peru. The church party, which vigorously opposed the public-works policy of the Government, blocked legislation to get pensions for the crew of the *Huascar*. Distracted from without and within the Government of Peru was not prepared to be of decisive help to Bolivia.

Chile controlled the ocean to the south and no war materials could be had from Europe, although eleventh-hour attempts were made. Materials were ordered from the United States to be smuggled across Panama.[2] Naturally in Lima and Callao there was plenty of war excitement, but in the interior it was not given much attention at first. It was by no means a popular war in Peru as it was in Chile where the "secret treaty" was considered sufficient *casus belli* in itself to say nothing of the revindication of the Desert of Atacama. The Peruvian decree of *casus foederis* was issued April 6, 1879, and hasty preparations were made for war.

Although the objectives of Chile in the war were, according to the ultimatum given Bolivia, the revindication of Atacama to parallel 23°, leading Chileans seemed to realize that no halfway expansion up the coast could be possible—or at least desirable. The question was, Where is a good stopping point? And that

was the key to the difficulty of settling the recent
Tacna-Arica case. If that had been thoroughly appreciated, a plebiscite surely would never have been attempted. If Peru should have won Tacna-Arica, Chile
feared a revindication of Tarapacá and perhaps of
Antofagasta, the geese that are still laying golden
eggs. The Arica-for-Bolivia policy on the part of Chile,
it will be remembered,* entered the negotiations when
the Treaty of 1866 was being drafted. The proposition
was again made to President Daza before hostilities
had fairly begun and if he had been as unworthy as
most South American writers have pictured him he
would have acceded if possible. At about the time he
was showing a belligerent attitude toward Chile and the
latter was preparing to occupy Antofagasta, two
prominent young men from Chile had approached two
Bolivian former officials with a proposal to overthrow
President Daza and to prevent Bolivia's going to war
with Chile over Antofagasta, saying that Chile would
aid Bolivia in taking Tacna-Arica from Peru. These
officials, Casimiro Corral and General Rendon, had been
exiled by Daza and were then at Puno, Peru. Naturally, they would be expected to listen to such a proposal.

This policy was rather widely favored by Chileans of
high position. When Chilean forces occupied Antofagasta and Cobija, a Bolivian soldier, Colonel Canseco,
who had been taken prisoner, was given his liberty under the condition that he take similar proposals to
enemies of Daza in La Paz.[3] Besides trying to break
the alliance by means of the political enemies of Daza
an attempt was made to get Daza himself to break the

* See pp. 6, 14, 46.

alliance. The following letter, written by Justiano Sotomayor, brother of the Chilean Chief of Staff, and former consul to Bolivia, who evidently was acquainted with Daza, shows pointedly how Bolivia was and is related to the Tacna-Arica question.

I have been here for a month and you will not need me to tell you why I have come.

The rupture of relations between Bolivia and Chile had been very painful to me, because I have always been of the opinion that there should not be any other countries in South America that should cultivate closer relations of friendship.

Peru, on the other hand, is the worse enemy of Bolivia, she is the one that holds her under the weight of her customs regulations, the master of the commercial, industrial and to a certain point political liberty of Bolivia.

Chile has taken to Bolivia industry and capital. With that impulse mining has taken on considerable growth, that activity has had to affect the agriculture and wealth of the country.

Chile is the only country that can free Bolivia from the yoke which Peru imposes on her.

Chile is also the only nation which allied with Bolivia can give her what she lacks to be a great nation, namely, her own ports and free communication.

Can Bolivia hope to find in Cobija and the other ports of her littoral an outlet for her commerce? Profound error.

The only natural ports for Bolivia are Arica, Ilo, and Mollendo or Islay.

Allied with Peru and making war on Chile, what will happen to Bolivia if Chile is conquered? She will fall into the hands of Peru and suffer as before under the weight of her duties. And if Chile should triumph, what would the allies gain? Bolivia, conquered or conqueror, will remain without ports and handicapped as a nation.

On the other hand, with Bolivia united to Chile, wouldn't she be sure of conquering Peru? Wouldn't she have it in her power to possess a door to the street which she lacks?

One thing here I have noted since my arrival. There is no hatred whatever of Bolivia, the persons and property of Bolivians have been respected, the war with Bolivia has not stirred the country; except for some movement or other of troops we would seem to be in peace. But when the moment arrived to declare war against Peru the country arose en masse, as one man, and all have known that Peru has filled the measure with her intrigues, ingratitudes and disloyalty, and all that is talked of is punishing her terribly.

Against Peru we will fight to the death; Bolivia, we cannot hate her.

Why are we going so out of the way making wars that we do not like and alliances even that we do not want?

Would there still not be time to put things in order? Why not?

Now or never Bolivia ought to think about gaining her place as a nation, her real independence, which certainly is not in Antofagasta but rather in Arica.

After this war it will be too late, Chile as conqueror would not consent to it, at least unless Bolivia does her part. Peru as a conqueror will impose the law on Bolivia her ally and on Chile her enemy, and Chile weakened would not be able to aid Bolivia if she should ask it.

The man who should give to Bolivia her independence from Peru, would be greater than Bolivar and Sucre, be-

cause they only gave her an imitation of liberty and he
would be giving her real and true independence.
Was not such a colossal enterprise reserved for you?[4]

Belief in this policy was not confined to free-lance
diplomats, for President Pinto expressed the same idea
in a letter dated three days after the above, April 11,
1879, to Rafael Sotomayor, his confidential agent on
the field. He said:

The most satisfactory solution of the question in which
we find ourselves compromised [*comprometidos*] would be
an alliance with Bolivia, with her taking the southern departments of Peru and leaving us the coast to the river
Loa. Bolivia separated from Peru, the war would not last
long. This chance will not come twice and Bolivia ought
to seize it.[5]

President Daza did not cease preparations for a
campaign to the coast, but answered the proposals of
Chile evasively asking for more details. On May 22 official proposals were drawn up by the Chilean cabinet
which embodied about the same provisions as suggested
by Justiano Sotomayor. When Daza received these he
answered by making them public and made great manifestations of loyalty to Peru. It was evident that the
Bolivia-Peruvian alliance could not be broken, at least
without a test of arms. In Argentina there were demonstrations in favor of Peru, and since the Patagonia
question was not settled, Chile was in danger from that
direction, so a decisive military move against Bolivia
and Peru was imperative if Chile were to reap the results expected of its occupation of Antofagasta.

From a military standpoint little was known then of
the relative strength of the belligerents, but Peru was

traditionally more powerful. This proved to be erroneous. By the nature of the country naval units would be
the deciding factors in the contest. Chile had two ironclads, the *Cochrane* and *Blanco Encalada,* built in
England in 1875, which were the deciding factors.
They were of the latest model in construction, armored,
shooting projectiles, and displacing 3,500 tons. There
were two lesser ships, the corvettes *Chacabuco* and
O'Higgins, a wooden corvette the *Esmeralda,* and a
wooden gunboat the *Covadonga.* A few other ships and
numerous transports were soon added. Opposed to this
navy Peru had six craft, only two of which were very
effective. The *Huascar* was a turret ship of 1,130 tons
built in 1866 and was the best. The *Independencia,* a
ship of 2,000 tons, was built about the same time, but
was an old-type ironclad. The *Union* and *Pilcomayo*
were wooden corvettes of 1,150 and 600 tons. These
were all British built. Then there were two old monitors
built in the United States, the *Atahualpa* and the
Manco Capac. These were unseaworthy and were used
only for harbor defense.

Neither country possessed large standing armies, but
each had some regiments. Chile began preparing earlier
and accumulating forces and supplies at Antofagasta.
Chile had two advantages in her army, good artillery
and cavalry. While she was preparing to move northward from Antofagasta, Bolivia and Peru were assembling forces in Arica and Tacna to support what defenses there were in Tarapacá. Chile hoped to strike her
decisive blow by destroying the Peruvian fleet at Callao
without which the forces of the allies in the south could
not be maintained for there were no longitudinal railroads.

On May 16 the Chilean fleet, under Admiral Wil-

liams leaving the *Esmeralda* and *Covadonga* to maintain the blockade of Iquique, feigned an attack on
Arica and sailed for Callao. Coincidentally, the two
Peruvian ironclads were sailing south reconnoitering
and the fleets missed each other. Arriving at Iquique
one of the Peruvian ships, the *Huascar*, sank a smaller
Chilean warship that had remained there to keep up the
blockade. The *Independencia*, pursuing a small Chilean
ship close to shore, ran aground and was lost, a costly
loss because it was one of the two really effective vessels owned by Peru. This action which took place on
May 21, 1879, is one of the classics of school histories.
The *Huascar* rammed the *Esmeralda*, whose commander Captain Pratts, having given the command to
board when the impact came, leaped to the *Huascar's*
deck with a lone follower, for the ships quickly separated, and refusing to surrender was killed after slay-
ing an enemy. Every year this event is celebrated with
great patriotism. The Peruvian ship which grounded,
the *Independencia*, was commanded by an Anglo-
Peruvian, Captain Moore, who was so chagrined that
he doffed the uniform of an officer and later died as a
private on the Morro of Arica.

When Admiral Williams reached Callao and learned
of the departure of the Peruvian ships south, he sailed
south at once, but missed the *Huascar*. For several
months Captain Miguel Grau of the *Huascar*, who was
soon made an admiral, boldly cruised up and down the
coast eluding capture, carrying defense to Arica and
Tarapacá, and raiding Chilean ports.

While these events were occurring, friends of peace
were also active, as well as were international meddlers
with various "axes to grind." Before hostilities between
Chile and Peru had begun, the British Minister in

Lima, Spencer St. Johns, had tendered the good offices
of his Government to prevent a trial at arms. Colombia
very soon appointed a commissioner, Dr. Pablo Arosmena, to visit the belligerents and attempt mediation.
Ecuador made a similar move. In Argentina there were
public demonstrations in favor of the allies and the
Patagonia question again became acute.

Mediation and meddling came simultaneously. Hor-
ace Fisher, a former colonel in the Union army, who
was acting as Chilean consular agent in Boston when
war was declared, at once got an interview with President Hayes and Secretary Evarts through recommendations of his former generals. Telling them he was going immediately to South America and offering to take
any dispatches the Government wanted to send, he got
a special passport as bearer of dispatches. He then
sailed for South America *via* Panama with a number of
messages on routine affairs to consuls and ministers
along the way. At Panama he did Chile a good turn by
discovering that munitions of war were being smuggled
over the isthmus, and went on to Lima, where he gave
the impression of being an important messenger of the
United States State Department.

At the same time that Colonel Fisher was thus engaged the United States Minister to Bolivia, Judge
Newton D. Pettis, had taken steps toward the settlement of the question by mediation. He was prompted
by the double purpose of avoiding bloodshed and of
advancing the prestige of his Government. There were
rumors of offers of mediation by European powers and
Mr. Pettis, sharing the conceptions of the Monroe Doctrine held by our statesmen of that period, wished to
forestall such mediation. His principal motive, however, was a real desire to promote peace, for in no other

way could his unofficial and audacious mediation be explained. Being on close terms with the Minister of State of Bolivia, the subject of mediation was frankly discussed and a memorandum drawn up.

The war in Bolivia was so popular that within two months a division of seven thousand men was equipped, largely by public donation, and was on its way to the coast. Foolishly enough, it went to Tacna instead of to Calama with President Daza in command.

Likewise, President Mariano Prado of Peru led in person his forces then assembling in Tacna and Arica. Judge Pettis left for the coast as soon as he secured the memorandum of Bolivia's peace bases. The allies placed at his disposal the use of a boat over Lake Titicaca and the railroad and telegraph line to Mollendo. He cabled the United States Minister in Lima, I. P. Christiancy, to meet him in Mollendo. The latter not being able to come, Pettis came on to Lima, where he easily secured the approval of Sr. Manuel Irigoyen, the Peruvian Minister of Foreign Affairs, and Vice-President La Puerta who was acting in the absence of President Prado. He then went to Arica and found Presidents Daza and Prado at Tacna, and both were favorable to the bases of his memorandum. Knowing that it would take two months to consult Washington by letter and fearing to cable, he resolved to go to Chile "to visit his old friend Mr. Osborn, U.S. Minister in Santiago."

The Chilean ministry also seemed favorable to the proposals. About all the announced objectives of the war were tentatively offered by the allies, but it was held that Peru deserved thorough punishment. Of course, the difficulty with any halting of the war then, or any time after it started, was that there could be no safe place to stop. Chileans knew better than anybody else that even the Antofagasta region could not be retained if Peru and Bolivia were not both crushed. The destruction of Peruvian predominance on the coast and the capture and retention of Tarapacá was the least that would satisfy Chilean peace conditions if the whole truth had then been known.

At the time of this war, European commercial interests in South America greatly exceeded those of the United States. The British minister at Lima had formally tendered the good offices of his country to avert war, and various diplomats had let it be known that their respective governments were willing to mediate. After the great destruction of property in the bombardment of cities, built up largely by European capital, and when the blockade began to threaten the supply and price of guano, European governments were disposed to intervene forcibly, if necessary, to stop the war. However, they would not take that step without the coöperation, or at least the consent, of the United States.

Accordingly on June 14, Lord Salisbury sent a telegram to Sir Edward Thornton, which was taken personally to Secretary Evarts by Mr. Henry Howard of the British legation. The message stated that Germany and Great Britain regretted the war which was being waged largely at the cost of neutrals, and desired to know if the United States would join those powers to offer mediation for the purpose of concluding the war. Secretary Evarts replied that his Government was ready to assist in the restoration of peace when its offices could be usefully proffered, but that it did not favor a premature effort, nor an effort in combination with other powers which could carry an impression of coercion.[6]

Coincident with the failure of the Pettis efforts, Dr. Arosmena was made to understand privately that mediation was not wanted, and did not officially tender the offices of Colombia, but soon returned home. Colonel Fisher remained in Chile a year and his motives were not known, even to Secretary Evarts, to whom he sent voluntary and voluminous reports, which were very accurate. He was pro-Chilean and did various small services such as securing from the United States War Department copies of our rules of warfare and creating good feeling for Chile in the United States.

The result of these peace moves was to demonstrate that there would be no peace without a serious trial at arms. Both sides prepared feverishly for a hard struggle. Peru endeavored to secure ships of war, since the *Huascar* was the only unit in her navy at all comparable to the *Cochrane* and *Blanco Encalada*. For five months Admiral Grau maneuvered the *Huascar* about the coast attacking Tocopilla, Antofagasta, Taltal, and Caldera, captured a transport, and blocked the campaign against Tarapacá. The Chilean fleet was overhauled and a new admiral named, with the result that the *Huascar* was captured near Angamos in a battle on October 8, in which Grau and all senior officers were killed.

The naval battle of Angamos was the decisive battle of the war. It was a heroic effort and also a remarkable engagement from a naval point of view. It was the first struggle between ironclads designed after the lessons of the battle between the *Monitor* and the *Virginia*. On October 7 the Peruvian ships, *Huascar* and *Union*, under Admiral Grau, appeared at Antofagasta and finding no prizes sailed north. The officers of the Chilean fleet, having learned from Arica of the cruise south-

ward of the enemy, were on that date holding a council
of war at Mejillones near by, planning how to intercept
Grau. Aided by advice from Antofagasta, the Chilean
commander discovered the two ships cruising northward in the night. At dawn the long-pursued *Huascar*
accompanied by the wooden, but fast, *Union*, sighted
some of the enemy's ships. The *Union*, capable of making perhaps thirteen or fourteen miles an hour, tried
to draw off the new Chilean cruisers, but two lesser
ships were sent in pursuit of it and the *Blanco*, capable
of about nine miles, followed the *Huascar* to its trap.
The latter could make eleven miles an hour and expected to escape, but was intercepted by other Chilean
units led by the *Cochrane*, which was slightly faster.
English and Peruvian witnesses state that the *Huascar*
attempted to ram, but it is denied by Chilean historians. The Peruvian vessel had five and a half inches
of armor and the Chilean ships nine. The *Huascar*
opened fire first from its turret guns with shells of
three hundred pounds. The second discharge struck the
hoisting gear of the anchor, and the third, the armor
plating of the main battery. This hit produced a great
shock to the *Cochrane* whose engines blew off steam.
Thinking the machinery might be disabled before he
would be any closer, the captain of the *Cochrane* gave
the order to fire, the distance then being about two
hundred yards, and the fight of ironclads was on. It
must have been a strange spectacle to the inhabitants
of Mejillones, who witnessed from the cliffs this three-
cornered duel of iron ships on the placid waters of a
coast, hitherto disturbed only by the screams of the
gulls, cormorants, and pelicans, who innocently had
been the cause of a mighty combat—mighty for 1879.
The fire of the *Cochrane* was deadly, the first projectile

NITRATE PRODUCTION ON THE CHILEAN DESERT

GUANO-PRODUCING BIRDS

striking the *Huascar's* fighting tower and another destroying the steering gear, while within a few minutes one exploded on the bridge blowing Admiral Grau to fragments. The second and third officers in command were also killed, but the crew continued the struggle. The *Blanco* came up and both tried to ram the *Huascar*, narrowly missing it and each other. Both then raked the *Huascar* with shrapnel and projectiles at close range until someone lowered the colors. When a boarding party came on the decks, the *Huascar* was on fire in several places, and the valves had been opened in an attempt to prevent it from falling into the hands of the enemy. The ship was saved by Chilean sailors and after being refitted was added to their navy. It took part later in the attacks on Arica and other points where its missiles doubly damaged Peru,—first materially and then sentimentally.

The *London Times*, in describing the Battle of Angamos, gave an extensive account of the history of the *Huascar*, comparing it with other famous ships. It might be said here that many of the engineers and artillerymen on both sides were British sailors, the nitrate-paid galley slaves of two nations misguided into a nitrate war.

Now master of the sea, Chile landed an expedition, November 2, at Pisagua in Tarapacá, and fought a hard battle with the allies at San Francisco [or Dolores] near Iquique, defeating them decisively. The armies were about equal in numbers, but that of Chile had superior cavalry and had, above all, the latest Krupp artillery manned by German officers experienced in the Franco-Prussian War. The allies were allowed to withdraw, however, and some of Bolivia's troops returned directly home while others retreated

with the Peruvian army, which fought a brilliant rear
guard action and retired to Tacna.

With Tarapacá in their possession the question of its
disposition had to be discussed. The Chilean Minister,
José Santa María, stated the question well in a letter
to General Sotomayor, November 20, the day he received the news of the victory at San Francisco. The
first part was written before the news came and the rest
after receiving it. The reference to Argentina is about
the old Patagonia trouble. Very fortunately for Chile,
mediation of the United States was acceptable to Argentina and the question was left to arbitration.

Minister Santa María's letter follows:

November 20. We can say that Tarapacá is ours, but
the hard thing, my dear Rafael, is to know what we
should do next, if victories do not help to define the situation. Shall we continue fighting? Shall we halt in Tarapacá? Shall we fortify ourselves there and there await
Peru to destroy her if she presents herself again to combat us? Shall we go to Lima, by that means to compel the
government to come to peace terms? And so I could continue with a series of questions which could not be
answered.

And this situation can become more difficult if the Argentinian negotiations should take a disagreeable turn.
Since a spirit of conquest is attributed to us, since it is
believed that we are bent on annihilating Peru and dividing up the Lord's garments, not only shall we not have
sympathies of the Americas, but Argentina will also fear
for herself, she will suspect that we, powerful and proud,
will try to take Patagonia from her without ceremony or
preliminaries. This is an error, but overexcited people do
not escape easily from their errors. I think and think

about our subsequent action [*conducta posterior*], but I am very much afraid that opinion in this country is misled to the extremity of embarrassing the prudent action of the government.

I am breaking the seal of this letter because at this moment I am overcome with the enthusiasm of the news which we have just received. We possess the *Pilcomayo* and are owners of Tarapacá. Now after the diversion of the triumph we must think seriously on what is incumbent on us to do. I consider Peru as vanquished [*rendido*] and the alliance ended; now enters the hardest phase of the question, listening to the exaggerations of patriotism and the benefits which triumph suggests. Shall we go to Lima? Think about it a moment; there are two ways to take; one is to remain in Tarapacá awaiting there for them to seek us to dislodge us, and the second, to march rapidly upon Lima to impose the terms of the conqueror.[7]

While Santa María was not wholly correct, his insight into the future was almost prophetic. There was no good stopping place for Chile's northward expansion once it was begun. It is hard to believe that Secretary Hughes was cognizant of the above described roots of the Tacna-Arica question or he would not have proposed the Protocol of Washington.[8]

REFERENCES

1. *British State Papers*, 1876–77, pp. 744–767. García y García, Aurelio, *El Monitor Rebelde.* [Official report of the Secretary of the Navy.]

2. Charles R. Flint, *Memories of an Active Life,* chap. viii.

3. Daniel S. Bustamonte, *Bolivia, su estructura y sus derechos en el Pacífico,* p. 157.

4. Prescott, *El problema continental,* pp. 287–290. [Note: President Coolidge's advisers seemed never to have heard of this doctrine.]

5. Bustamonte, *op. cit.*, p. 158.

6. *House Executive Documents,* Forty-sixth Congress, third session, Doc. 1, Part I, p. 490.

7. Gonzalo Búlnes, *Guerra del Pacífico,* I, 729.

8. *Opinion and Award of the Arbitrator,* p. 1.

CHAPTER VI

ON TO LIMA

WITH the Battle of Angamos which ended the naval power of Peru the outcome of the war was decided, but there was no way to make peace. True, the entire nitrate coast was now in the hands of Chile and she was mistress of the sea excepting for the fortified ports of Arica and Callao which were now blockaded. But the war had not been close to home in Bolivia and Peru where many thought that it had not been properly conducted and that there was still hope for victory.

President Daza, with the Bolivian division, had started to make a juncture with the Peruvian army in Tarapacá before the Battle of San Francisco, but pretending that he had a report of a Chilean force about to attack President Prado at Tacna, he had returned there. A few of his followers had rebuked him and continued south arriving in time to tell of their chief's withdrawal and to take part in the struggle at San Francisco. From that date Daza's followers sought a new leader. When the allies all fell back to Tacna, President Prado left Admiral Montero in command and returned to Lima. There he tried to reorganize the ministry and continue the war. He offered the portfolio of finance to Nicolás Piérola who had been a critic of the Government for many years. Piérola refused in a remarkable open letter that sounded like a bid for a dictatorship. Although there was bitter disappointment in Lima at the defeat of the allies, Prado was not generally blamed and was well received so there was great

surprise when on December 18 he abdicated and sailed
for Europe ostensibly to secure ships.

With the abdication of President Prado the way was
now open for Nicolás Piérola who seemed to desire the
presidency although the occasion was inauspicious. For
that reason there must have been much patriotism
intermixed with his ambition. He had been attorney
for the large Dreyfus guano concern in Peru, had been
minister of finance, and after disagreeing with the
former administration on guano policy he had resigned.
He will be remembered as having revolted, seized the
Huascar, and taken part in a quixotic duel with two
British ships. He had ability and energy and probably
no one else could have done more than he in the crisis.
The trouble was that he represented the bitter opposition, politically and financially, to the civilist party.
General Manuel La Cotera, who remained loyal to the
civil party, was induced by high church officials to cease
resistance and Piérola entered the palace.

While this revolution was taking place in Peru and
a similar one was fomenting in Bolivia, Chile was
divided between celebrating its great successes and de-
bating on what move to take next. Preparations went
steadily on however for an expedition against Tacna
and Arica. Raiding expeditions were carried out to destroy the guano-loading facilities all along the coast
of Peru with the double object of shutting off its financial income and stopping competition with the guano
now being shipped by Chile.

Coincident with the military and political crises in
Peru and interwoven with them was a clash of huge
financial interests. Agents of the Prado government,
Francisco Rosas and Marciano Goyeneche, signed a
contract with a company representing a large block of

French interests organized under the name of the Crédit Industriel.

Holders of mortgages on Peruvian guano and owners of certificates for the dispossessed nitrate mines in Tarapacá represented interests of different types. These bondholders lived in various countries of Europe and organized, taking a name, usually that of the country in which they lived, and designating a committee such as "Committee of Peruvian bondholders in France." The most important of these were the British, French, Italian, and German committees in about the order named. Dreyfus & Company of Paris had the largest single claim, but since they were trying to make a separate arrangement, backing Piérola, they are not included in the above statement, although they should in a sense be counted for they were cautious and agreed to the Crédit Industriel plan also.

The complex economic motives underlying the political moves of this period cannot be treated at great length here. However, there was a large group of bondholders who were now disgusted with the titanic struggle in this industry for favor at the hands of either Chile or Peru, and wished to have a powerful nation intervene.

The Crédit Industriel was a company organized in Europe to liquidate all the varied claims against the guano and nitrate deposits of Peru and to pay the indemnity of war which Chile would logically demand; it was then seen that she would win. According to the plan of this company a neutral nation or several powers would be needed as international trustee. Since Secretary Evarts had made it clear that the United States did not care to see European intervention it was hoped that his Government would assume that responsibility.

Important agents were soon dispatched to the United States to have the matter laid before Secretary Evarts. This plan, which will be discussed later, was frustrated for a year.

President Piérola attempted to save the nation from both bankruptcy and loss of territory. He settled all debts owed for internal improvements by transferring railroads and other government-owned property to the claim holders. He then attempted to realize cash payments on all guano then stored at government account in Europe, and to devote the income to the purchase of war materials with which to retake the captured guano deposits and the nitrate region of Tarapacá.

The principal difficulty that he encountered was in securing warships. His guano credit was sufficiently good to purchase ships, but it was impossible to evade neutrality laws. In view of the very efficient diplomacy of the Chilean Minister in London and Paris, Blest Gana, and the aid of certain bondholders, Peru was unable to buy a single ship. Her army was still about equal in numbers to that of Chile, but it was a war in which by the circumstance of the long coast, a navy was the deciding factor. The British-owned steamship lines carried munitions rather impartially to both belligerents and Peru tried to break Chile's naval power by the use of torpedoes smuggled into the country, but was unsuccessful. President Piérola's efforts were heroically supported by his people, but his was a hopeless task.

Piérola had cabled to Rosas and Goyeneche to make no contracts except *ad referendum;* instead they signed the Crédit Industriel agreement January 7. On the same date, Piérola issued a decree disposing of all stored guano to Dreyfus. The two agents, wealthy men of the former guano *régime*, soon had their estates in Peru confiscated by the same decree that annulled their contract. The minister of finance who authorized the contract also suffered the same penalty and was imprisoned besides, although the decree was made retroactive in doing so. The backers of the Crédit Industriel however did not accept Piérola's program as final and worked on their plan, sending agents to see Secretary Evarts. They were prepared for any misfortune that might befall Piérola.

Thus while soldiers were called in to Lima for the defense of the country against what they supposed was a struggle of national and racial antipathies, and soldiers from Chile embarked for the north to punish what they thought was a treacherous foe, three giant economic groups were really clashing and using them as pawns. One group was of those bondholders who were putting the nitrate wealth under a different flag; another group represented those favored by the civilian government of Prado and represented in the Crédit Industriel; the third group, personified in Piérola, represented Dreyfus.

The group of bondholders who backed Chilean expansion was more fortunate. After the capture of Iquique and the occupation of Tarapacá, the city was placed under the military governorship of Gen. Patrick Lynch, a British soldier of fortune who had taken service in the Chilean navy. He facilitated guano development by fortifying the headlands, protected deposits, and gave the city a thoroughgoing administration.

On February 23, 1880, Gen. J. A. Villagran, commander of the region of southern Peru occupied by Chilean armies, issued a military decree which for its importance is quoted. It should be noted that the chairman of the committee on arrangements mentioned in the last article of the decree is Mr. Proctor, the same man mentioned by Minister Matte previously quoted in connection with this guano politics.* Another interesting fact is that although the war had started because Bolivia broke a contract with an Anglo-Chilean company by putting a tax of ten centavos a quintal on its exports, Chile by this decree put a tax of thirty shillings a ton on guano from Peru's deposits which were mortgaged to European bondholders. But these bondholders for the most part did not object to the tax, for after all other expenses of shipping and sale were deducted the proceeds were divided between all the bondholders who subscribed to that arrangement. Those who did were fortunate. However, many, like the Crédit Industriel group, sought a neutral mandate. The military decree is as follows:

The province of Tarapacá being occupied by the Chilian army, and in virtue of the powers conferred upon me by the Supreme Government, I decree:

That as the foreign holders of Peruvian bonds have solicited due permission from the Supreme Government to ship guano from the Peruvian deposits occupied by the arms of the republic, and there being no impediment to granting this permission, I decree:

ARTICLE 1. The foreign holders of Peruvian bonds are hereby allowed to extract guano from the Peruvian deposits occupied by the arms of the republic, under the following conditions:

1st. The bondholders shall name a committee or responsible business house to direct the operations;

* See p. 76.

2d. The Chilian Government reserves the power of intervention and of naming one or more functionaries to inspect, and if it be thought opportune, to direct the operations of extraction and shipment.

3d. The functionaries referred to in the foregoing paragraph shall dispatch the loaded ships to Valparaiso, whence they cannot sail to a foreign port until the sum of 30s. per ton of guano on board has been paid into the custom-house.

4th. This payment shall be made in bills of exchange upon London, in favor of the Chilian Government and to its satisfaction; this payment shall be lowered to 20s. per ton, in case that the price of guano falls below £6 per ton.

ART. 2. The papers of the ships sent off shall be made out to the order of the firm of Messrs. Baring Bros. & Co., or to some other equally respectable firm, in case consignation is not arranged with them.

Until a contract of consignation be signed, the ships' papers shall be made out in favor of the Chilian minister and plenipotentiary in Europe, and of James Croyle, esq., and Sir Charles Russell.

ART. 3. The consignee or consignees of the guano shall proceed to sell the cargoes, and, after deducting the sums expended, be it in the obtaining of this permission, be it in payment of the debts referred to in article 1, or be it to repay the shipping expenses, or in other similar objects, the remainder shall be divided between the foreign holders of Peruvian bonds, in whose favor the guano deposits have been mortgaged.

PROVISIONAL ARTICLE. Until the committee, mentioned in article 1, be named, Mr. John Proctor is authorized to arrange provisionally the mode of shipment, he being em-

powered to use for that purpose the material in possession of the government.[1]

By March, 1880, the War of the Pacific and the
international repercussion resulting from it caused
Secretary Evarts to take steps to safeguard the policy
of no European intervention in America. The com-
plexity of the situation with regard to foreign bond
and certificate holders, and the curtailment of the
supply of fertilizer for European countries, together
with the destruction of so much foreign property and
some lives, caused interpellations of at least two European ministries and talks of a coalition of powers to
intervene in South America.

In order that his ministers to the belligerent countries might be prepared to forestall any move in conflict with the policy of the United States in American
political affairs, Secretary Evarts sent them instructions which were virtually discretionary orders to offer
mediation.[2] The offer of mediation was to be contingent
upon European efforts at mediation that might tend to
be "coercive." This contingency did not arise during
the spring of 1880, but the ministers of the United
States to the belligerents were prepared.

While revolutions in Bolivia and Peru were over-
throwing the governments of those countries, both military and diplomatic campaigns were being prepared
in Chile. By the end of February an army, transported
from Iquique and Pisagua and disembarked at Ilo, began to advance into Tacna where the allies were making
a stand, while the fleet blockaded Arica.

By the terms of May 22 of the previous year Chile's
proposal to Bolivia to exchange allies did not offer very
definite territory in compensation. Now with the suc-

cess of Chilean arms practically certain the terms were summarized in the following note sent by the Minister of Foreign Affairs, Santa María, to the Chilean Minister in La Paz, Eusebio Lillo.

May 8th. Santa María to Lillo. The principal bases from which we should not deviate are these:

1. That Antofagasta is ours.

2. That all the territory to the Loa is also, as a necessity created by the war which Bolivia made against us.

3. That the eastern boundaries shall be fixed later, in order not to have another point that might disturb the peace to be signed.

4. That in order to maintain the Bolivian autonomy, Arica, Tacna and Moquegua be annexed to Bolivia.

It was well understood that this has its difficulty [*bemoles*, i.e., flats], but it is necessary to insist on it, as a means of giving Bolivia a frontier and placing her between Peru and us. Here is for me the hard part of the question, because Peru will forever resist such extensive cession and because Bolivia can consider herself insecure and insist that we become a protector. This demand once accepted would put us in the difficult situation of always having to keep an army ready, and thus to prepare or become used to militarism, which would turn out to be the real profession in Chile.

We have recently thought much on this point, but I see a difficulty in giving you concrete instructions, since we don't know which physiognomy the political parties in Bolivia will present nor what men may be interested in its destiny. But you don't need instructions. You know the thoughts of the government, for in our conversations I haven't concealed from you the fact that I look upon peace with Bolivia as a necessity to arrive at peace with Peru.[3]

This was a good prophecy in most part. The only error was regarding Bolivia's insisting on Chile's becoming her protector. She has, despite all temptations and pressure, adhered to Peru. That this question in the large was intimately bound up with Bolivia is one of its basic facts, and it is strange that President Harding and his advisers, and President Coolidge and his first advisers thought that the Tacna-Arica question was merely one concerning Chile and Peru. The Bolivian phase of the question is emphasized all through this work because of the conviction that no just nor permanent solution would be possible without attention to Bolivia's rights.

On July 29, 1880, Secretary Evarts, aware of steps taken by the representatives of the powers, telegraphed [to Panama to be mailed from there] to urge mediation on the belligerents, sending identical instructions to Mr. Osborn in Santiago, Mr. Christiancy in Lima, and Mr. Charles Adams who had taken the place of Mr. Pettis in La Paz.[4]

While the powers of Europe and the United States may earnestly have desired peace in the summer of 1880 the people of Chile did not. Confident that the victories of their arms were only in proportion to the justice of their cause, that Peru's losses were well deserved for "having made the secret treaty" against Chile, and that a haughty Goliath was being slain by a little David, the cry, "On to Lima" was insistent. The Government was no longer bankrupt. The riches of guano had begun to roll into her treasury and we have the strange spectacle of a government beginning a war bankrupt and each year accumulating a surplus.

On August 6, Mr. Osborn, who now had received the message of July 29 from Secretary Evarts, formally offered the mediation of the United States. After consulting his cabinet, Pinto on August 9 accepted reluctantly and secretly the mediation. Osborn telegraphed to Christiancy on the seventeenth to sound the Peruvian Government, but the latter did not get the message, for he was then on his way to Santiago. A letter from Pinto to the Chilean admiral, Riveros, dated July 25, stating that he would be favorable toward peace if some neutral power would offer the way was intercepted by Peruvians and came into Christiancy's hands. After waiting a week to hear from Mr. Osborn and fearing that some other power might be selected to mediate he decided to go to Chile, leaving quietly on board the *Wachusett*, one of the three American vessels cruising in belligerent waters.

As the war spirit was high in Chile and the ministry had virtually promised to push the expedition on to Lima the arrival of Minister Christiancy was embarrassing. President Pinto was of the opinion that the capture of Callao and even Lima would not insure peace and quoted history to show that Peru could resist from the fastnesses of the Andes. However the administration, faced with an election the following spring, was politic. On September 11 Congress interpellated the ministry on the question of foreign intervention. The ministry temporized by replying that there had been some extra-official inquiries.

Not only was Secretary Evarts' attempt at mediation predestined to failure by a victory-intoxicated Chilean war party which desired to annihilate the Peruvian nation, but his instructions were not understood in the same light by his three ministers intrusted with carrying them out. Mr. Adams understood his instructions to mean more than mediation, in fact forced arbitration, similar to that proposed by Mr. Gladstone. When he conveyed Secretary Evarts' message to the Bolivian Chancellor, Sr. Carrero, the latter stated that since it was practically certain that Chile would hold out for Tarapacá and Peru would not cede it he wished to know if the United States contemplated mediation by forced arbitration. Mr. Adams stated that he did not presume that Secretary Evarts intended his representatives to be mere spectators at a conference the opinions of whose representatives were already well known.

Furthermore, both Minister Adams and Minister Christiancy presumed that active military campaigns would cease during the conference while Mr. Osborn, the senior minister, seemed to see nothing unconformable to international practice in the vigorous prosecution of the war by Chile during the conference.

A conference was arranged to take place in October on board the U.S.S. *Lackawanna* off Arica. The delegates from Peru attended, with much reluctance owing to a sense of injured pride at the continuing of devastating expeditions in the productive valleys north of Lima.

In Chile where few men wished to be associated with pacifists in that victorious moment it was difficult to secure delegates. Two of them wrote that they saw no advantage in attempting peace parleys. A third, Eusebio Lillo, not only had no faith in the conference, but carried instructions to treat separately with the Bolivian delegates, which he tried to do, holding several interviews.

The conference was begun October 22. Mr. Osborn opened the session by a few remarks in which he stated that the United States had a profound interest in the welfare of the nations engaged in the war for it had inaugurated republican government in America, that republican institutions were on trial, and that he begged the envoys to labor earnestly to bring about peace. He doomed the conference to failure, nevertheless, in his opening speech by defining the position of the American representatives saying, ". . . they do not propose to take any part whatever in the discussion of the questions which may come before the conference." Before the session adjourned the following terms of peace were submitted by the plenipotentiaries of Chile:

First, Cession to Chili of such territory of Peru and Bolivia as extends to the south of the valley of Camarones and to the west of the line of the Andean Cordillera which separates Peru and Bolivia, as far as the valley of the Chacarilla, and to the west also of a line which, being prolonged from this point, would strike the Argentine frontier, passing through the center of Lake Ascotan.

Second. Payment to Chili by Peru and Bolivia jointly of the sum of twenty millions of dollars, four millions whereof are to be paid in cash.

Third. Return of the properties of which Chilian citizens in Peru and Bolivia have been despoiled.

Fourth. Return of the transport Rimac.

Fifth. Abrogation of the secret treaty made between Peru and Bolivia in the year 1873, leaving at the same time the steps taken to bring about a confederation between the two nations void and of no effect whatever.

Sixth. Retention on the part of Chili of the territory of Moquegua, Tacna, and Arica, occupied by Chilian forces, until the obligations to which the preceding conditions refer have been complied with.

Seventh. An obligation on the part of Peru not to

fortify the port of Arica when it shall be given up to her, nor at any time, and an undertaking that in future it shall be an exclusively commercial port.[5]

At the next session which met on August 25 the delegates of the allies rejected most of the seven articles of terms and proposed that the matter be submitted to the arbitration of the United States. Long speeches were made in which the whole question of events leading to the war was discussed, and the delegate from Bolivia summed up the effort at mediation by stating that it was understood by his Government that mediation meant arbitration. Mr. Osborn then had to state the position of the United States. He said that his Government "does not seek the position of arbiter in this question. A strict compliance with the duties inherent to that position would involve much trouble and great labor. . . ." He said that his Government doubtless would act as arbiter if requested, but that its present representatives did not court that distinction. Another session was held two days later but as the lines were sharply drawn and Mr. Osborn did nothing to save the peace efforts, the conferences adjourned, having availed nothing for the belligerents and nothing but criticism for the mediators.

Mr. Adams and Mr. Christiancy were disappointed at the turn the conference of the *Lackawanna* took. They wanted Mr. Osborn to telegraph Secretary Evarts that Chile had refused the arbitration of the United States, but he wired simply, "Conference failed." Further effects of the difference of opinion of these ministers on our effort at mediation will be seen in the later correspondence with Secretary Evarts. It was expensive to cable to Washington as the only cable

then was *via* Paris, but being urged by the Peruvian
delegates Mr. Christiancy wired at their expense
($66) a longer message than Osborn's, stating that
Chile had refused arbitration. The reactions of the
Chilean delegates are shown in extracts from their accounts of the conference. October 25, J. F. Vergara
wrote in part to President Pinto:

With this motive they pronounced many discourses and
much was said of civilization, fraternity of these republics, similarity of origin, institutions, customs, religion,
etc. They called out modern principles, American law,
equity, and whatever arguments that come to the conquered in defense of a cause which they see hopeless. We
held firm in our propositions, maintaining its justice and
the necessity of consolidating the peace which we seek.
The situation was a little bit painful for those of us who
are not used to seeing these moral executions which also
have their agonies, but pressing our hearts a little bit, re-
membering the causes of this war and thinking about the
obligations which the interests of peace impose, all weakness disappeared and our spirits remained inflexible.

. . . .

Our relations with Baptista [one of the Bolivian pleni-
potentiaries] have had a certain character of insinuation
and personal deference which should not be overlooked.
You should know now by the communications of Lillo,
how this distinguished politician expresses himself on the
pending question, and I am sure that he cherishes the idea
of obtaining for his country compensation for the lost
littoral, acquiring the natural and necessary appendix for
his country. He does not deny that their littoral of the
desert is an eccentric territory of Bolivia, that never
could be populated nor governed, and is suited only to

Chile, but he needs some cause or other to justify their separation from Peru not to clash so with sentiments of national honor and the duties of an ally.[6]

Regarding the attempt at this conference to arrive at a secret understanding with the representatives of Bolivia the three Chilean delegates were not in accord and, indeed, Chilean statesmen have never agreed on the Arica-for-Bolivia doctrine. Eulogio Altamirano wrote on the second day of the conference that while the Bolivian delegates were prudent and might play the part of friends, "they follow the Peruvians." He said, "Let us leave this business of peace which is a joke and talk of war."[7]

Besides the delegates to the conference men high in Chilean diplomacy had no faith in the conference, men such as José Balmaceda, prominent member of the cabinet. He wrote in terse style to a colleague his views on the peace, and advocated a way of securing Tarapacá which suggests the famous doctrine of *spurlos versenkt* of the World War. A paragraph of his letter follows:

The peace went to the devil, as it should have, for it was an illusion of timid souls to imagine it possible under these circumstances. The Peruvians and Bolivians gain diplomatically. There is a great difference in presenting to the world the cession of Tarapacá as an annexation consented in and authorized as an arrangement of peace, and in presenting it as an attempt at annexation which will cause a cry of war of conquest. It should be presented as a consummated act, never as a frustrated tentative that will make the war more bitter and will hold us up to our jealous neighbors as a certain and inexcusable menace.[8]

War preparations and active campaigns were not abated during the peace conference on the *Lackawanna*. The determination of President Piérola of Peru to continue the struggle, and his sale of stored guano in Europe to Dreyfus & Company, were answered by raids on loading piers and by expeditions to the coast valleys north of Lima. Patrick Lynch, former military governor of Iquique, devastated rich sugar estates and levied heavy war contributions, while the cry in Chile, "On to Lima," became more insistent.

Mr. Adams and Mr. Christiancy felt that Mr. Osborn had failed to make our mediation effective. Osborn made of the American representatives on the *Lackawanna* mere spectators by his interpretation of the mediation instructions of Secretary Evarts. The Secretary of State also was disappointed and in asking for an explanation gave a mild rebuke to Mr. Osborn. He said, "If, however, it was your purpose to convey the impression that we would not cheerfully assume any labor and trouble incident to arbitration in the interest of peace and the service of justice, you have not correctly appreciated the views and wishes of this government." He further said that the President "will shrink from no effort or responsibility which can properly tend to the accomplishment of such a desirable end." The ministers to each of the belligerent countries were instructed to show a copy of this letter to the respective chancelleries to which they were accredited. This interpretation of the scope of the mediation which the United States intended to offer in the *Lackawanna* Conference was not received by the ministers until three months later after the conference closed. Some writers in Bolivia and Peru state that the war might have been ended in 1880 had Mr. Osborn taken a dif-

ferent attitude in the conference of the *Lackawanna.*
Of course what could have been accomplished would
have depended on how far the President and Congress
of the United States would have gone in intervention.

There were two great forces behind the demand to
move against Lima—the guano policy of Piérola and
the war fever in Chile. The effects of the guano policy
will be apparent in what followed later and the Chilean
attitude was apparent in the tenor of their press when
Mr. Pettis wished to have the United States mediate.
When Mr. Christiancy arrived in Santiago before the
Lackawanna Conference he was suspected of having
peace designs. Congress questioned the ministry, which
appeased its inquisitors by denying any peace dealings
with the American minister. When the offer came
shortly afterward it was explained that the attempt
was useless, but owing to the prestige of the United
States it would be difficult to refuse its tender of good
offices. The following editorial statements regarding
the efforts of Minister Pettis, besides giving another
view of the Monroe Doctrine, will serve to gauge the
height of the war excitement in Chile and will excuse
somewhat Minister Osborn who did not know exactly
how far his Government was prepared to go in intervention.

Intervention of the Yankee Government[9]

It is hard to believe that the North American Government that has always looked with the most absolute indifference on the contests of the republics of this continent
should to-day want to enforce itself as mediator in a contest perhaps the most justified (it is so understood on our
part) of any that have stained with blood the New World.
Since when so much humanitarian zeal, after having

looked quietly upon the slaughter in all the South American countries except Chili?

Yesterday only did not Misters Yankees see Paraguay perish after a heroic combat against three adversaries, of which the least strong was a thousand times superior to herself? Well! Why then, did they not use their friendly influence or their coercive threat? When the Spanish squadron bombarded Valparaiso the Great Republic had in the bay the formidable Mounadnok nevertheless, Admiral Mendez Nuñez proceeded as if he were the absolute master of the seas. Minister Seward would not even listen, in compliment to Neutrality, to the complaints of the Chilian representative, who, in an unhappy moment, believed that the so-celebrated Monroe doctrine extended so far as to protect a feeble country, a victim of a powerful European nation.

Now, then, if the Monroe doctrine could not cross the Isthmus of Panama whilst a poor American country was being chastised by one that had been its master in the bygone times of colonization, why, then, shall we allow today, to the principle of intervention, a principle only used against the weak, so violent an interpretation, founded, it may be, on a humanitarian basis or upon financial interests?

A Mediation as Absurd as Dangerous[10]
[Extract from *La Patria*]

Conjointly with our colleague of this port, we received yesterday the advice that there had been presented to our government, in an imperative manner, a proposed forced mediation, tendered by the great Republic of the United States.

We will ingenuously say the truth; we gave no credit to the news, reserving to ourselves to qualify it as being of the worst character, and, above all, of more evil consequence than many of the false news which every day some people, with wicked designs rather than a spirit of intervention, spread about the streets.

Even to-day, and notwithstanding the honor it has merited from "El Mercurio" by finding place in its columns, we insist upon denying not only its existence but also its verisimilitude. And, in truth, foundation is not lacking in proof of our systematic incredulity.

It is an established fact, as it is opportunely put forth by El Mercurio, that the benevolent intention of the Northern Confederation and the purposes of the Monroe doctrine have never passed the sphere of beautiful theories in favor of any of the Latin-race countries of the South American continent. The Monroe doctrine was invented solely for Saxons and in favor of Saxons.

To the real and indisputable examples set forth in aid of this thesis by El Mercurio we can properly add other examples, if possible, to those already mentioned.

What has the Monroe doctrine done for Cuba? Has Spain not prosecuted with tenacity her implacable war under the nose of the United States? Has the case of the Virginius been forgotten, from on board of which Spain took out, by means of the Tornado, citizens under the protection of the starry flag, shooting them afterwards, notwithstanding the protest of the commander of the vessel?

What did the United States do for Mexico when the Imperial Eagle was making a prey of the heroic and intrepid Puebla? What did it do for Texas? What has it done for the Republics of Central America in their conflicts with Germany and other European Governments? To fold her arms, and if not co-operating, allowing, at least, the realization of the known maxim *la force prime le droit,* or, let us call it, the right of the strong is the only one possible right.

. . . .

. . . For this reason we limit ourselves to repeat with him to-day and with the entire country to-morrow: "The *Chilian flag that waves in the Bolivian territory cannot be hauled down* until the Peru-Bolivian army succeed in defeating ours. In this way only could it retire; in any other way, never! never!!"

. . . .

We repeat for the thousandth and last time, there is not, there cannot be, there will not exist the mediation of which we speak. If we should be mistaken, if such news became a fact, we say it ingenuously, we believe that the country, rising like a single man, would make a solemn "auto de fé" of the treaty of mediation, and God grant they stop there and do not incur the temptation of feeding the flames with the authors of the idea. For if it is true that people forgive many mistakes after glory has been obtained—for example, in France Henry IV, Louis XIV, and Napoleon—it is equally true that they are implacable with those that lead them foolishly or carelessly to degradation and shame.

The opening of the third year of the war found no abatement in its prosecution. The same causes which had existed to prevent peace continued to exist and that was what made the question of Tacna-Arica. There was no good stopping place. Tarapacá was scarcely occupied by the Chilean army before a measure was introduced in Congress to incorporate the department into the Chilean nation. It was clear to officials, press, and public that if Chile were to keep one foot of the coast she had captured from Bolivia she would have to preclude any possibility of a war of reconquest and revenge by Peru, a nation much larger and potentially stronger than Chile. If Tarapacá were not kept Peru would use it as a base and a source of revenue from which to reconquer the coast captured by Chile and to secure revenge. Peru would not then give up Tarapacá. Therefore when Secretary Evarts sought to restore peace it was far off and the advance against Lima destined.

Thus it is seen that the cry, "On to Lima," came from the desire to find a stopping place for this war of nitrate expansion. It was not found in the Treaty of Ancón which technically ended the war; Article III, the plebiscite article of that treaty, was not the crux of the question as had to be demonstrated by the attempted plebiscite under the Coolidge award. And even after the Treaty of Santiago and the reincorporation of Tacna into Peru, with that much recession to find a good stopping place for Chile's northern limits, who can say if the question raised in this chapter has been settled?

REFERENCES

1. *Senate Executive Documents,* Forty-seventh Congress, first session, Vol. IV, Doc. 79, p. 106.
2. *Ibid.,* p. 107.
3. Gonzalo Búlnes, *Guerra del Pacífico,* II, 281, 282.
4. *Senate Executive Documents,* Forty-seventh Congress, first session, Vol. IV, Doc. 79, p. 116.
5. *Ibid.,* pp. 406–414. Also William Jefferson Dennis, *Documentary History of the Tacna-Arica Dispute,* pp. 141–151.
6. Búlnes, *op. cit.,* II, 504–506.
7. *Ibid.,* p. 506.
8. *Ibid.,* p. 507.
9. *El Mercurio,* Valparaiso, Chile, August 14, 1879, quoted from *Senate Executive Documents,* Forty-seventh Congress, first session, Vol. IV, Doc. 79, p. 265.
10. *La Patria,* Valparaiso, August 15, 1879, quoted from *Senate Executive Documents,* Forty-seventh Congress, first session, Vol. IV, Doc. 79, p. 267.

CHAPTER VII

THE CAPTURE OF LIMA

WHILE the Lynch raid and the campaign against Lima are of more importance from the standpoint of their bearing on peace and peace terms, they have some rather interesting features from a military point of view. They had to be made sixteen hundred miles from home. Of course, depots for provisions were established at the intermediary points which had been captured, but nothing was produced in them. During the campaigns in the Atacama and Tarapacá deserts, Chile had developed a system of tank and distillery ships, for no dependable water supply existed within a thousand miles. For the size of Chile the expedition against Lima was very large, consisting of some twenty thousand men with sufficient transports and supplies. There still remained the fast old *Union* in the Peruvian navy and a launch or two which had been converted into torpedo craft, so there was the necessity of convoy.

Recognizing the inferiority of her navy and being unable to secure more ships, Peru hoped to accomplish much with torpedoes, which at the time were largely in the experimental stage. These, however, caused great concern in Chilean naval circles. During the first year of the war the Chilean admiral retaliated by bombarding a town, whether fortified or not, each time he heard that attempts had been made to use torpedoes. This brought many protests from neutral diplomats.[1] Peru had little success with this mode of warfare. The torpedoes were secured in the United States through Mr.

Flint who was at the same time Chilean consul in New York and Peruvian financial agent. Mr. Flint relates that before he could turn over the consulate to a Chilean, he, as Chilean consul, received a letter from an employee of a telegraph company over whose wires he had sent messages concerning munitions, offering for a consideration to disclose to him certain activities of Charles R. Flint in buying munitions for Peru![2] The principal difficulties involved were in getting contraband of war transported across the Isthmus of Panama, which belonged to a neutral country, Colombia. Some boats were smuggled across in sections labeled "carriages," and torpedoes were sent in rolls of oilcloth and barrels of lard. A former Confederate soldier by the name of Read had charge of the torpedoes, but according to the statement of Mr. Flint, did not get much chance to use them because of the ambition of Peruvian officers who wished to monopolize the glory.[3]

Some damage was done in the war with the new implement of destruction, although it sometimes reacted on the ship that was trying to use it. The *Huascar* at one time launched a torpedo at the *Abtao*, but it turned around and came back directly toward the *Huascar*, which was saved by the quick work of a Peruvian officer who dived overboard and turned the bomb aside.[4] Chile also experimented with new weapons. An Irish pig boat was bought and fitted with a dynamite gun which carried eight thousand yards, much farther than any of the Peruvian coast batteries. Before it had been used very often, the gun, when being fired, recoiled with so much force that it went overboard. Chile lost two boats which were destroyed by dynamite bombs. The *Loa* was sunk with half its crew by a bomb hidden in a sack of grain bought along the coast. The *Covadonga* picked up what was apparently an abandoned gig near Chancay, but what was in reality a dynamite trap which exploded and sank the ship with the loss of a number of men. The hatreds engendered by this new and terrible form of slaughter outweighed any advantage secured in its use.

The Lynch expeditions to the northern valleys of Peru, which had been objected to by Christiancy as being a slap at our mediation, also did more harm than good, so far as ending the war was concerned, and even brought the criticism that the purpose of Chile was not to end the war, but rather, to continue it indefinitely. Lynch, himself, who wrote to the President of Chile proposing the expedition, stated that it would stimulate resistance, but he seemed to advise it on the ground of securing contributions of war.[5] The expedition landed at Chimbote, destroyed the railroad and great sugar estates near there, levying contributions ranging from 100,000 soles ($50,000) down, according to the size of the town or plantation. Much of the property in this region was owned by neutrals and this raid brought out the usual protests from diplomats.

The Chimbote railroad belonged to a North American concern, the manager of which was unable to prevent its destruction. He protested to the general in command who detailed troops to guard the property, but the guards were found selling at public auction the property they were left to guard. It was a repetition of the sacking of Mollendo. In warfare it is impossible to prevent raiding parties from looting, even among the most civilized nations. When an international expedition went to the relief of foreign legations at Peking during the Boxer uprising the troops, representing highly civilized nations, engaged in shameful looting of stores. If these troops could not be restrained we could not expect General Lynch to restrain his, although as an Irishman and soldier experienced in British discipline, he did much to keep his forces in hand. Búlnes and other Chilean historians claim that he prevented looting and personal stealing, but nevertheless, most of the Chimbote railroad disappeared under the protection of his troops, and in his *Memoirs* Lynch gives large inventories of loot later sent from Lima to Chile.

These acts and the mutual hatreds they engendered caused grave concern as to what might happen if an expedition came to Lima. The U.S. Minister in Chile reported that one reason the Government there hesitated was the fear that its army might get out of bounds and bring disgrace upon itself if Lima were taken. Chilean historians say that in the army were "20,000 of the most arrogant and conceited volunteers, anxious to get in the front line." The expedition consisted of at least twenty-four thousand men and corresponding naval and transport elements. Counting reserves and troops left on the Araucanian frontier, Chile had under arms over forty thousand men—a large force for such a small country.

As stated, preparations had continued during the *Lackawanna* Conference in October, and in November and December the expedition moved up the coast by stages from Arica to Pisco, and by marches along the coast to Lurin and Cerro Azul, the fleet and transports coming along the coast. Some little opposition was met near Lurin the middle of December, but it was not serious, and by January 12 the army was below the foothills of San Juan near Chorrillos, a suburb of Lima. A blockading fleet had been bombarding Callao from time to time and it now aided the advance of the army. On

January 13 the outlying defenses at San Juan, Santa Teresa, and Morro Solar were stormed by the invading army in a sanguinary battle lasting over half a day and Chorrillos was taken a block at a time. There was a delay the next day in following up this advance. During the afternoon a committee of the diplomatic corps of Lima visited General Baquedano, the Chilean commander, seeking an armistice. This was granted on the fifteenth to last until midnight.

The dean of the diplomatic corps, Sr. Pinto of Salvador, stated that that action was taken in view of the very great interests of neutrals involved, which interests had suffered much already in the war, to lessen the risk of exposing to danger the large foreign colonies in Lima, to furnish diagrams of the location and markings of the various legations, asylums, and deposits of goods of neutrals, and to suggest that in case Lima were occupied only a small garrison at a time be allowed to enter. Before this date diplomatic representation had been made to the Chilean Government at Santiago that in case Lima were taken it would be expected that neutrals would be protected. Assurances were always given that the General in Chief would attend to the matter, and that he was instructed to confer with the diplomatic corps of Lima.

In the conference of the morning of the fifteenth the diplomats inquired what terms the Chilean commander would accept. These were given and Piérola was asked to attend a meeting at two o'clock in the afternoon.[6] The meeting was held at Miraflores, another sea resort north of Chorrillos and about five miles from Lima. By the terms of the truce, military officers were not to fire before midnight. However, various divisions were being shifted when the afternoon conference was to take place. Mr. Pinto, Mr. Christiancy, and the ministers of England and France arrived at Miraflores at two o'clock. Shortly afterward some officers were coming out from breakfasting and Piérola was about to come out when suddenly a heavy gun boomed and in less than a minute a battle broke out along the entire line which was but about eighty rods away. The Chilean fleet in Miraflores Bay opened simultaneously; the parley was broken up suddenly and unceremoniously. Both General Baquedano and Sr. Piérola were equally taken by surprise for the starting of the battle was evidently caused by a spontaneous clash in moving troops to new positions. The diplomatic corps fled toward its train, but some missed it and had to make their way to Lima on foot dodging falling shot and shells. Mr. Christiancy was among those who missed the train and stated that he had to travel eight miles to get to Lima, and there found his legation overflowing with refugees. Besides United States interests his legation at the time was caring for Swiss and Colombian interests so that by nine o'clock twelve hundred people were in his care.

Much should be said for the work of neutral authorities and citizens in connection with the capture of Lima. When all Peruvian troops were thrown out of the city to occupy the defense lines at Chorrillos and Miraflores, a foreign legion called the Urban Guard was formed and policed the city. It was ordered to disband though later, for stopping a minister one night. The neutral fleet formed an asylum under their guns at Ancón, a little port north of Callao, and issued rations to two thousand refugees who feared to stay in Lima. General Baquedano accepted all of these precautions and permitted two naval officers from each foreign country represented by a warship, to be assigned as observers with the various divisions of the Chilean army.

The Chilean forces were victors in the Miraflores battle of the fifteenth and the Peruvian troops were badly scattered. Some of the stragglers entered Lima the next day, and without officers or other restraint, began to help themselves in stores, owned largely by Chinese. Some resistance on the part of the merchants led to a riotous attack on the Chinese quarter followed by pandemonium in the streets. The riot lasted during the night in which the glare of burning buildings added terror to the situation. Fortunately, the mud construction of the buildings prevented a general fire and during the night the Urban Guard was reorganized. On the sixteenth representatives of the municipality surrendered the city and arrangements were made whereby it was to be occupied the following day at 2.00 P.M. It was feared in Lima that the drunken element that had plundered the Chinese might fire on the Chilean forces sent to take possession of the city and cause its destruction. However, during the forenoon the Urban Guard got the rioters in hand after a sharp clash in which several guards and many rioters lost their lives.[7] After order was restored a picked body of three thousand Chilean troops quietly entered Lima, January 17, 1881, and the city was not destroyed as many neutrals had expected. Later, most of the Chilean forces were marched through the city and encamped outside.

Here the war should have terminated, but it did not. Most foreign observers thought it would, and the diplomatic corps was expected to offer its services to arrange terms. There were several reasons why peace was not made. In the first place, unconditional surrender of Lima and the complete dispersal of Piérola's army left

to Chile the initiative, and Chile had no well-defined
policy as to what plan of action would be followed when
Lima should be taken. All, from the highest officials to
the most wretched hangers-on of the army, were determined to exact a hard and vindictive peace, and last but
not least, the hand of nitrate and guano was to be
played. Before the surrender of Lima the diplomatic
corps was told that no mediation would be accepted.[8] A
policy not having been formulated, much now would
depend on events which are always very uncertain in
tense times. Although at first, great efforts were made
to keep up discipline, it was impossible to keep a victorious army, intoxicated with success and other stimuli,
from wanting some of the spoils of war. When the rich
watering places—Chorrillos, Barranco, and Miraflores
—were taken fine furniture and other loot were sent
out to the ships and these places were burned. The
Chilean general, Saavedra, who was appointed governor of Lima, tried to prevent misbehavior on the part
of his soldiers, but there were murder and looting for
several nights.

Piérola retreated over the cordillera to Tarma and at
first signified his intention of continuing the fight, but
later wrote to the diplomatic corps that he would treat
for peace. But previously, January 20, his Secretary
of State had addressed a letter to the diplomatic corps
in which he charged the Chilean army with the breaking of the truce of the fifteenth, the killing of Peruvian
wounded, and the burning of the suburbs. At the same
time General Baquedano was harping upon the treachery of the Peruvians for opening the battle. A considerable incident was made of this and the diplomatic corps
tried to arrive at the truth. It seems that General
Baquedano had stated that he would not open fire until

midnight, but had not promised not to move troops into position. When the Chilean fleet moved into position off Miraflores and artillery was moved up almost against the Peruvian lines, a Peruvian regiment mistook the rapidity of the movement for an attack. That a Chilean force came into contact with the Peruvians first and the latter fired the first gun, seems to be what happened. Undoubtedly, there was no intended treachery on either side.[9] The incident, though, had important results, for the Chileans now would not treat with Piérola unless he withdrew his letter of the twentieth.

The refusal of Chile to treat with Piérola evoked from his secretary, García, a letter of protest to Mr. Christiancy, March 1, in which was expressed the hope that the United States would now intervene.[10] Events of the war were again summarized from Peru's point of view. García's protests were confined to Chilean methods of carrying on the war, the military government and the possible protectorate which he suspected that Chile intended to impose. On March 9 the Chilean civil governor of Lima issued a decree imposing contributions of one million pesos a month on the cities of Lima and Callao. This was imposed by list on prominent residents supposed to be wealthy.[11] As a chronological, if not financial, sequence seventy-seven leading residents of those cities held a meeting and named one of their number, Francisco García Calderón, as the provisional president of Peru. This group had the support of the Chilean occupational force and its motives as voiced through *La Actualidad*, a paper published by Chileans in an appropriated Lima plant, were to secure peace with Chile and to get back to constitutional government. It was early stated that Chile would recognize no government that had not the approval of a congress. It might be noted here that Mr. Calderón was a young Lima lawyer of good standing who was the agent in Peru for Goyeneche, a Peruvian dealer in guano who resided in Paris, and whose operations had been declared null by a Piérola decree, but who now came to act as Peruvian ambassador in Paris.

At this time Christiancy received a letter from Secretary Evarts who had heard of the capture of Lima and was considering peace. The secretary describes an interview by Count Montferrand for the Crédit Industriel and infers that, while his proposition seems sound, peace was the first consideration; that finances were important only so far as they were conducive to peace. He inquired, moreover, why Mr. Christiancy had not sent him any peace news. Mr. Evarts did not know how far off peace was. Shortly after the setting up of the Calderón government, Mr. Godoi who had been so effective in bringing on the war, called on Mr. Christiancy, and said very knowingly that peace was a long way off. He knew the situation better than most people. Christiancy soon came to the opinion that Chile did not mean to adopt any peace policy, and he even thought they might be playing Calderón's government against that of Piérola with the purpose of further humbling Peru. He was probably strengthened in that belief by reports from speeches in the Chilean Congress which voiced the idea that Peru must be rendered impotent, that the very railroads must be torn up, that there should be a protectorate, and even that Peru should be annexed to Chile.

Although the statesmen of the invaders had formulated no policy to follow after the capture of Lima, other than to make it impossible for Peru to invalidate the result of Chilean victories, the financial interests involved did have definite ideas about what they wanted. The first official information that was received in Washington of the fall of Lima came from agents of the Crédit Industriel, and Lima had scarcely been occupied when guano shippers were on the ground seeking contracts. It will be recalled that the program of the Crédit Industriel was suppressed by the decrees of Piérola annulling the contract made by Goyeneche in Paris, January 7, 1880. With the retreat of Piérola to the interior of Peru and the naming of Calderón, attorney for Goyeneche, as provisional president in Lima, the company began actively to assert its claims. It was not to be expected that Chile would favor the "program," the European powers could not intervene in America without incurring the opposition of the United States and, therefore, it was hoped that the United States would intervene in behalf of the great number of neutrals involved financially in the war. The essence of the program of the Crédit Industriel is as follows:

I

The neutrality of the guano and nitrate deposits, so as to avoid ill-feeling between the two nations, which would result from a surrender of the territory, and at the same time to guarantee to the creditors said deposits (pledged to them), against all future difficulties or competitions.

II

The working of the neutral deposits to be entrusted to an institution of credit, offering a financial basis of unquestionable standing and ability to assure public confidence in any engagement it shall undertake in regard to all the interests.

III

THE BASIS OF THE TRANSACTION

The contract of the Crédit Industriel, dated at Paris, January 7, 1880, so modified as to give satisfaction to every interest, allowing, namely:

First. *To Chili.*—The royalty claimed by her of £1 10s. per ton, or £450,000 per annum, which would permit a loan of £4,000,000 to be raised to pay a reasonable war indemnity.

Second. *To Peru.*—The amount which she has declared indispensable for her internal budget, £450,000 per annum.

Third. *To the bondholders.*—The balance, which represents 3⅓ per cent. on the principal of the standing debt.

IV

The funding of the nitrate debt in order to permit the redemption of the guano Peruvian debt, and to increase, if necessary, the royalties appropriated to Peru and Chili.

V

To lay a cable from Panama to Peru (Callao), to aid the development of commercial relations with the last-named country, and assist in the restoration of her credit. There could be appropriated for the benefits of said cable a subsidy to be derived from the funded nitrate debt.

We can assert that this programme, should it be proposed by the United States, would be endorsed by the great European powers whose subjects are the creditors of Peru, mainly England, France, Belgium, and Holland.

Included in the program was a financial statement of the obligations and remuneration specified in the contract which was summarized as follows:

The foregoing will therefore permit regularly to be appropriated each year:

I. *To Chili*, £550,000; that is to say, an amount more than sufficient to raise a loan of £4,000,000 to £5,000,000.

II. *To Peru*, £550,000; that is to say, more than the treasury has ever regularly received.

III. *To the bondholders*, £1,200,000. This is an income less than the one originally promised, £2,600,000; but it will be perfectly sure, as it will be protected against all chances by the neutrality secured.

It is sufficient to read the foregoing programme and the figures attached to it to acknowledge:

A. That said arrangement is acceptable to both nations, since it will permit them to settle peace without any sacrifice to their national pride, and securing to each one a large pecuniary compensation.

B. That said arrangement is acceptable to the creditors of Peru, since it gives to them a security which they have never had, in return for abandonment of a portion of their interests.

C. That said arrangement would be acceptable to any mediator, since it does not impose a sacrifice of any interests, and it permits the restoration of the credit of two nations, whose ruin will cause trouble in the commercial world.

This was signed by A. Guillaume, President of the Peruvian Bondholders' French Committee.[12]

The "program" of the Crédit Industriel also contained a long list of banking and commercial firms in the leading countries of Europe who were supporting that plan of mediation. In the last paragraph of the document there is a plain attempt to appeal to the anti-European sentiment, then existing in government circles at Washington. It says:

It is pertinent to observe, that while Peru and Bolivia have from the beginning of the war turned their eyes towards the United States, Chili, on the contrary, has to the present moment endeavored to fortify her political and commercial links with Europe. She has attempted on different occasions to place the guano and the nitrate deposits under the exclusive control of English houses, but her efforts have proved unsuccessful, owing to the open declaration of the British Government and of the English courts of justice, which will undoubtedly become more emphatic and decisive as soon as it will be known that the United States has decided to mediate with the firm intention of settling the difficulties existing between the three sister republics, and adjusting every claim on equitable grounds to all parties.

It is doubtful if any other war in history, with the exception of the World War, has had so many international financial ramifications as did the War of the Pacific. On February 18, 1881, the Bolivian Minister, Ladislas Cabrera, submitted a proposal to Secretary Evarts for a financial intervention similar to that proposed by the Crédit Industriel.

Following the *Lackawanna* Conference, each of the belligerents had issued circulars placing the blame for the failure of the conference on the enemy. In the Chilean circular dated November 10, there was a financial item that caused a stir among the bondholders. Regarding the intention of Chile to retain Tarapacá it said, "The surrender of the territory furthermore involved on the part of the successful power a recognition of the mortgages and incumbrances created upon it by Peru to her foreign creditors." This aroused the hopes of hundreds of claim holders and the cupidity of divers financial ghouls. It created such a storm of protest in the press, however—and an interpellation by the Congress of Chile—that a special circular dealing with Tarapacá bondholders was issued December 24, 1880. In this statement it was explained that the recognition of debts was contingent on the acceptance by Bolivia and Peru of Chile's terms, but since the *Lackawanna* Conference did not result in the acceptance of those terms Chile did not recognize the claims and they would have to be settled by international law.

A company known as the Peruvian Corporation was organized in New York by one Jacob Shipherd, which put forth a claim to one-third of all the nitrate and guano ever sold in Peru. It was based on a claim bought from an illegitimate son of Alexandre Cochet[13] and its success depended also upon the intervention of the United States. While it was a wild scheme it was the direct cause of an investigation by Congress of the efforts of the Secretary of State to bring about peace in South America.

Returning nearer to the scene of hostilities, we find great activity on the part of guano shippers. General Lynch was soon made military governor of Lima and he contracted in the name of the Government of Chile to sell forty thousand tons of the guano of Peru to John T. North and H. R. F. Jameson, sometimes called the nitrate kings. This contract, hurriedly made, contained a time limit of one year for shipping, with a fine for each ton not shipped at the end of that period. Haste was needed for there was now the specter of intervention by the United States. Dreyfus & Company had tried to get this contract at a figure low enough to reimburse them for the bonds they owned against Peruvian guano.[14] Naturally, then, there would be no hurry on the part of Chile to make peace and evacuate Lima before a year had elapsed.

As soon as Secretary Evarts learned of the fall of Lima, he sent instructions to Minister Christiancy to use his influence to secure peace if possible. This was difficult, owing to the state of affairs in Peru, and the guano contract made by Lynch. Peru was helpless and almost hopeless. The only hope in continuing the war came from the fact that Argentina had finally consented to allow Bolivia to transport arms across her territory, and a Bolivian force was expected to coöperate with President Piérola in the Arequipa region, which as yet had not been harmed by Chile. While the allies could not expect to win the war, they hoped to prevent the annexation of the entire coast which they believed Chile intended. They did not know that guano exploitation, and not expansion beyond guano deposits, was the motive of the war.

Christiancy reported that residents of Lima had even approached him regarding the possibility of the United States assuming the protection of Peru, believing that a protectorate was preferable to annexation. The morals of Chile are frequently condemned for the conquest of so much Bolivian and Peruvian territory. Without excusing this policy it may be explained by calling attention to the helplessness of the allies, which offered great temptation to a victor, and to the commercial spirit of that epoch. In this connection, Christiancy, in commenting on the idea of a United States protectorate for Peru, stated that he would not wish us to possess it until we should have better assimilated the territory we had, but he was certain that if it were adjacent our settlers would soon colonize it and demand annexation. But we have not colonized and annexed below the Rio Grande.

At the request of the people of Lima the Chilean commander allowed a provisional Peruvian government to be set up at Magdalena, near Lima, to devise means for paying the contributions required by the Saavedra decree.

On March 10 Christiancy received a protest from the curator of the national library and museum in Lima saying that on February 26, although he had been promised immunity, the keys had been demanded and priceless manuscripts and books were being carted away. This appropriation of books and the taking of laboratory materials from the school of medicine, and the agricultural station, caused a protest from *El Orden*, the official organ of the new Calderón government. The semiofficial Chilean paper, *La Actualidad*, had the following answer which indicates the temper of the victors in 1881:

The Chilian authorities have determined to follow and will still continue to dispose of national property of Peru, with the indisputable right, conceded by all the nations of the world to the conqueror, when it is to repay himself the expenses of the war, and when he has at hand the means of coercion, which obliges the enemy to put an end to the war, in order to prevent worse evils.

This is, nevertheless, the protest of the gentlemen of *El Orden*, what the Chilian authorities have done with the work-shops of cartridges, the machines of the school of arts, with books and instruments of sciences, and with one historical picture.

They can do it to-morrow with all the public buildings, beginning from the palace of government and ending with the last sentry-box.[15]

In Lima, Christiancy was very close to reliable sources of information such as Sr. Godoi, who had returned to Lima, and to the British Minister, Spencer St. Johns. He wrote to Washington on March 21 that the war had reached such a stage that the influence of the United States on that coast upon any question connected with the war, or the question of peace, could only be secured by active intervention against the will of Chile. He thought that the Crédit Industriel plan might have been acceptable earlier in the war, but that nothing except hostile intervention by other powers would induce Chile to accept the plan suggested or any other for immediate peace.

While intervention by the United States, alone, or in conjunction with other American powers, as Secretary Blaine suggested, should have taken place at this time it would have been difficult for the critics of the United States ever to have seen in such a move anything else but material motives and financial aid to the Crédit Industriel, although that company was a European concern. As seen in his instruction to Mr. Christiancy, Secretary Evarts made it clear what was the attitude of his Government; namely, that this or any other liquidation plan was incidental and considered only as a means of settlement of claims growing out of the war and not as an end to be sought in intervention.[16] Chilean writers have persisted in the thesis that up to the appointment of Secretary Frelinghuysen, the United States held a brief for the Crédit Industriel. They are especially derogatory in their treatment of Secretary Blaine who is accused by the two leading Chilean historians of having given one set of formal instructions to Minister Hurlbut and different verbal instructions. Their source is entirely the report of the Congressional Committee which investigated the State Department, blocked United States mediation, and ended in exonerating Blaine. In the examination of witnesses, Blaine's political enemies tried to show that he practiced duplicity in instructing Hurlbut, but they lacked any proof.[17]

REFERENCES

1. *Senate Executive Documents,* Forty-seventh Congress, first session, Vol. IV, Doc. 79, p. 217.
2. Charles R. Flint, *Memories of an Active Life,* p. 85.
3. *Ibid.,* p. 87.
4. G. F. Scott Elliot, *Chile,* p. 219.
5. Gonzalo Búlnes, *Guerra del Pacífico,* II, 556.
6. *Foreign Relations,* 1881, p. 856.
7. From the diary of a survivor of the Urban Guard.
8. *Foreign Relations,* 1881, p. 860.
9. *Ibid.,* p. 905.
10. *Ibid.,* p. 882.
11. Tomás Caivano, *Historia de la guerra de América,* p. 75.
12. *Senate Executive Documents,* Forty-seventh Congress, first session, Vol. IV, Doc. 79, pp. 450–452.
13. F. B. D'Avricourt, *Les chemins de fer du Pérou,* p. 167.
14. Patrick Lynch, *Primer memoria de Lynch,* p. 162.
15. *La Actualidad,* Lima, March 21, 1881.
16. *Senate Executive Documents,* Forty-seventh Congress, first session, Vol. IV, Doc. 79, pp. 449, 450.
17. Note: In the examination of Blaine it was attempted to show that on the margin of a temperate instruction he had written in pencil, "Go it, Steve." This was supposed by his enemies to mean that Stephen Hurlbut was to "go it" intervening. Búlnes accepts this as historical evidence and leaps to the conclusion that Blaine intended to intervene in behalf of the Crédit Industriel: he must not have read the entire testimony or he would not have arrived at that conclusion. Other Chilean writers on the subject are mostly copyists of Búlnes. See Gonzalo Búlnes, *op. cit.,* Vol. III; and Anselmo Blanlot Holley, *Historia de la paz entre Chile y el Perú, 1879–1884,* pp. 95–125. For Congressional Investigation of Secretary Blaine see *House Reports,* Forty-seventh Congress, first session, VI, 217.

CHAPTER VIII

INTERVENTIONS OF THE UNITED STATES

PREVIOUS to the fall of Lima two attempts at mediation had been made by representatives of the United States. The efforts of our Minister to Bolivia, Judge Pettis, in August, 1879, were made on his own responsibility.* The State Department had termed his action "daring" and had withheld approval or disapproval. The attempt was barren of results except that in the memoranda of bases which he secured were seen the objectives of the belligerents at the beginning of the war and his activity was an index of the interest the United States would manifest in the struggle.

The first authorized attempt at mediation, that which resulted in the conference of the *Lackawanna*, has already been noted. It had no permanent effect upon the war or peace except to show that Chile was determined to annex Tarapacá and break the Bolivia-Peru alliance. Mr. Osborn thought that the prestige of the United States was not hurt by the attempt, but it certainly was not enhanced. It made evident at any rate that there would not be the possibility of effective intervention by European powers for that was to be prevented by the political interest of the United States whose financial interests in South America were as nothing then compared with those of Europe.

On March 4 the administration of President Garfield inherited the complex case. The new Secretary of State, James G. Blaine, gave it more than usual atten-

* See *supra,* p. 92.

tion. In April there was an unsuccessful attempt to reinstal in Lima the constitutional City Council as it had existed before the Piérola revolution. President Calderón's government gained power slowly, the support given it by the Chilean army of occupation being of doubtful value because the masses looked upon Piérola as a hero for defying the Chileans from his mountain retreat. Calderón issued a call for a congress to meet May 15, and Chilean safe-conduct was given for representatives to assemble. Piérola issued a countermanifesto calling a congress to meet at Ayacucho, June 4. Secretary Blaine had advised Christiancy to recognize Calderón as soon as he thought it advisable. The call for the Ayacucho Congress now delayed this recognition until the outcome of the dual Congress could be seen.

Representatives of Great Britain, France, and Italy now tendered to Chile their offices to help negotiate for peace but were refused. Mr. Osborn in April counseled the Chilean Government to give more support to the Calderón government by restoring the capital to him. He again states to Secretary Blaine that Chile will certainly demand Tarapacá and possibly Moquegua. Osborn's vacation, now long overdue, was granted and he was followed by Gen. Judson Kilpatrick. Christiancy in Lima was also to be relieved August 3 by Gen. Stephen A. Hurlbut. On June 15, 1881, Secretary Blaine sent both ministers instructions which indicated his policy.

Blaine recognized that any intervention of the United States was already embarrassed by the failure of the conference of the *Lackawanna* and that Chile was prepared to "dictate and not discuss" terms. In order that the United States ministers at the capitals of the belligerent countries might be prepared he gave them an outline of policy. Recognizing the right of Chile to indemnities and guaranties of future peace he said:

   . . . it would seem natural that Peru and Bolivia should be allowed to offer such indemnity and guarantee before the annexation of territory, which is the right of conquest, is insisted upon. If these powers fail to offer what is a reasonably sufficient indemnity and guarantee, then it becomes a fair subject of consideration whether such territory may not be exacted as the necessary price of peace.

But at the conclusion of a war avowedly not of conquest, but for the solution of differences which diplomacy had failed to settle, to make the acquisition of territory a *sine qua non* of peace is calculated to cast suspicions on the professions with which war was originally declared. It may very well be that at the termination of such a contest the changed condition and relation of all the parties to it may make readjustment of boundaries or territorial changes wise as well as necessary; but this, where the war is not one of conquest, shall be the result of negotiation and not the absolute preliminary condition on which alone the victor consents to negotiate. At this day, when the right of the people to govern themselves, the fundamental basis of republican institutions, is so universally recognized, there is nothing more difficult or more dangerous than the forced transfer of territory, carrying with it an indignant and hostile population, and nothing but a necessity proven before the world can justify it. It is not a case in which the power desiring the territory can be accepted as a safe or impartial judge.[1]

This doctrine of "no territorial indemnities" when

the territory carried a hostile population, Blaine hoped
would be an American doctrine. Regarding the "difficulties in a forced transfer of territory," the Tacna-
Arica difficulties furnish ample example. The reader
may find justification for the interest of the United
States in securing peace in a statement regarding the
helpless condition of Peru which could neither "enforce
order within nor peace without." That the Monroe
Doctrine was always in mind in the policy of Secretary
Blaine may be seen in the final paragraph of his instructions. It says:

> The Government of the United States seeks only to per-
> form the part of a friend to all the parties in this un-
> happy conflict between South American republics, and it
> will regret to be compelled to consider how far that feel-
> ing might be affected, and a more active interposition
> forced upon it, by any attempted complication of this
> question with European politics.

In May Gen. Stephen A. Hurlbut was appointed by
President Garfield as minister to Peru. In the meantime Christiancy was in a quandary as to whether and
when to recognize Calderón's government. Piérola's
Congress was postponed to July. Calderón made a
clever bid for recognition by inviting the members of
the diplomatic corps to attend the installation of his
government, April 30. Christiancy was the only member who thought that the note of invitation could be
acknowledged without recognizing the Government.
The watchword in Chilean circles in Lima was indefinite
occupation.

Coincident with the entry of Mr. Hurlbut into this
question was the ill-starred rise of the Peruvian Company in New York which was to prove the nemesis of

Hurlbut if not of Secretary Blaine also. In the history of this El Dorado of nitrates, many names of wealth were created such as North, Jameson, Dreyfus, and Meiggs, but there were also many others who should have received more of the fruits of that bonanza than they did. Among the latter figure the names of two Frenchmen, Landreau and Cochet. The former, Jean Theophile Landreau, as a guano prospector, located thirty-four new deposits for the Peruvian Government when its credit was low and reports of exhausted guano beds had made it difficult for the administration to secure new loans. Since Cochet, who was the real discoverer of the value of the stream of wealth that later flowed from nitrates, *caliche*, and guano, had got nothing out of it, Landreau had made a contract with the Government of Peru by which he was to receive 10 per cent of the returns of his discoveries, aggregating a million tons. Since the yield was much more than that, he formally asked a settlement. After a long legal contest he was unable to collect his share and so gave his brother, John Landreau, a citizen of Louisiana who had "grubstaked" him in his prospecting tours, a half interest in his claims. John Landreau then appealed to the United States Government and Congress passed a joint resolution February 20, 1880, granting him the good offices of the President and the Secretary of State in the settlement of his claim.[2] The matter was given the attention of our minister in Peru and effective results were expected.

Jacob Shipherd and his Peruvian corporation also entered the lists to realize a fortune out of Peru. Besides owning the Cochet claim, he had an understanding with Landreau to liquidate his claims also. In fine, Shipherd's plan was to establish a claim to one-third of all the vast nitrate wealth of Peru and liquidate all war claims and private claims of good standing. He also expected to be backed by the intervention of the United States. Before Hurlbut left for Lima, Shipherd tried to take him into his scheme offering him stock in the company. He claimed to have inside information of Secretary Blaine's plans for intervention and was obsessed with the idea that the State Department would back his plan as an American policy. The Secretary's enemies tried to prove him involved in financial diplomatic freebooting in South America and much of their suspicion was based on the wild propaganda of Shipherd.[3]

When General Hurlbut was named minister to Peru he was given instructions similar to those given the ministers to the other belligerents and in addition was asked to report whether Peru could meet an indemnity without the loss of territory. Of course Secretary Blaine may not have known that the provisional President of Peru was intimately related to the agent who made the contract in Paris with the Crédit Industriel which was anxious to liquidate the war. It can readily be seen that Minister Hurlbut entered upon a difficult mission. With Peru and Bolivia disorganized, and Chile in an undecided and inflamed state following her conquest, and with great international financial interests involved, the man who represented the only power from which possible outside intervention might come, would naturally be a storm center in the question. Besides being sought out and tempted by Shipherd before he left his home in Illinois, he was accompanied to the boat when he sailed by agents of Calderón and the Crédit Industriel. But he was absolutely unimpeachable and died a soldier of diplomacy as he had lived a general in war.

On June 16 Mr. Christiancy had a conference with the Chilean Minister in Lima, Sr. Godoi, and with Admiral Lynch, Military Governor. These men did not wish foreign countries to recognize the government of provisional President Calderón until Chile did. He also learned from other sources that Chile had sent emissaries to treat secretly with President Piérola. On the nineteenth Godoi called and talked over the subject. When Mr. Christiancy stated that he probably would recognize President Calderón if the latter's Congress secured a quorum or returned to constitutional government, Godoi remarked that peace was a long way off. He did not know that Christiancy had word that Chile was treating with President Piérola, too, and that Christiancy was convinced that Chile was playing Calderón and Piérola against each other. Christiancy however did not know about the one-year time limit on the guano contract made by the commander of the army of occupation.

Christiancy soon resolved to recognize the government of Calderón although his judgment told him it would be better to wait until the results of President Piérola's Congress were known. He heard that his successor, Hurlbut, had been named, but was not to relieve him until after the recognition, so in order to avoid the appearance of withholding recognition in order to retain his post longer, he recognized the Calderón government June 26—just fifteen days after its Congress secured a quorum.

On August 10 Mr. Hurlbut made a comprehensive report to Secretary Blaine. He said that war as such was over, that Chile had destroyed all organized resistance and occupied the capital and principal ports, sold guano and nitrates and collected the duties, which in June amounted to $400,000. He hoped that one of the two congresses would give way and that Peru could secure peace, and still be a nation. He said that Peru was ready to pay any sum to $40,000,000, according to President Calderón, and that since the Government of Chile had estimated the cost of the war at $30,000,-000, a money indemnity should be satisfactory. Little did he know of the big prize in Tarapacá, or of the deposits of guano on the islands of Peru to be shipped before peace was made, for, when the contract for forty thousand tons was filled, another was let for a million tons. He closed his report with an opinion of what course the United States should pursue in the case. He said:

It is, in my deliberate and carefully considered judgment, the proper time for the United States to act as a friend to both parties, and to say very kindly, but very firmly, to Chili, that war has fulfilled all its legitimate purposes; that longer continuance of the state of war would be disastrous to both countries, and an unnecessary invasion of the rights of neutrals, engaged in commerce or owning as they do, large properties in Peru; and that a peace honorable to both countries should be concluded as soon as possible, on fair terms as to indemnity. It will be remembered that Chili in the Arica conferences denied any purpose of acquiring territory by conquest, and placed her demand for cession of territory solely upon the ground that Bolivia and Peru had not the means to pay a money indemnity.

Inasmuch as Peru offers to pay and can pay a money indemnity, the forcible annexation of territory ought not to be permitted. By such action on the part of our government we would gain the highest influence in South America, we should subserve the purposes of a truer civilization, and inaugurate a higher style of national and international law on this continent.

In whatever form this may be done, if done at all, it ought to be done very speedily, and as a very serious emergency may arise at any time, I should be happy to receive from the Department by telegraph, some indication of approval or disapproval of my views.

Following the recognition by the United States of President Calderón and the arrival of new ministers to each country there was acute interest in the attitude of the United States on peace terms. Reports from Chile indicated that milder demands would be made on Peru. Hurlbut was confident of the efficacy of our influence and apparently expected an early settlement. Full of patriotism and military efficiency he lacked tact and soon exploded a bomb in the delicate situation.

He wrote to Secretary Blaine that Christiancy had been in the questionable habit of calling the diplomatic corps together to consult on all matters. He said that that "practically emasculated the United States and deprived them of their leadership." He held aloof and soon Admiral Lynch came to ascertain, for his "own personal guidance and not in any diplomatic sense," what the sentiments of the United States were. Hurlbut was glad to give them and offered to reduce them to writing in the form of a memorandum. Lynch went directly to the British legation and within three hours the British and French ministers visited Calderón and offered their good offices. Previously they had steadfastly advised President Calderón that it would be impossible to make peace with Chile without cession of territory. They now faced about and said they believed they could arrange it through Admiral Lynch. A reading of the memorandum does not reveal at once anything very inflammable, but it created a *furore* in Santiago and brought a protest from the Chilean legation in Washington which considered the memorandum obnoxious and officious.

It summarized the views contained in his instructions, but in very direct language using such terms as "violent dismemberment of a nation" and "war for the purpose of territorial aggrandizement." He practically said that war was over and should cease both for the good of Chile and the great neutral interests involved. Before taking up the further activities of General Hurlbut, all of which were of a military type of diplomacy, the efforts of his colleague in Santiago, Gen. Judson Kilpatrick, should be noticed. These two men were of exactly opposite types, the former burly and frank to bluntness, while the latter was sickly and tactful to a fault. They had in common, though, the desire to serve their country and both died at their posts at about the same time. Neither lived to know the results of his efforts as peacemaker.

When General Kilpatrick arrived in Santiago and received the instructions of Secretary Blaine he had a difficult task. He had to learn the views of the outgoing administration of President Pinto and those of the President-elect Santa María. It is often stated in Chile that had not Secretary Blaine virtually espoused the cause of Peru by advancing the doctrine of no territorial indemnities at that time, President Calderón of Peru would have accepted the terms of Chile. Because of this assertion which could not be proved without knowing the intentions of Sr. Calderón, and because the essential part of Mr. Kilpatrick's statements were posthumously assailed in Chile it will be well to quote parts of the Minister's letter to Secretary Blaine.

I discovered later on that the President was alarmed at the views you advanced, delicately brought to his attention, and in all probability would not be inclined to accept them. I at once became satisfied that the President and his cabinet held not only other views, but were contemplating absolute peace with the Government of Señor Calderon. I therefore did not deem it wise to acquaint the Secretary of State and the President with the full purport of your dispatch. I adopted what I thought to be a wiser course; I called upon Señor Louis Aldunate, the first friend of the President elect, a gentleman of great ability, who, I have reason to know, will occupy the first position in the cabinet of President-elect Santa Maria. I read him your dispatch, and at the same time informed him of my belief regarding the intention of President Pinto. After a full discussion of each separate point, and explanations of what I believed to be the result of misinformation on your part regarding "annexation of hostile territory," (to which I will refer again) your views were substantially accepted as wise and just. Señor Aldunate immediately acquainted President-elect Santa Maria with the contents of your note, and both have assured me [this is the part denied later by the Chilean ministry]—"That not one foot of Peruvian territory will be exacted by force unless all efforts of diplomatic negotiations shall fail, and that in no case can Chili treat finally with the Government of Señor Calderon until it shall appear that his government is respected and obeyed throughout Peru, which does not obtain at this moment. That no doubt President Pinto would like to celebrate the last days of his administration by a proclamation of peace with Peru, with the Government of Calderon, a government without a single element that constitutes a real government, and that would fall at once but for Chilian protection."

I was invited to attend Congress the following day, when the government would be interpellated regarding its plans and purposes. I went, found the House crowded with people, and, amid great excitement, heard the cabinet of President Pinto questioned and worried by Señor Lira, the first orator of Chili. I intended to send you translations of the speeches in this debate, but am too unwell to attempt it. I have been confined to my bed the greater portion of the time since my arrival in Chili. This debate developed the fact that President Pinto was contemplating peace with the Government of Calderon—peace which, from the nature of the debate, I was satisfied, must of necessity include territorial annexation. Intimate friends of the administration not only confirmed this belief, but convinced me further that President Pinto was determined to accomplish his purpose; that he yet had time, and that the Government of Calderon was in no condition to refuse any conditions Chili might impose. How to prevent this without giving offense to President Pinto I could not satisfactorily answer. I had gained the incoming administration; this was not sufficient. I determined finally to approach the administration, and change its purpose if possible. I sent for Señor Aldunate and Señor George Huneens, the solicitor for the government whose name you will find frequently mentioned in the paper relating to the Arica [or *Lackawanna*] conference, and asked them to arrange for me a meeting with the secretary of state and secretary of war, the dominant members of the President's cabinet.

After some delay this was agreed upon, and a conference was held at my house last night between Señor Valderrama, secretary of state, Señor Vergara, secretary of war, Aldunate, and Huneens. The conference lasted from 7 p.m. till one in the morning. I am too ill to give you a full account of the meeting; the result is all I can forward at this time.

Your dispatch was read and fully considered, and its advice and suggestions pressed upon the secretary of state. He finally replied. "The ideas indicated by Secretary Blaine are in direct conflict with those held by the Government of Chili, and if we abandon our policy it is out of respect for the opinion of the administration at Washington. You may therefore say to your government, that every effort would be given by Chili to strengthen the Government of President Calderon, giving to it the most perfect freedom of action, considering the Chilian occupation. That no question of territorial annexation would be touched until a constitutional government could be established in Peru, acknowledged and respected by the people, with full powers to enter into diplomatic negotiations for peace. That no territory would be exacted unless Chili failed to secure ample and just indemnification in other and satisfactory ways, as also ample security for the future, and that in no case would Chili exact territory save when Chilian enterprise and Chilian capital had developed the deserts, and where to-day nine-tenths of the people were Chilians; and finally that Chili would never consent to submit her rights gained in battle to the arbitration of any European power."

Mr. Kilpatrick seemed to think he had secured the concessions desired by Secretary Blaine, but in reality the promises were so conditioned that they were capable of various possibilities. The specific thing that was stated and afterward caused trouble was that Chile would not exact territory unless ample and just indemnification in other ways was not secured. Of course a question might arise over "just" and "ample" indemnification.

The unfortunate Minister was also confronted with a new difficulty originating with Mr. Hurlbut. Admiral Lynch, the Chilean military governor of Lima to whom Hurlbut had given his famous memorandum, telegraphed to the Secretary of State of Chile that the latter had told Calderón that "the United States will under no circumstance permit annexation of territory to Chile," and had repeated the assertion to outside parties. Lynch stated that "it is now the subject of conversation here, complicates and endangers our occupation." Kilpatrick was questioned by the Secretary of State of Chile who naturally wished to know if it were true. Kilpatrick explained his instructions regarding the annexation of territory and said that he could not twist them into meaning what Lynch had attributed to Hurlbut, and further stated that he believed that Hurlbut had no instructions that he himself did not have. In the absence of a key for communicating with Hurlbut which had not yet arrived he practically denied the statement attributed to Hurlbut.

It is not probable that Hurlbut made the statement for on September 21 he wrote another summary of the situation and suggested that if the United States were going to press the no-territorial indemnity policy "such insistence on our part should pass directly from the Secretary of State to the Chilean Minister at Washington, and thus come with the highest authority." He further said that if the Department of State was not prepared to take that step he did not see how he could exercise any wholesome influence upon the belligerents. He called attention to the fact that since the United States had cut Peru off from European aid, "it would seem that a duty was, by its own act, imposed upon the United States, to render effective and positive aid to the solution of this question."

Upon learning of the recognition of Calderón by the United States and of the arrival of a new minister who gave strenuous promises, Piérola's secretary García y García wrote a note to Hurlbut claiming that Piérola was the legal president of Peru. Hurlbut answered in vigorous style (in English) not characterized by any excess of diplomatic diction, saying that Piérola was a dictator and the acts of his assembly were illegal, that Peruvians were worse enemies of Peruvians than the Chileans could be, and that the efforts of the friends of Peru were paralyzed by their intestine dissensions. He urged all Peruvians to unite in restoring peace.

While Hurlbut was boldly doing his duty as he saw it, he had to fight back at Shipherd of the Peruvian Company in New York who was alternately urging him to support the Cochet claims, and threatening him with removal for supposed support of the Crédit Industriel. Hurlbut answered by returning Shipherd's correspondence to Blaine with the statement that he had no confidence in the Cochet claims and little in Shipherd. It would not be too much to say that the activities of Shipherd and the accusations he made against Hurlbut when he found that the Minister could not be bribed were the chief cause of the investigation of the State Department by Congress.*

* See *infra,* pp. 170, 173.

Hurlbut then made a mistake somewhat difficult to understand, which brought a deserved rebuke from Secretary Blaine. In September he drew up a protocol for the lease of a coaling station at Chimbote and for the purchase of the Chimbote railroad. The latter was to be bought by some company to be formed in the United States and Hurlbut was to be the trustee until the company could be formed. The lease was valueless owing to conditions stipulated, and the purchase an improper procedure for a diplomat, as Secretary Blaine forcibly told him.

In the fall of 1881 there was a peculiar indefiniteness about this war that was not really a war, except for some little guerrilla warfare in the interior. Peru and Bolivia were hoping for help from Argentina who was arming. In Chile the ministry asked their Congress for appropriations for twenty-four thousand men in spite of the fact that much of the expeditionary force had returned from Lima, and for full naval equipment on war footing. All kinds of rumors were afloat in Peru, the most hopeful of which was intervention by the United States.

Secretary Blaine was not deterred from his peace policy in South America although his efforts had been frustrated by the "shirt-sleeve" diplomacy of General Hurlbut, by General Kilpatrick's virtual disavowal of Hurlbut, and by Kilpatrick's fatal illness. The Secretary of State left the two men at their posts to attend to the ordinary legation duties after a merited censure of both and appointed, November 30, a trained diplomat, William Henry Trescot, to go on a special mission of mediation to the belligerents.

Besides Secretary Blaine's well-known policy of Pan-Americanism there were other motives prompting the sending of the special mission. On August 11 the United States Minister to France, Levi P. Morton, wrote that President Grévy suggested that the United States should intervene in the war; that French subjects were suffering because of the undue demands of Chile on Peru and that some kind of intervention ought to take place. Secretary Blaine replied that he also deplored the situation, but that the United States could not enter into any joint intervention with European powers. He stated in his reply a conception of Pan-Americanism that should be accepted as more of an ideal than a reality as events were soon to prove. He said:

. . . Their proximity of situation, similarity in origin and frame of government, unity of political interests on all questions of foreign intercourse, and their geographical remoteness from Europe have naturally given to American states close and especial relations to each other, and in the course of time removed them further from the European system.

This was said when the only cable connection between Washington and South America was *via* Paris and the quickest and cheapest steamship lines *via* Liverpool. Mr. Morton had another interview with President Grévy who expressed his approval that the United States should intervene alone.

Intervention was also in line with Secretary Blaine's South American policy. He was planning an American Congress to meet in Washington, and to further this project as well as to lend dignity to Trescot's mission he commissioned Walker Blaine, Third Assistant Secretary of State, to accompany him and present the invitations to the proposed American Congress, a forerunner of the present Pan-American Union. The Congress was to meet in November, 1882, which he supposed would give ample time for terminating the war. After summing up the efforts of Hurlbut and Kilpatrick, and recalling that Chile had stated to Kilpatrick that she would not take territory from Peru if it was possible to avoid it, he enumerated points of procedure and instructions.

Where Secretary Blaine was under a wrong impression was in connection with the arrest of provisional President Calderón by Admiral Lynch. After Mr. Hurlbut so strongly backed the Calderón government Piérola's followers fell away. In early October the Department of Arequipa declared in favor of President Calderón, and Admiral Montero who commanded remnants of the army in the south and General Cáceres who was a strong leader of the center offered to support the provisional President. Accordingly Sr. Piérola issued a decree November 28 abdicating the presidency. In direct proportion to this strength accruing to Calderón's government the Chilean authorities began to curtail his power. He had been allowed to borrow money from the Bank of Mexico, Peru, and London, and had issued 8,000,000 pesos of paper money. Two or three countries other than the United States had recognized him. On September 26 Chilean officers seized his treasury and forbade his government to collect taxes. A report had been circulated widely that President Calderón was making a treaty giving the United States a mandate over the country, and Chilean officers ruthlessly searched his house and family for the treaty. A decree was issued by Admiral Lynch calling upon Sr. Calderón to cease his functions and to surrender his archives. Upon the advice of Mr. Hurlbut,

President Calderón refused to do so and left his records at the United States legation. Acting upon suggestions from the same source a quiet session of his Congress had elected a vice-president, Admiral Montero, so that the Government would have legal succession in case of accident to President Calderón.

It was a military and financial necessity to have Sr. Calderón removed. If strong governments recognized him, the very profitable indefinite occupation by Chile might be interrupted; the Lynch-North-Jameson contract for the sale of great quantities of guano at over two pounds sterling a ton might be broken; while at the same time the port of Callao was yielding over a half million pesos a month indemnity; and the paper money with which Calderón was paying war contributions was deflated. Admiral Lynch was remitting shiploads of plunder from Peru to Chile—his diary contains curious inventories of animals from the Lima zoo, plants from the botanical gardens, and statuary. The war fever had not yet sufficiently abated, and the guano importers as well as the Chilean Government were not ready for peace at the time that Secretary Blaine sent his special mission.[4]

In Secretary Blaine's instructions to Mr. Trescot is seen an able appraisal of a difficult problem. Regarding the arrest of President Calderón in face of his recognition by the United States, the hope was expressed that Chile had meant no insult and that there was some explanation that would relieve the impression of "an intentional and unwarranted offense," and if there was no such explanation to break off diplomatic relations. But Blaine did not expect that relations would have to be broken. Any explanation was to be accepted that did not require as a condition the disavowal of Hurlbut. Regarding this point he said:

. . . Whatever may be my opinion as to the discretion of all that may have been said or done by Mr. Hurlbut, it is impossible for me to recognize the right of the Chilian Government to take such action without submitting to the consideration of this government any cause of complaint which it was prepared to allege against the proceedings of the representative of the United States.

Regarding the territorial indemnity he restated his policy as expressed in instructions to the resident ministers to the belligerent nations. He said:

. . . But this government feels that the exercise of the right of absolute conquest is dangerous to the best interests of all the republics of this continent; that from it are certain to spring other wars and political disturbances; and that it imposes, even upon the conqueror, burdens which are scarcely compensated by the apparent increase of strength which it gives. This government also holds that between two independent nations, hostilities do not, from the mere existence of war, confer the right of conquest until the failure to furnish the indemnity and guarantee which can be rightfully demanded.

Regarding the fall of the Calderón government and the possible extinction of Peru, Secretary Blaine formulated the nearest to a real Pan-American policy that the United States approached before President Wilson permitted the A.B.C. powers to mediate in the Mexican imbroglio growing out of the occupation of Vera Cruz. It was a plan to appeal to other American republics to join in an intervention. This was Pan-Americanism, not United States tutelage. It is unfortunate that Secretary Hughes did not adopt such a policy when the Harding mediation was sought in 1922. Mr. Blaine said:

The practical prohibition of the formation of a stable government in Peru, and the absolute appropriation of its most valuable territory, is simply the extinction of a State which has formed part of the system of republics on this continent, honorable in the traditions and illustrations of its past history, and rich in the resources for future progress. The United States, with which Peru has for many years maintained the most cordial relations, has the right to feel and express a deep interest in its distressed condition; and while with equal friendliness to Chili, we will not interpose to deprive her of the fair advantages of military success, nor put any obstacle to the attainment of future security, we cannot regard with unconcern the destruction of Peruvian nationality. If our good offices are rejected, and this policy of the absorption of an independent state be persisted in, this government will consider itself discharged from any further obligation to be influenced in its action by the position which Chili has assumed, and will hold itself free to appeal to the other republics of this continent to join it in an effort to avert consequences which cannot be confined to Chili and Peru, but which threaten with extremest danger the political institutions, the peaceful progress, and the liberal civilization of all America.[5]

If, however, Chile received in a friendly spirit the representations of the United States, Mr. Trescot was instructed to urge Chile to negotiate without the necessity of territorial indemnities. The instructions indicate that Secretary Blaine neither favored any special financial program for settling the financial complications of the war, nor wished the United States to be the umpire. In closing his instructions he says:

If negotiation be assured, the ability of Peru to furnish the indemnity will be a matter of direct interest. Upon this subject we have no information upon which definite instructions can now be based. While you will carefully abstain from any interposition in this connection, you will examine and report to this Department promptly any plans which may be suggested.

You will not indicate any wish that the Government of the United States should act as umpire in the adjudications between the contending powers. Should an invitation to that effect be extended, you will communicate by telegraph for instructions. The single and simple desire of this government is to see a just and honorable peace at the earliest day practicable, and if any other American government can more effectively aid in producing this auspicious result, the United States will cordially sustain it and lend such co-operation as the circumstances may demand.[6]

When Mr. Trescot arrived in South America he found a difficult situation. The Calderón government was provisional and permitted to exist in a small neutral zone within territory under Chilean military rule. Generals Cáceres, Montero, and other leaders of Peruvian groups, spurred on by hope of intervention by the United States, held out.

The news of Mr. Hurlbut's activities in Lima had reached Santiago and Mr. Trescot found the press there very bitter. The Chilean minister in Washington was also objecting to Mr. Hurlbut, whom he considered officious and pro-Peruvian.

Not only was Mr. Trescot's mission difficult, but

coincident with its beginning the Secretary of State, who provided him with his instructions, found his own power crumbling and his South American policy bitterly denounced. Political opponents of Secretary Blaine had seized on the financial scandal which the activities of Mr. Shipherd and the Peruvian Company suggested, and were trying to show that our intervention was to be turned to financial profit for men high in the Government. Enemies of Secretary Blaine united with financial interests opposed to the Crédit Industriel to make the most of the accusation. The New York papers, particularly, attacked Secretary Blaine's South American policy and no effort was spared to injure his reputation. The matter came to a head in Congress. The Senate and House requested the President to communicate to them all correspondence of our diplomatic agents in Peru and Chile. At the death of President Garfield and the coming of Arthur to the presidency, Secretary Blaine found himself working with a cautious and vacillating executive and menaced by a congressional investigation of his department. Confident that no tarnish would be found on his record and that history would vindicate his policies he resigned.

Peru, with her provisional president imprisoned and her leaders scattered into three main camps, found herself at the mercy of an unrelenting conqueror which, although it had spent but $30,000,000 in waging the war and was granted Bolivia's coast, could accept nothing less than the cession of Tarapacá as an indispensable condition for peace discussions. Argentina had ratified the treaty of boundaries with Chile, thanks to the good offices of the United States, and no help could come from that source. Bolivia had armed a small force, but did nothing. Now the United States was to about-face after arousing great hopes among the leaders of the allies and thereby unwittingly prolonging the struggle. Peru was to be left to whatever settlement Chile would make, with the latter's temper raised again by the Calderón government and United States intervention. Copies of Shipherd's plan and Hurlbut's letters to Admiral Lynch and Piérola had preceded Trescot to Chile and feeling there ran high. President Arthur's message to Congress of December 6 also reached Chile ahead of Trescot and by its mild helplessness with reference to the South American war weakened the force of Trescot's mission in the eyes of the clever ministers with whom he was to deal.

Blaine was superseded by Frederick T. Frelinghuysen, January 1, 1882, and Trescot's instructions were changed before he arrived at his post. A telegram started after the envoy January 3 urged him to exert "pacific influence" and avoid any issue leading to withdrawal from Chile. The next day another message was sent saying the President wished to extend friendly offices impartially to both countries, to avoid issues leading to offense, that the Calderón affront would be explained in Washington, and that Mr. Trescot should not return by way of Buenos Aires.

This sudden change of policy by Secretary Frelinghuysen became known to the Chilean Minister in Washington, M. Martínez, as soon as the former took office. The Peruvian Minister did not learn it for three months and Trescot did not know about it until January 31, when he learned of it from the Chilean Minister of State. Minister Martínez had sent a cablegram *via* Paris while Secretary Frelinghuysen's dispatch to Mr. Trescot was sent *via* Panama and by boat. The promptness with which the interview giving this information was secured and cabled to Chile is one of many brilliant pieces of Chilean diplomacy in this war. The following is the cablegram which graphically tells of the complete change of front in the Pan-American policy of the United States as a result of the Stalwart-Liberal political fight, of demagogic newspaper attacks seeking to discredit Secretary Blaine, and above all of the death of President Garfield whose continuance in office would have prevented the change:

Instructions Blaine to Trescot published. They ask explanation over suppression of Calderón; I gave them here. Frelinghuysen says in writing he is satisfied. The latter [*éste*] in new instructions to Trescot, very favorable, revokes instructions Blaine relative using interventionalist good offices. He orders him to limit himself to friendly suggestion in neutral attitude, saying not to be offended if Chile refuses. Doesn't dictate nor promote peace. Doesn't question justice nor consider exigencies, offers of terms, nor alterations of frontiers, nor who shall be president of Peru. American Congress [Pan-American] will not be called.—M.[7]

It is difficult to understand how the Secretary of State could have failed to have availed himself of the quickest means of advising his envoy of his change of policy. Trescot began to carry out his first instructions before receiving the modifications sent while he was *en route*. He had secured explanations of the Calderón affair, of the tampering with our minister's mail, and had treated the Kilpatrick veracity question. His remaining instructions were to insist on no territorial indemnities and milder peace terms. He was pressing these matters when he received a diplomatic humiliation which does little credit to Secretary Frelinghuysen.

With respect to the invitations to the American Congress Trescot thought it would be better not to present them for a time and had so written to the ministers in Bolivia and Peru, but before his letter arrived General Hurlbut had already issued the invitation to Peru, and his act increased the expectations in that country of mediation. It was then necessary that the invitation to Chile should be extended at once. He advised Minister Adams at La Paz to present the invitation to Bolivia and asked Walker Blaine to accompany him on an interview which had been arranged for January 31, with Minister Balmaceda, there to present formally the invitation to Chile to attend the American Congress. After discussing a draft of a protocol Trescot explained the purpose of Blaine's visit. What happened is better told in the envoy's own words:

To my great surprise, he expressed the wish that Mr. Blaine would not read the communication, and then, turning to me, he said, "It is useless. Your government has withdrawn the invitation." Seeing, I suppose, an expression of astonishment, which I did not pretend to conceal, he added, "Your own instructions have been changed. Your instructions from Mr. Blaine have been published, and others are on their way to you modifying your original instructions in very important particulars. The whole question about Calderón is out of the way, and you are told to be entirely neutral."

I replied, "I do not understand that there is any such thing as a Calderón question between us," and then said, "Do you mean, Mr. Secretary, that both my original in-

structions and the instructions from the present administration are published?"

He added, "Yes, they have been published, and will be
soon published here in *La Patria* (a newspaper)." He
then went out of the room and returned with a telegram,
which, he said, had come from Paris only two days before,
and of which he read me the first line, which, as I recol-
lect, was, "The Blaine-Trescot instruction has been published," and then paused, smiling and looking over the
telegram, as if he were uncertain whether he should communicate the rest. I said, "As you say that all this is confidential, don't make a half confidence of it. If I am to
receive my instructions through you let me know them in
full." He smiled, shook his head, and folded up the telegram, saying, "This, however, will not interrupt our
negotiation," and then proceeded, at some length, to
state why and to explain what he considered the advantages of the condition of things under the new instructions.

I said to him, "That may all be so, Mr. Secretary, but
I think that a diplomatist of ordinary experience would
conclude, when he learns that his instructions have been
communicated to the government with which he is nego-
tiating, before he receives them himself, that it is time
for him to be silent until he does receive them. I think
there must be some mistake about all this, but at any
rate I must decline to say a word more until I learn from
my government what it has done and what it means me
to do."

He said that he hoped that I would receive my instructions very soon, that the position was strained and could
not be maintained for an indefinite time, that is, Chile
could not wait much longer for the United States to decide what action it would take, and then, for the first

time in our conferences, his manner became excited and his language somewhat too demonstrative.[8]

After some complaints about Mr. Hurlbut who was trying to get permission for the American railroad from Mollendo to Puno to import coal, the interview ended. Mr. Trescot was diplomatically "scooped" and further chagrined within a few days when mail from Lima brought word that the full text of the invitation of Peru to the Pan-American Congress had been given out and published there. He had a saving sense of humor, however, and did not take the matter as seriously as did the successor of Mr. Hurlbut who was soon to make another *faux pas* for the United States in this famous question.

When Trescot finally received his new instructions embodying a "hands-off" policy for the United States he drew up a protocol with Minister Balmaceda at Viña del Mar in which it was stated that the Calderón incident was closed, the armed intervention of the United States eliminated from discussion, and that Chile would accept the good offices of the United States in securing peace with Peru on terms named by Chile, with the understanding that if those terms were not accepted the action of the United States should terminate. Chile further agreed in case of the use of such good offices to facilitate the communication of Trescot with all Peruvian representatives beyond the military lines except with Sr. Calderón, then a prisoner in Chile. This protocol was signed by Trescot, conditionally on the approval of his Government, which was not secured, and it is mentioned only because in its terms appear for the first time peace conditions relative to the ten-year captivity of Tacna-Arica. Tarapacá was to be definitely ceded to Chile, Tacna and Arica were to be occupied by Chile for ten years at the end of which time Peru should pay Chile twenty million pesos. If Peru should not pay the sum Tacna and Arica were to be incorporated into Chile, and if Peru redeemed the provinces she was to leave Arica forever unfortified. Chile was to occupy the Lobos Islands as long as there was guano there, and the proceeds from guano sales from both those islands and Tarapacá should be divided equally between Chile and the creditors of Peru.

The failure of our fourth attempt to mediate in this question has been given many interpretations by South American writers. It has been termed everything from impertinent officiousness to well-meant blundering.

It will be remembered that as soon as Secretary Frelinghuysen entered upon the duties of his office he also abandoned the idea of the American Congress which Secretary Blaine had planned. He said that it was untimely and might cause jealousies in Europe and he implied that it was merely Blaine's idea. Former Secretary Blaine came out in a vigorous open letter to the President defending his Latin-American policy.[9] He said that both presidents, Garfield and Arthur, had read and approved the invitations. Much of the Blaine opposition was the natural result of the politics of the period, echoes of the Blaine-Conkling feud. The congressional investigation not only gave him a clean bill, but his Pan-American policy was heartily approved in twenty-three petitions looking toward closer relations with South America which were introduced in Congress during the summer. However, Secretary Frelinghuysen's policy had destroyed any influence we might have exerted on peace negotiations in the War of the Pacific.

The most charitable appreciation of the failure of

this intervention and at the same time the most correct was given by Judge Elmore, Peruvian Minister at Washington, in a letter to his Government. It is in part as follows:

Today at 12.30 P.M. there was executed in the capital Charles J. Guiteau, the assassin of President Garfield . . . thus has this perverse man expiated his crime.

I was, on July 2, 1881, on board the boat that was to convey Minister Hurlbut from New York to Colón to take leave of him, when the news was received by telegraph of this atrocious and unexpected crime. We entertained the deepest hopes that the mission of General Hurlbut would save Peru, putting a prompt and honorable end to the iniquitous war that Chile wages against us. The assault of July 2 destroyed a great administration, demoralized the chief secretary of the cabinet, Blaine, who lost his place, and to conserve it and himself adopted a hesitating policy, not knowing how to save Minister Hurlbut (trying to sustain himself), and after a year of the most extraordinary events and no little humiliation for the United States we are convinced that the greatest damage caused by the ball of Guiteau (next to that done the family of the noble victim) has been to the Peruvian Republic.[10]

Two days after the signing of the Protocol of Viña del Mar, Trescot received instructions that obliged him to communicate to Balmaceda that the United States could not tender its good offices under the terms of the protocol. Chile was now no longer molested by the aid of the United States in settling its war, and on March 8 there was given in the official Chilean newspaper a denial of Kilpatrick's statements, which had been quoted by Secretary Blaine to Trescot in the latter's instructions. All of these had become generally known through the congressional investigation.

The Government of Chile had to make its peace with the public. There is no doubt, however, as to the accuracy of Kilpatrick's statements because he understood Spanish well. Senator Huneens, speaking English perfectly, was spokesman for the Chilean administration then and later, and was anxious to have it denied. The explanation is this. The statements were really so worded that each understood that the result would be as he interpreted it.

Trescot arriving home stated frankly the following opinion:

If the United States has the intention of intervening effectively to prevent the disintegration of Peru, now is the time to declare so openly. If it hasn't this intention it is even more necessary that Chile and Peru know exactly where the action of the United States ends.

He further stated that if the United States would withdraw its efforts European powers would intervene effectively and establish peace.

If our efforts had ended completely here we should have been relieved entirely of the blame for the final impossible peace conditions that were exacted in the Treaty of Ancón, and no doubt Great Britain would have mediated and obtained better terms for Peru. Her interests in Peru were very great and her diplomacy efficient. The policy of Secretary Frelinghuysen, now, was to avoid anything that would appear to be intervention in South America, yet to aid in bringing about peace by "good offices" and "our influence." He had not yet encountered and felt the impact of great capitalist interests coupled with victory-intoxicated national expansion in which as former Secretary Blaine said in the congressional investigation the spoils "were shared fifty-fifty."[11] During the rest of the war, whatever part that was taken by the ministers of the United States offered no obstacle to the reaping by Chile of the full benefits, and liabilities, of her victories, other than to state mildly disapproval of the Treaty of Ancón, and withhold for some time the recognition asked by the Government that made this famous treaty which technically ended but did not settle the War of the Pacific.

REFERENCES

1. *Senate Executive Documents,* Forty-seventh Congress, first session, Vol. IV, Doc. 79, pp. 157–159. [Full text of Secretary James G. Blaine's instructions.] Also pp. 511, 598, and 178.

2. *Congressional Record,* Forty-sixth Congress, second session, p. 1046. Also Charles A. McQueen, *Peruvian Public Finance,* p. 69.

3. Note: In the congressional investigation Shipherd was absolved from responsibility on the presumption that he was mentally unaccountable.

4. *Hispanic-American Historical Review,* V, 673. Note: This contains much bibliography of the Blaine phase of our policy in South America at this period.

5. *Senate Executive Documents,* Forty-seventh Congress, first session, Vol. IV, Doc. 79, pp. 176–179. [Text of instructions to Mr. Trescot.]

6. Gail Hamilton, *Biography of James G. Blaine,* p. 503. Note: This reference is to the universality of Blaine's foreign policy.

7. Tomás Caivano, *Historia de la guerra de la América,* p. 162.

8. *Senate Documents,* Forty-seventh Congress, second session, I, 67–69.

9. *New York Tribune,* February 4, 1882.

10. Caivano, *op. cit.,* p. 160.

11. *House Reports,* Forty-seventh Congress, first session, VI, 217.

CHAPTER IX

THE FATAL TREATY OF ANCÓN

SINCE the validity of the Treaty of Ancón which ended the War of the Pacific was the principal issue in the Coolidge arbitration, the antecedents of that agreement should be considered. Fortunately, the United States had nothing to do directly with the making of the treaty, and in fact disapproved of it. The bases on which the treaty was made, however, are closely related to negotiations carried on by the United States minister in Santiago after the return of Mr. Trescot and those negotiations show the evolution of the terms of peace set down the following year in the Treaty of Ancón.

Shortly after the death of General Kilpatrick in Santiago, General Hurlbut died suddenly in Lima, so the United States was soon represented by new men. James Partridge was sent to Lima without instructions and without knowing to which president he was accredited. What seems stranger, for his instructions could follow, is the fact that he was not given the benefit of the experience of Trescot who had returned and could have interviewed the outgoing minister. Dr. Cornelius A. Logan who had been named for the post at Santiago, and who during the year had been laboring to bring about peace, was asked by the Chilean administration to give a summary of the various peace proposals that had been submitted through him. Of course, this statement was not asked for to supply any lack of record on the part of Chile, but to learn the probable attitude of the United States regarding peace.

Much criticism, especially by Peruvian writers, has been made of the efforts of Dr. Logan to secure peace and some explanation should be made of his attempts. It may be said that more importance was attributed to Logan's activity by the leaders of Peru and Bolivia and even by many in Chile than it merited. This was due to the fact that but few people, those near the ministry of Chile, knew of the changed policy of Secretary Frelinghuysen. The Chilean ministry and the nitrate kings knew the true instructions under which Dr. Logan worked. Logan also knew that Chile not only held a free hand in dealing with Peru, but that she was about to conclude a separate peace with Bolivia. Being anxious to save something for Peru he sought to secure an early agreement before the terms demanded were even more severe. Of course, there was always the possibility that Secretary Frelinghuysen might change his policy and so, on October 17, Minister Logan was asked for a summary of his efforts to secure peace. The following day, the day on which bids were to be accepted for the sale of a million tons more of Peru's guano, Dr. Logan made a report, a summary of which is here given:

First. In order to remove the difficulty regarding the sale of Tacna and Arica, I proposed a treaty on the basis of ceding Tarapaca, with a separate article presenting the question of Tacna and Arica, to the Peruvian Congress for its own decision, without any recommendation from Señor Calderon. This proposal was declined, both by your excellency and Señor Calderon.

Second. I proposed to make the river Azufre the boundary line, giving Arica to Chili and Tacna to Peru. This proposal was not accepted by either party.

Third. This suggestion came from your excellency's

Government, and was made into a formal proposal by myself. Owing to a mistake of my own, as to one of the conditions, the proposition was first made to Señor Calderon as follows: Chili to have military occupation of Tacna and Arica for five years, at the end[1] of which time a vote to be taken by the people of the territory to determine whether they would attach it to Chili or to Peru. If the vote took the territory to Chili, the latter was to pay Peru $10,000,000 in compensation. Chili was to pay Peru $3,000,000 as a loan, upon the ratification of the treaty, and if Chili afterwards obtained the territory by a vote of the people thereof, this amount was to be deducted, leaving Chili seven millions still to pay. If the territory went to Peru, the latter was to repay the three millions with 6 per cent interest, and Chili was to retain possession of the territory until the whole amount was paid.

The mistake made by me above referred to, was that your excellency's Government, while being willing to pay $10,000,000 for the territory, if voted Chili, also expected to receive $10,000,000, if voted to Peru.

Señor Calderon, however, refused the proposal in its more favorable form, and it was useless to present it to him in the other form, even if I had felt authorized to commit my own Government to it in that shape.

Fourth. I proposed to Señor Calderon that Chili should have military occupation of Tacna and Arica for ten years, and then evacuate it. He declined this, and it was not presented to your excellency.

Fifth. I proposed to submit the following question to the President of the United States, in the capacity of a friendly arbitrator:

"Shall the Chilian Government as a measure growing out of the necessities and manner of settlement of the war have the right to purchase the Peruvian territory lying between the river Camarones and the river Sama, for the sum of $9,000,000, with the stipulation that Bolivia shall be given the perpetual right to the free and innocent passage over said territory, with perpetual freedom from export and import duties, upon the conclusion of a satisfactory treaty between the latter Republic and the Republic of Chili?"

Señor Calderon accepted this proposal, but your excellency declined it, chiefly for two reasons; firstly, because to refer such a question at this time to a foreign ruler would be practically to place the results of the war in the hands of a foreign state, which would be an infringement upon the sovereignty of Chili; and secondly, because to admit the possibility of a decision against Chili, would be to yield all claim upon the district in question, a claim which she has constantly made since the conference of Arica.

Sixth. I then proposed to Señor Calderon that Tacna and Arica should be ceded to Bolivia. This proposal he declined, and it was not presented, therefore, to your excellency.

Seventh. I then proposed that the following question be submitted, *not* to the head of a foreign Government, but to a diplomatic representative friendly to both parties, who should simply be regarded in the light of an impartial referee:

"Shall Chili have the right to purchase the territory embracing Tacna and Arica for $9,000,000, or shall she have military occupation of the said territory for a period of fifteen years, being obliged to evacuate it at the expiration of that period?"

As this proposition removed your excellency's objection to a foreign ruler, and also secures either the purchase of the territory or its occupation for fifteen years, your ex-

cellency consented to accept it, in substance, as the basis
of a negotiation. Señor Calderon also consented to it, and
I rejoiced in the belief that we were to have peace at
last.[2]

When they came to the arrangement of details of
procedure, however, negotiations reached an *impasse*
over the question of settlement with Peruvian creditors
and Mr. Logan's efforts failed to result in the hoped-
for peace.

At the close of 1882 the peace situation in Peru was
still indefinite. Calderón was a prisoner of Chile. Vice-
President Montero had some following at Arequipa,
and Gen. Andrés A. Cáceres, who was a strong leader
of Indians in the interior, had a group in the center
disposed to continue the war. In the north Gen. Miguel
Iglesias was expected to favor peace with Chile even at
great loss in order to secure Chilean evacuation.

In a special session of the Chilean Congress reports
from the President and Minister of Foreign Affairs indicated the usefulness of Logan to Chile in peace negotiations. He served though merely as an intermediary. A great change had taken place in one year in
the diplomatic policy of the United States: the American minister now became merely a messenger in the
dismemberment of Peru instead of her moral defender.
What brought him the most criticism was a letter to
Vice-President Montero on November 18, for which he
was later accused of being the unwitting tool of the
Chilean Government. But Logan knew that Bolivia was
on the point of signing a separate peace with Chile and
believed that once that were done so much harder terms
would be exacted that it was imperative for Peru to accept the terms then offered. Some of his arguments were

untactful, but his intentions were good. The reason for writing to Montero was that on October 14 the latter had called a congress to meet in Arequipa which act might indicate that the authority of Calderón was not recognized in Peru.

The essence of the Montero letter was a strong recommendation for the acceptance by Peru of the sale of Tacna-Arica for $10,000,000 and the cession of Tarapacá. Montero was urged to send a power to Calderón to treat on this basis. The hopelessness of Peru, the need of peace, the improbability of outside intervention, and the probability of worse terms were pointed out. It was even bluntly suggested that $10,000,000 would be a fair price for Tacna-Arica in comparison with what the United States paid to Mexico for much more valuable territory. However, Logan overlooked the number of Peruvians in Tacna-Arica as compared with the number of Mexicans there had been in California and the rest of the Mexican cession, and their hostility to Mexico.

Early in 1883 the movement of Miguel Iglesias who favored peace gathered strength, and he assembled a provisional congress at Cajamarca which named him supreme chief with the title of "Regenerator." A peace club was formed in Lima and after the distribution, probably by the Chilean authorities, of copies of Logan's letter to Montero, the following manifesto was issued:

As truth can no more be bettered by falsehood than was Salmoneus able to imitate the rays of heaven, the hour of truth has at last arrived. For this reason we have decided to reproduce the letter of the American minister, Logan, to Rear-Admiral Montero.

This reproduction is for the people, because the journal in which it appeared has been exhausted, with the notable circumstance that to-day not a single copy is to be found.

In order that the Peruvian public may read, meditate, and resolve quickly, we insert it.

[Then follows the note of Mr. Logan to Montero.][3]

Whoever studies this document cannot do less than clearly see where lies truth; where lies error, where is safety, and where ruin.

Those who entertained placid illusions of all which was to come of the American legation, to-day that the same legation presents the naked truth, find it necessary to attack it with vigor and pertinacity.

Upon this account the advocates of the conclusion of the war do not need more persuasion than the authorized word of the American minister.

And all those who preserve love of country, of home, of dignity, and of liberty, will enthusiastically hasten to augment the ranks of the advocates of peace.

Because in this alone is to be found the tranquillity, the pacification, and the resurrection of Peru.

Without peace there exist only ruin and prolongation of slavery for a people who by so many titles are called to a higher destiny.

When the Montero note became known publicly Peru was finally disillusioned regarding the intervention of the United States.

The Treaty of Ancón was strictly the work of Chilean diplomacy and its ratification was disapproved and protested by numerous governments. But why should it not be the work of Chile since her arms were victorious; how did it concern the rest of the world? That was a fair question in 1883 so soon after Prussia had summarily dictated terms of peace to France and exacted territorial indemnities. It was even a fair question after the United States retained valuable possessions of Spain as a result of the Spanish-American War. But if any lessons have been learned from the experiences of various nations in forcibly annexing areas containing hostile populations, it can be seen now that Chile made a mistake. Many of her own statesmen saw it, but the problem, then, was how to conserve without danger of recapture the vast desert of nitrate wealth south of Tacna-Arica without retaining these provinces, and, retaining them, the question was how to provide Bolivia with an outlet to the sea, and keep her from being a perpetual ally of Peru in schemes for recapture of their territories lost in the War of the Pacific. This is most important. Furthermore, should nitrates be found in Tacna-Arica they would furnish competition with an industry which the war had placed exclusively under Chilean control. But Chile had to make a peace. Indefinite occupation was impossible. All the guano of Peru would be exhausted in the million tons now contracted. Also yellow fever was reported in Lima. Peace would now be made, on Chile's terms without any outside intervention.

Although the United States had definitely concluded its efforts at peacemaking between Chile and Peru, there was an unofficial quixotic anticlimax to these, made by the new United States Minister in Lima. Minister Hurlbut had died in Lima. His death was so sudden and the times so bitter that his widow had an autopsy held on board a United States warship, which, however, resulted in a finding that death was caused by angina pectoris. His successor, James Partridge, whose appointment was mentioned in the previous chapter,

was without any definite instructions and was technically accredited to the Montero government at Arequipa, but he actually resided in Lima.

In January, 1883, he asked permission to go to
Arequipa where Admiral Montero had his headquarters
to secure exequaturs for some consuls, saying that he
would while there urge Montero to accept peace terms.
He did not go for various reasons but suggested to Sr.
Novoa and Admiral Lynch that peace be made on the
basis of the cession of Tarapacá, the sale or cession of
Tacna-Arica to Bolivia or the neutralizing of Tacna-
Arica. He advised the belligerents to negotiate directly
without the intervention of any other country. Novoa
did not take well the suggestions regarding Tacna-
Arica, or the inclusion of Bolivia in peace discussions
with Peru, for Chile was at that moment making separate terms with Bolivia.

Mr. Partridge now took a strange course. He called
a secret meeting of the diplomatic corps which was attended by the representatives of England, France, and
Italy (those of Germany and Spain did not accept), at
which it was the consensus of opinion that the interested neutral powers should intervene. Some of the ministers spoke with great feeling of the long occupation
by Chile of Peru, but the British Minister while agreeing with the rest as to the necessity of peace stated that
he did not know with whom Chile could treat if she
wished to. The Italian Minister was named to make a
report of the sense of the meeting to be sent to the several home chancelleries. This abortive move for European intervention made at the initiative of the Minister
from the United States caused quite a diplomatic stir.
Secretary Frelinghuysen immediately disauthorized
Partridge and granted him a leave asked for, effective

on the next boat to Panama. The unfortunate Mr. Partridge took his humiliation very seriously. He went to Spain where, brooding over this incident and the loss of relatives, he committed suicide.

Secretary Frelinghuysen was ruffled by this affair. He explained to foreign chancelleries and to an inquiry from the Senate that the Partridge meeting was unauthorized. He then asked for an interview with Sr. Godoi who was now representing Chile at Washington. Godoi's predecessor, M. Martínez, had made in a note of leave-taking an impertinent criticism of Mr. Trescot's efforts in Lima, and Secretary Frelinghuysen demanded that the note be withdrawn. Following the Partridge episode the Secretary plainly informed Godoi that Chile was "on the carpet" in various chancelleries and that the pernicious prolongation of the war might cause an intervention, much as such a step would be repugnant to him. Of course, the answer of Chile to this was that there was no government in Peru with which to treat.

When Chile began in earnest to make peace it was a difficult task. Calderón would not sign away the territory required for peace. Admiral Montero had stated publicly that he would burn off his right arm before he would sign such a document, and General Cáceres could not be caught in the mountains, much less treated with. Chile now turned her attention to General Iglesias, a wealthy planter of Cajamarca, unattached to any guano group, who was willing to make peace. Lynch secured a defection of part of General Cáceres' men in favor of General Iglesias who had but four hundred men, who were paid with his own money. Later money was furnished him by Chile. No constitutional requirements were placed on him as they had been on Calderón. He was carefully backed by Chile for leadership.

Owing to the fact that President Coolidge in his opinion which accompanied his award took a hypothetical basis for the Treaty of Ancón, it will be necessary to see what was in the minds of the men who made it in order to appreciate properly the arbitration.

At the first discussions between Iglesias and Novoa, which were private and were not taken as a recognition of the new government which Iglesias was trying to create, Novoa presented tentative bases for peace, or rather for withdrawal from Lima of Chilean troops. Unsigned proposals were made on the basis of: (1) Unconditional ceding of Tarapacá to Chile; (2) sale of Tacna-Arica for ten million pesos on payments; (3) Chile was not to assume any indebtedness of territories received but would complete the guano contracts made by the Chilean Government; (4) Chile would continue administering the Lobos Islands until the one million tons of guano were shipped, but as soon as the treaty of peace should be ratified she would give Peru 50 per cent of the money received—the sum Chile was applying to Peruvian mortgages; (5) later treaties would be made to settle commercial relations and private war claims.

March 27 at Chorrillos, a suburb of Lima, the first formal conference was held. Sr. Novoa represented Chile and Srs. Lavalle and Castro Zaldivar, the latter a brother-in-law of General Iglesias, represented Peru. In a letter to General Iglesias on March 28, 1883, Sr. Lavalle tells of the birth of the Treaty of Ancón. He said:

Here I opened the discussion and Señor Novoa followed me in it on these two points: foreign debt and Tacna-Arica.

With respect to the first I stated categorically that Peru should perish rather than save herself by abandoning the rights of those who had trusted in her honor; that to pay Chile the war indemnity with what was not hers would be an infamous act on the part even of an obscure individual, and much more so for a nation; that I would never sign a peace that did not protect the rights of the creditors of Peru, and that, although I should wish to, I could not for the only authorization which we have, the only instruction which we had from you was to protect those rights, in support of which my colleague handed to Sr. Novoa your admirable letter to which I have referred and which visibly affected Sr. Novoa.

With respect to the second point I stated that the sacrifice of Tarapacá and of Iquique which did not represent more than riches, although immense ones, didn't matter to me, but that of Tacna-Arica horrified me; a man can sell his house or his lands or give them away, but a man cannot sell or cede his brothers; I discussed the necessity or convenience to Chile of obtaining those provinces and finally I showed him that there might be formulas for all which without changing the essence of things might save injuring all those sensibilities [*salvasen todas las susceptibilidades*]. Señor Novoa accepted the discussion on these points and after a very long and detailed discussion I concluded by proposing to him (I was surprised at my own audacity) the following modifications to the ultimatum which by the way now is not one.

"Peru cedes to Chile in payment of war indemnity the provinces of Tarapacá and Iquique with all the deposits of guano and nitrate which they contain, fifty per cent of the product of which Chile will apply to the foreign debt of Peru until it is paid, and as the product of the Lobos Islands are also involved, Peru cedes to Chile said deposits (not the islands) in order that their products may be applied to her creditors in equal proportion.

"The provinces of Tacna and Arica will remain in the power of Chile for ten years, at the end of which [*al fin de los cuales*] a plebiscite will be held by which their inhabitants will decide if they wish to return to Peru or be annexed to Chile or to another nation."

This is not a formal copy of articles for no text was prepared, just the bare ideas. Sr. Novoa objected at length to both conditions, but he didn't refuse them, agreeing finally to telegraph to his government for instructions upon points so different from those accepted by it and which he had supposed would never have to be discussed again.[4]

In answer to a request for instructions regarding the proposals of Lavalle, President Santa María refused the proposal regarding the debts of Peru, but accepted the plebiscite proposal for Tacna-Arica. He said Chile had suggested the plan in negotiations with Calderón carried on through Logan, and Calderón had rejected it, but that if Peru were now suggesting it they should seize upon it because, "it is evident that after a possession of ten or fifteen years there would scarcely be anything in Tacna that would not be Chilean. The plebiscite would hardly be necessary, the verdict would already be written in plain characters." Here he was mistaken. No nitrates were found as had happened in Tarapacá to bring many Chilean settlers.

At the second conference held at Chorrillos, April 9, Lavalle withdrew the proposal regarding the nitrates of Tarapacá, and proposed that Chile apply 50 per cent of the proceeds of the sale of the one million tons of guano to Peruvian debts until they should be paid or the deposits exhausted. Regarding Tacna-Arica he asked that if a plebiscite held at the end of ten years should give the region to Chile that Peru be paid ten million pesos. There was a delay in which the delegates might ask for instructions. Novoa had raised the question of why Chile should pay ten million pesos for Tacna-Arica if the people should vote to belong to her. In replying to this Santa María expressed the doctrine later famous in the case known as "disguised sale." He said he recognized the justice of Novoa's position, but that Chile should accept the proposal of Lavalle, making it reciprocal so that whichever country was favored in the vote should pay the loser the ten million pesos. He considered the plebiscite an invention to avoid the objections that would be raised to a straight sale. He said:

If the plebiscite is no more than a circumlocution [*rodeo*], an invention to disguise the sale, there is no reason why the payment of the quantity offered should be rejected, since it is certain that a plebiscite held within ten years [*dentro de diez años*] is going to give to Chile the region under dispute today.

These were discussed again in another conference on April 22, and on May 3 a protocol was drawn up and sent to Iglesias containing approximately the terms of the treaty in its final form, embodying the application of 50 per cent of the proceeds of guano to Peruvian debts and providing for a reciprocal plebiscite in Tacna-Arica. In this protocol appears for the first time the language, "*Espirado este plazo*" or "This term being expired," which was a pivotal phrase in the arbitration award of President Coolidge.[5]

When the negotiations with Iglesias became known to
the other leaders in Peru their resentment was great.
The Montero government at Arequipa declared for a
continuation of war to the end, but attempted, nevertheless, to make a peace with Chile which included
Bolivia. It is interesting to note that all of the negotiations of the year had completely disregarded Bolivia.
In the center General Cáceres assumed the offensive
and a Chilean army was sent against him. At Hua-
machuco in July he was defeated and all effective resistance of Peru broken. General Iglesias then moved
down to the coast and securing a port at Trujillo set
up a government and asked recognition. Novoa who
was Chilean commissioner saw humor in the fact that
General Iglesias cabled to the United States announcing the installation of his government at Trujillo.

Before Iglesias was treated with, in any formal way
that would imply official recognition, he was obliged to
sign a contract agreeing to make peace, on the terms
demanded by Chile. In other words the Treaty of Ancón was not the result of deliberations by any self-con-
stituted Peruvian body, but the direct carrying out of
a contract. On May 12, Iglesias wrote agreeing to sign
the terms desired and carry them out in return for
recognition; if he had not, then the Chilean envoy, generals, or the unnational nitrate dealers would have
found and set up somebody who would have done what
they wished.

The terms of this contract are virtually the same as
the treaty, they deal mostly with nitrate, guano, and
debts, but, of course, the matter of Tacna-Arica had to
be included. In order to make complete the story of the
evolution of Article III of the famous treaty it is well to
notice how it read when it was in the form of a contract

with Iglesias, in which contract or protocol it was Article II. It reads:

2d. The territories of Tacna and Arica, actually in possession of Chile will be subject to the legislation and laws of Chile for the term of ten years, reckoning from the date when the treaty of peace shall be celebrated. This term once elapsed, a plebiscite will be convoked to decide by popular vote whether the territories shall remain under the sovereignty of Chile or return to that of Peru. That one of these two nations, in whose favor the definite annexation shall be decided, shall pay the other 10,000,000 silver pesos in Chilean coin or in Peruvian soles of equal fineness.

An additional paragraph provided for the election protocol as it did in the final form of the treaty. Now that Iglesias signed the contract to make the desired peace, he had a chance to make peace as neither Calderón nor Montero had, for they did not acquiesce in the nitrate expansion program. It must be remembered that Tacna-Arica was incidental and connected only as possible deposits of a competing product and the strategic key to Bolivian diplomacy and nitrate frontiers.

On October 18 Chile recognized formally President Iglesias although he represented a small fraction of Peru—his army was paid with Chilean money and the officers had to lock the privates up at night so they would not desert. The final draft of the famous treaty was made at Ancón which name it bears, but it was signed in Lima, October 20, 1883. The Chilean troops withdrew from Lima October 23, 1883, and it was occupied by General Iglesias the same day. Callao was turned over to the new *régime* also. Chilean forces were stationed in nearby suburbs, and certain hospitals in Lima were left for their use. Three hundred thousand pesos a month were to be paid for the maintenance of those troops, and that sum proved embarrassing to the new Government. Iglesias has been severely condemned by his countrymen for accepting such terms, but with the growing desire of the officers of occupation to hold the country indefinitely, he was probably much more of a patriot than a tool of the country's enemies, for he could not have remained in power a week nor could the treaty have been signed without the Chilean troops near by.

While the United States did not immediately recognize President Iglesias, and Secretary Frelinghuysen thought the 50 per cent clause of the treaty was contrary to international law, our new minister to Peru, Mr. S. L. Phelps, was instructed not to hinder ratification "although the terms were at variance with those the United States had counseled." The Minister was instructed to express the opinion unofficially that Chile should recognize all the debts of the territory conquered. Eventually, mixed commissions settled most of the claims except the Dreyfus claim, which was but recently settled. The exactions of that house seem somewhat hard when it is remembered that the first prominent Dreyfus had been a clerk in a store in Lima and made his wealth from exporting Peruvian guano.

News was now received that there was probability of a European intervention; the powers protested the Treaty of Ancón. Chile determined to invade Bolivia and force peace, a move that would be a convenient continuation of the campaign against Arequipa, which was then being pushed forward. The Bolivian commissioners then accepted the truce.

In evacuating Peru the Chilean army remained in possession of a part of Tarata on the ground that it was a part of Tacna. They held that the river Chaspaya was the river Sama named in the treaty. When Chile refused to move out of Tarata, Iglesias protested, and the fulfilment of the treaty and its ratification seemed threatened. When the United States Minister in Lima inquired about it he was assured that there had been some little misunderstanding, but that all was settled. Under Peruvian administration there was a Department of Tacna comprising the provinces of Tacna, Arica, and Tarata. Tarata contained six districts and when Peru went to occupy it after peace was declared Chilean forces held the districts of Tarata, Tarucachi, and Estique which lay south of the river Chaspaya and which Chile maintained belonged to Tacna. Peru was thus obliged to see three of the districts of the province of Tarata kept by Chile as long as Tacna was held. These were returned to Peru by the Coolidge Award.

The ratification of the Treaty of Ancón was not secured without great difficulty and good fortune on the part of Chile. The most formidable obstacle was the attitude of foreign governments whose citizens would lose money invested in Peruvian guano and nitrate loans. Many bondholders refused to accept the arrangement to receive in payment 50 per cent of the sale of a product when they had been secured by a full mortgage. Formal protests against the treaty were made by France, Italy, England, Holland, Belgium, and Spain. The United States Minister was instructed to object unofficially. While we had recognized the Calderón-Montero government, nevertheless Secretary Frelinghuysen said we would not refuse to acknowledge the

Iglesias government if it seemed an advance toward an amicable adjustment of the difficulty. The protests by so many powers would doubtless have prevented the ratification of the treaty had not France insisted on a preference for a claim of seventy million francs for the house of Dreyfus of which President Grévy had formerly been counsel.

The treaty was approved by the Chilean Congress in January and by the Peruvian assembly in March, 1884, and it was ten years from this date that the plebiscite was to be held in Tacna-Arica. The fatality of the whole matter lay in the failure to include the special protocol provided for, before the treaty was ratified. President Santa María said he feared that no agreement could be reached regarding details of elections and a discussion of them would jeopardize the ratification of the treaty.[6]

Thus the War of the Pacific was ended, technically, and the boundaries of Chile expanded northward seven degrees. However, the echoes of this struggle and its imperfect treaty were to reverberate for forty years and the problems growing out of it were to occupy the statesmen of many generations and countries. Since the Treaty of Ancón resulted in the later phase of the Tacna-Arica question, the entire text appears in the Appendix, and Article III the famous plebiscite clause is given also in Spanish. It should be noted that of the fourteen articles in the treaty, nine refer to guano or nitrates. It was the "fifty per cent" stipulations in Articles IV, VII, and X that led Secretary Blaine to say that it was a war in which the bondholders and the Government of Chile went "fifty-fifty."

REFERENCES

1. Note: This phrase is the original form of stating the ten-year period of the plebiscite clause. See *infra*, pp. 196, 217–220.

2. *Executive Documents,* Forty-eighth Congress, first session, Vol. I, No. 1, Part 1, pp. 77–79.

3. William Jefferson Dennis, *Documentary History of the Tacna-Arica Dispute,* p. 211.

4. Gonzalo Búlnes, *Guerra del Pacífico,* III, 414.

5. Note: There was no intention of changing the meaning of the treaty in using *"Espirado este plazo,"* because the Chilean Minister of Foreign Affairs in reporting this treaty used *"Al fin de diez años."*

6. Búlnes, *op. cit.,* III, 526. Note: See also note 8, p. 226, *infra.*

CHAPTER X

THE HARDING-COOLIDGE MEDIATIONS

FOLLOWING the War of the Pacific each of the nations involved experienced stirring times in reconstruction. By the terms of the Truce Pact between Bolivia and Chile they agreed to an indefinite truce during which time Chile would keep all the Bolivian littoral; other seized property on both sides was to be restored; Bolivian damages were to be paid from a portion of the customs duties of Arica on goods bound for Bolivia through that port, and the truce would have to be ratified within forty days. It was twenty years before this truce was followed by a definite treaty of peace.

During the ten years before the plebiscite was due both Chile and Peru witnessed exciting occurrences. In Peru after Iglesias entered Lima and hoisted the flag over the *palacio* trouble began at once. A civil war over the form of government resulted between Iglesias and Cáceres. In December of the following year both surrendered their claims and a council of ministers governed until 1886 when Iglesias left the country and Cáceres was elected president.[1] During his administration the nation began to recuperate somewhat from the war. The country was without industry, money, or spirit.

Toward the end of his administration the immense public debt amounting to upward of $250,000,000 was consolidated and an arrangement made to syndicate it; bondholders and debtors taking stock in a company for their claims, and the company receiving all state railroads and other considerations.[2] The arrangement was long a source of dispute in domestic politics, the company and the Government often being at logger-heads. Recently a new contract was made by which the former retained the railroads it had and the latter received back the guano islands. It must be said, though, that the Peruvian Corporation, as the company is called, provided a *modus vivendi* for a very sick nation.

Since Cáceres' administration Peru has been slowly improving in industry, education, and progress. The shadow of the Peruvian Corporation is always near and there have been a few revolutions, but much progress has been made. Alternating with her domestic problems has been the ever present question of Tacna and Arica and the efforts looking toward its solution will be discussed later.

Chile following the War of the Pacific experienced great commercial growth.[3] Millions of dollars were invested in public works, railroads were constructed, public buildings built, and great armaments bought.[4] Since Chile paid off $240,000,000 of Peruvian debts with the 50 per cent of the sale of guano captured it is apparent that an equal sum could be spent for her own purposes. This had its dangers. A large official family was created which soon came to live in discord. Various combinations came into friction, and the trouble came to a head, during the administration of President Balmaceda, in a great civil war between the executive and legislative branches of government. It resulted in military operations and costs larger than the War of the Pacific. The "*Baltimore* affair" which narrowly missed involving the United States with Chile grew out of the Balmaceda revolution.[5]

Ironically the news of the overthrow of the Balmaceda government was received in the United States by private citizens before it was received by the Chilean Minister. A cable had been constructed down the west coast and news of the victory of the rebels was cabled from Valparaiso long before Balmaceda was able to wire to Buenos Aires and have a message cabled to Washington.[6]

With these events taking place in Peru and Chile at the end of the ten-year period it can be seen that it was not a propitious time for the holding of the Tacna-Arica plebiscite. However as the ten-year period drew to a close, negotiations were started looking toward the holding of elections, and from time to time diplomatic efforts were renewed until the archives of the two governments were filled with notes and protocols, but deadlocks always resulted. The only time that any serious endeavor was made by Chile to hold the plebiscite previous to the Harding mediation was in 1898 when the Billinghurst-Latorre Protocol was signed. This was due to a recurrence of the Patagonia dispute with Argentina. The protocol provided for an arbitration by the Queen Regent of Spain. Peru approved the protocol as did the Chilean Senate. The Government was anxious to conclude the matter, for strong notes had been sent to Argentina. In September a government supporter demanded on the floor the ratification, saying, "The international situation demands the approval of the protocol, and whoever opposes it would be acting as a traitor to his country."[7] Before the House approved it the Argentine crisis passed and the protocol was tabled. There was great disappointment in Peru. Preparations for holding the plebiscite, including a national salt monopoly for raising revenue, had been made and hopes had been aroused.

Regarding the general attitude in each country toward the holding of the plebiscite the best summary was made by the leading Chilean historian, Búlnes, about twenty years after the making of the Treaty of Ancón. He said:

Peru has had a live interest in holding the plebiscite. To deny it would be placing one in a bad situation, because she could prove it by merely exhibiting the diplomatic documents. The reason for this interest can be condensed thus:

"1. Chile was in possession of the thing in dispute and the only means Peru had of recovering it was to insist on the fulfillment of the treaty provision. Therefore it is natural that Peru should have the initiative and active part, Chile the passive.

"2. Peru has been hearing the clamor of the inhabitants of those provinces to be reincorporated into their old nationality, and because of patriotism or even decorum she could not be indifferent to the pressure.

"3. Peru has had a blind confidence in the plebiscite. The Peruvian policy has been fixed since the beginning of the debate, and ours has had all kinds of curves and vacillations. The objective of Peru could not vacillate, because her old aspiration has been to recuperate her former provinces, working for the plebiscite to be presided over by a foreign power and trying to secure the best facilities for the payment of the ransom."

On the other hand Chile has worked one day to get a plebiscite favorable to it, another day to give the territory to Bolivia, another to give it to Peru, and naturally, its action has been weak and has made declarations contradictory and dangerous.[8]

During these years no definite peace had been made

between Chile and Bolivia. Many notes and conversations had taken place. Bolivia had been given to understand that the matter was to rest until Chile should receive Tacna-Arica as a result of the plebiscite and then it would be ceded to her. Bolivia had many financial and other obligations with respect to her lost littoral that needed settlement. As time had elapsed she began to insist on terms that would in a measure recompense her for the loss of territory. It was during exchanges of this nature that Bolivia received the famous König note which represented the climax of Chile's extreme policy—not approved by the better element. Abraham König was the Chilean plenipotentiary at La Paz. In a long note he said in part:

It is a common error and one that is reported daily on the street and in the press the opinion that Bolivia has the right to demand a port in compensation for her littoral.

There is no such thing. Chile has occupied the littoral and has taken possession of it with the same title with which Germany annexed to the empire Alsace and Lorraine, with the same title by which the United States of North America has taken Porto Rico. Our rights are born of victory, the supreme law of nations.

That the littoral is rich and worth many millions, that we already know. We keep it because it is valuable; if it were not worth anything there would be no interest in its conservation.

This note seems to be too harsh even for the most exacting and Chile soon attempted to make a livable arrangement with Bolivia. A settlement called the Treaty of 1904 was made which gave Chile permanent ownership of Atacama, now called Antofagasta, thus sealing the loss by Bolivia of a coast province. Chile assumed certain debts against the region, agreed to build a railroad from Arica to La Paz which should become the property of Bolivia at the end of fifteen years and to permit free duties at the ports of Arica and Antofagasta. This technically closed the War of the Pacific between Chile and Bolivia, but did not settle the "question of the Pacific." Periodically, Bolivia sought to have the Treaty of 1904 annulled and a new arrangement made by which she would have a zone to the sea—the only permanent solution of the Tacna-Arica question.

During the long period between the Chile-Bolivia settlement of 1904 and the Harding-Coolidge mediation, the question of Tacna-Arica policy disturbed the governments of Peru and Chile and to a lesser extent that of Bolivia. For some time Chile was not specially concerned about the settling of the question, playing Bolivia and Peru against each other with respect to Tacna-Arica. It did not occur to Chilean congresses and cabinets that the friendship of Peru would be very valuable. Of course a few statesmen saw it.

At the time of the Billinghurst-Latorre Protocol a book was published by Javier Vial Solar showing that Chile's future lay on the sea, that her maritime possibilities with a long coast and fine traditions as sailors should make Chile the Venice, the Genoa, the England of South America, and that a definite peace should be made. He was obviously advocating the Billinghurst-Latorre program of settlement for his book was dedicated to those two envoys. However, he saw clearly the ill effect of the unsettled "Problem of the North," as he entitled his book. Besides taking the above advanced view of future peace he succinctly characterized

Chilean policy concerning Tacna-Arica, in a manner
that is worth adding to Búlnes' statement. He said:

> . . . Chilean politicians had imagined that the victor
> of the War of the Pacific was a fat and sentimental papà
> who carried Bolivia and Peru in his arms like two babies
> with whom he passed the time amusing himself playing
> the most naïve of games; that is, alternately taking the
> sweet "sugar-pap," Tacna-Arica, from the mouth of one
> and putting it into the mouth of the other.[9]

That seems to be a correct, if homely, summarizing
of Chilean policy with respect to Tacna-Arica and the
plebiscite clause of the Treaty of Ancón. Her need was
to hold these provinces in order to hold Tarapacá, the
El Dorado of nitrate, for she knew her neighbors well
enough to be certain that Peru's feelings toward her
lost provinces were the same as those of France toward
Alsace-Lorraine.

Meanwhile, both before and after the end of the ten-
year period, Chilean administration of Tacna-Arica
led to Peruvian charges of official Chileanization.
Article III of the treaty provided that the territory
should "continue to be possessed by Chile and subject
to Chilean legislation and authority for a term of ten
years, etc." Chile not only held it subject to her authority and administrative legislation, but colonized,
built a railroad, and subsidized factories. These acts
Peru always protested. In the difficulties attending
these acts Peruvians had their schools closed, their
priests removed, and their press silenced. As a result
diplomatic relations were broken by Peru. She recalled
her minister in 1901 but renewed relations in 1905. In
1908 relations were again broken, but there were some

direct negotiations between their ministries in 1909, 1912, and 1914.

In the awakening of national consciousness during and following the World War, there was a reawakening of the question. Owing to the idealistic utterances of President Wilson regarding the rights of lesser nations, hope for a settlement was renewed in Peru, and even Bolivia revived her aspirations for a port on the Pacific. There were demonstrations in pro-Peruvian clubs in Tacna-Arica and even in definitely ceded Tarapacá. Some of these clubs were stoned and demonstrators were warned to leave. The usual diplomatic flirtation with Bolivia took place and sentiment was divided in that country on whether to expect a port from Chile or from Peru.[10]

Of course this ever present foreign problem affected domestic as well as international politics and hindered real progress in both countries. Peru, under the administration of Dr. José Pardo, had adhered to the allies during the World War, had allowed the United States to take over interned German ships, and had protested against submarine warfare, but had not declared war against Germany. Although Germany had sunk a Peruvian bark and popular sympathies were generally with the allies, Dr. Pardo said it would be almost "despicable" to declare war on a nation eight thousand miles away when his country lacked the means of being effective in the war.[11] It was understood that the allies wanted a contingent of fifty thousand men and offered to arm and train them. Opponents of the administration accused Dr. Pardo of losing a unique opportunity of participating in a world peace conference which might restore Tacna-Arica or at least give Peru military prestige and training. Without commenting on the proposition it is sufficient to say that it had a great effect on domestic politics. The Minister of Foreign Relations was interpellated by the Senate,[12] and the situation was a contributing factor in the overthrow of Dr. Pardo before his term had expired.

In Chile also domestic reforms were complicated with the Tacna-Arica situation. One instance is typical. After the disturbances took place in Peruvian clubhouses in Tacna-Arica an army of thirty thousand men was mobilized in northern Chile. Since it was well known that Peru did not have a complete regiment in any one garrison outside of Lima it was evident that the military gesture was made for its effect on domestic issues. In a speech in the Chilean Congress on April 20, 1921, a deputy condemned the costly mobilization and charged that it was an attempt at intimidation of the party that had elected Arturo Alessandri to the presidency.[13] Opponents of Alessandri used the Tacna-Arica issue to defeat his candidacy, and his desire to be free to deal with domestic issues may explain partly his direct and unexpected negotiations with Peru which resulted in the Harding mediation.

The question also was a menace to the peace of South America and contributed to international whisperings and talks of balance of power. In May, 1921, a Chilean mission, called the "Matte Mission," went to Brazil avowedly as a return courtesy for a visit from a Brazilian diplomat made many years previous. A Brazilian daily commenting on it stated that the mission had, in its opinion, three objects: viz., to sound Brazil on the question of the Pacific, to discover what coöperation could be secured from Brazil, and to see if it were possible to galvanize the corpse of the A.B.C. policy.[14] Another instance of the international aspect of this question was occasioned by the visit of Gen. Charles Mangin who represented France at the Peruvian centennial the same year. Owing to his renown he was entertained with military reviews by the countries visited *en route* and had an opportunity to observe military affairs. On returning to Paris he stated in answer to a question in an interview that Chile had the best army he saw. As soon as the French paper was received in Argentina the Congress of that country interpellated its Minister of War.

The extremity of feeling to which Chile and Peru have gone was demonstrated in 1921 in connection with the celebration of the Peruvian centennial of its independence. Of all the nations of the world only Chile and Ecuador, her supposed ally in the balance of power, did not take part; Chilean dispatches to Argentinian papers furnished derogatory accounts of the celebration. Among the many special ambassadors at the celebration was the United States Ambassador, Albert Douglas, who in a speech at a banquet made the statement that "might does not make right, . . . that treaties solemnly made cannot, with impunity, be treated as 'mere scraps of paper.' . . ." He also made some generalizations about the moral accountability of nations to the world. The reports of this speech caused Santiago to request an explanation from Washington, and Douglas said he *had not referred especially to Chile.*[15]

The same year, on September 13, the President of Chile promulgated a law incorporating Tarata into the Department of Tacna after it had been administered as a separate unit for forty years. The Peruvian Minister of Foreign Affairs addressed a note to foreign chancelleries in which he charged Chile with trying to "hide the fruits of her crime," feeling the hour approaching of "great historical reparations in the new world."[16]

There is no doubt that the universal awakening following the World War hastened the bringing about of the Harding mediation. There was also an important economic motive besides the domestic political ones made soon after the above-mentioned incidents of the centennial. Previous to the completion of the Panama Canal and the advent of the World War, the nitrate industry was the great predominating influence in Chilean economic policy. There was no other big industry contributing any considerable tax to the Government or requiring economic policies of the state. But the Panama Canal rerouted commerce. Chile, owing to its coast and naval traditions, has always had great maritime possibilities. The opening of the canal was soon followed by the German blockade, so Chile made the most of her opportunities and became an important carrier in South America as had been predicted by Vial Solar. Business at once felt the effects of the Tacna-Arica trouble. Not only did the long unfriendly coast of Peru give most of its business to American and Japanese lines but, whenever there was a disturbance arousing fresh anger at Chile, Peruvian longshoremen refused to load or unload Chilean cargoes. That Tacna-Arica was a "white elephant" to Chilean commerce became more and more evident and this factor increased the desire of President Alessandri for a settlement.

Although both presidents were determined to terminate the Tacna-Arica question there was strong opposition at home. The opposition in Chile to President Alessandri has been mentioned. There were three principal reasons for objecting in Chile to the holding of the plebiscite other than purely political opposition to the President. If Chile should win, little would be gained as it already had possession and exercised all the privileges of sovereignty. If Chile should lose Tacna-Arica the "ambitions of old and irreconcilable enemies would be whetted" and Peru might then want Tarapacá back. And if "Chile were generous with Peru, Bolivia and many others would interpret this as a weakness and would feel inclined to press their demands."[17] In Peru the opposition held that a political arbitration would not be so advantageous as a juridical settlement by The Hague, the World Court, or some other judicial body. The opposition feared that by arbitration a Solomonic decision might result and believed a juridical verdict would give them the provinces whole.

From the foregoing, something of the magnitude and acuteness of the question on the eve of its submission to arbitration may be gathered. In 1920 the President of Chile authorized Minister Puga Borne to negotiate informally with the President of Peru, but nothing was done. Near the close of the following year, in which, as related above, the question had been in a state of more or less constant ferment, the step was taken which led to the Harding mediation. On December 12 the Chilean Chancellor, Barros Jarpa, sent a cablegram to the Peruvian Chancellor, Alberto Salomón, inviting Peru to hold the plebiscite, agreed upon in the Treaty of Ancón, to determine definitely the nationality of Tacna-Arica. The message, frank and friendly in tone, stated that the invitation had been agreed upon by the heads of political parties, and it caused a little sensation in Lima.[18] As diplomatic relations did not exist the Peruvian Government inquired through a neutral embassy as to the authenticity of the cable, evidently fearing a hoax. The result of several weeks of negotiations by cable was an offer of Peru to "submit jointly the entire question of the South Pacific that divides us to an arbitration, agreed to through the initiative of the Government of the United States of America."[19]

Very soon after this offer came the invitation of President Harding to have the negotiations brought to Washington where the question might be arranged or its arbitration agreed upon.[20] Copies of the invitation were delivered to the two governments on the same date, January 18, 1922, through the United States embassies in Santiago and Lima. When deliberations were transferred to Washington, the Chilean delegation maintained that the only question needing settlement was the manner of fulfilling Article III of the Treaty of Ancón; i.e., the plebiscite clause. Peru held that a plebiscite arranged for under conditions existing in 1883 would be invalid now and that the ownership of Tacna-Arica should be determined by the arbiter taking into consideration the whole question of the South Pacific. The deliberations were long and difficult and the repercussion in Peru and Chile great.[21] Not until July 20, 1922, was the protocol of submission and supplementary act agreed upon.*

Bolivia had on November 1, 1920, appealed to the League of Nations for a seaport on the grounds that the Treaty of 1904 was null and void. Chile challenged the appeal and secured good lawyers who said the league had no jurisdiction in the case.[22] Bolivia withdrew and adhered to Peru in not entering the League of Nations when it was seen that the United States was not entering. When Peru's case was intrusted to Washington for solution Bolivia asked to sit in the con-

* Text in Appendix VIII.

ference, but was denied the privilege by President Harding.

At the conferences in Washington, Chile again won a diplomatic victory. It was clear from the beginning that Peru would ask the arbitrator to declare the plebiscite clause invalid and arbitrate the disposition of Tacna-Arica on historical grounds; Chile would ask merely that the manner of holding the election be decided by arbitration. Each government had to give its constituency to understand that the mediation of the United States would take its view of the scope of the arbitration or neither Senate would have ratified the protocol. When the conferences came to a deadlock over this point Secretary Hughes in order to avoid the failure of the attempt took a course that rendered our arbitration practically innocuous.

Chile secured an early advantage in the statement of the question, viz.:

It is hereby recorded that *the only difficulties* arising out of the Treaty of Peace regarding which the two countries have not been able to reach an agreement, are the questions arising out of the unfulfilled stipulations of Article III of said Treaty.[23]

On May 27 Dr. Melitón Porras representing Peru proposed the following:

. . . for the purpose of determining the manner in which the stipulations of Article III of the Treaty of Ancon shall be fulfilled there shall be submitted to arbitration the question whether, in the present circumstances, the plebiscite shall or shall not be held.

This was naturally followed by the following questions: "If it is not to be held, to which country will belong the final dominion of Tacna and Arica and under what conditions?" "If it is to be held, under what conditions shall the plebiscite take place?"

Chile rejected this as being outside of the offer contemplated in President Harding's invitation and unacceptable to Chile. As soon as Secretary Hughes was advised of this deadlock he offered the following substitution:

For the purpose of bringing about a solution of the long standing controversy between the two countries having to do with the unfulfilled provisions of the treaty of Ancon, they agree to submit to arbitration the questions arising out of the unfulfilled stipulations of Article III.

This was a happy suggestion so far as saving the conference was concerned for each side thought it had won. Secretary Hughes unfortunately went farther and suggested that the parties include in another exchange of notes the statement that any decision of the arbitrator would not change the status of the territory, i.e., if the arbitrator held the plebiscite clause invalid it would not change the actual status of the territory under discussion; its future would be determined by the parties in later negotiations. The Chilean representatives hastened to recommend to their government the acceptance of that step of the negotiations for they said:

Here we considered that, the only point having been eliminated which placed the fate of Tacna and Arica in the hands of a foreign arbitrator, submitting a popular referendum for [instead of] the decision of a third party, and expressly recognizing the fact that the declaration of the lack of foundation for the plebiscite did not alter the rights which, up to the present time, we have exercised in these territories, and which are given us by the Treaty, the proposition was acceptable and thus it was accepted.

The plan of Secretary Hughes did not bind Chile technically to accept arbitration except as to the manner of holding the plebiscite, but morally it bound her to accept our good offices for a settlement in case the plebiscite clause was held invalid by the arbitrator. In fine, whatever decision President Coolidge would hand down Tacna-Arica would still be in the undisturbed possession of Chile. This ineffective formula was strongly recommended to Chile by Secretary Hughes who was oversanguine as is indicated in his address opening the parley, when he referred to the success of the disarmament conference which had been held in the same room. Thus the agreement was to allow the President of the United States to arbitrate as to whether the plebiscite clause was still valid, and if so to fix the conditions under which the election should be held, but if it were not valid to accept his "good offices" in further negotiations. In case the plebiscite clause were held invalid, much would depend on the scope of the good offices; the question might resolve itself into whether a mediation or an arbitration was contemplated, just as at the conference of the *Lackawanna* the question was whether the United States was to mediate or intervene.

In securing the approval of their congresses to the protocol, the domestic politics of both presidents, Leguía of Peru and Alessandri of Chile, were important as both cause and effect. In Peru opposition to the negotiations was strengthened by the action of loyal Peruvians in Tarapacá and Tacna-Arica. Pro-Peruvians in definitely-ceded Tarapacá, whose hopes of reincorporation into Peru had been aroused, memorialized Peruvian officials in Lima and in Washington praying that no action be taken under the Treaty of Ancón. They urged that the treaty be held null in its entirety, saying that it would be better to hold the question open to future settlement on that basis than to give sanction to the treaty by complying with the plebiscite clause even to gain Tacna-Arica.[24] This Tarapacá group was not large, but opponents to the Washington negotiations were much affected by it. A committee from Tacna-Arica also presented a memorial to the United States ambassador urging against the division of the region.

Besides being confident of the justice of her contentions, Peru expected a favorable hearing on the part of the President of the United States. This was due to the fact that the United States had intervened ineffectively in the War of the Pacific advocating the policy of "no territorial indemnities." This had aroused in Peru a hope that had helped cause her to prolong the war to an extent resulting in the severe terms of the Treaty of Ancón. The policy of the United States had prevented European intervention. It was expected, therefore, that the arbiter should feel a measure of responsibility in securing a very fair, if not indeed favorable, settlement for Peru. While the United States could not be blamed for the death of President Garfield and the consequent downfall of Secretary James G. Blaine and the intervention policy, President Coolidge might in justice make some belated amends by effective intervention in the question. For these historical reasons and because of the lapse of time and the Chileanization of Tacna-Arica during the period, it was taken for granted in Peru that President Coolidge would hold the plebiscite clause void and determine the future of the provinces on other bases.

After delays in securing congressional approval to the protocol and in arranging the personnel of the delegations, the parties presented their allegations to the arbiter. The cases were presented by distinguished diplomats and counsel, among whom were Professor Edwin M. Borchard for Peru, and former Secretary of State Robert Lansing for Chile. President Coolidge, who inherited the arbitration from the late President Harding, handed down his "Opinion and Award," dated March 4, 1925, the last day of the incumbency of Secretary Hughes who had labored hard to bring about the settlement of the question.[25] It was made public March 8 and created a great sensation in South America.

REFERENCES

1. Teresa G. de Fanning, *Historia del Peru*, p. 142.
2. C. E. Akers, *A History of South America*, p. 542.
3. W. A. Smith, *Temperate Chile*, p. 11.
4. F. Valdes Vergara, *Historia de Chile*, p. 341.
5. J. D. Richardson, *Messages and Papers of the Presidents*, 5620.
6. Charles R. Flint, *Memories of an Active Life*, p. 65.
7. V. M. Maurtua, *The Question of the Pacific*, pp. 221–232. Also Sarah Wambaugh, *A Monograph on Plebiscites*, pp. 160–165.
8. Gonzalo Búlnes, Article in *El Ferrocarril*, Santiago, May, 1914.
9. Javier Vial Solar, *El problema del norte*, p. 21. Santiago, 1898.
10. Note: The statements in this paragraph are based on the tone of the press of the three countries and observations of the author who resided in South America from 1918 to 1921.
11. José Pardo, *Peru*, p. 6.
12. Mariano Cornejo, *La intervención del Peru en la guerra mundial* [printed copy of his speech delivered in the Senate].
13. *La Prensa*, Lima, May 28, 1921.
14. *Gazeta de Noticias*, Rio de Janeiro, May 10, 1921.
15. *The West Coast Leader*, Lima, August 6, 1921.
16. *Ibid.*, November 30, 1921.
17. Bishop D. Rafael Edwards, *Relations of Chile and Peru*,

Santiago, p. 21. Note: This booklet was secured from the Chilean embassy in 1922 in answer to a request for literature containing the Chilean point of view.

18. *The West Coast Leader*, Lima, December 14, 1921.

19. *Opinion and Award*, p. 16.

20. Tacna-Arica Arbitration, *The Case of the Republic of Chile*, pp. 2, 3. Note: Text of Harding invitation.

21. *Ibid.*, pp. 3–5. Spanish text, *Boletín de la Unión Panamericana*, October, 1922.

22. John W. Davis, "Two Judicial Reports" in the *Problem of the Pacific and the New Policies of Bolivia*, p. 178.

23. *Tacna-Arica Arbitration, Appendix to Case of the Republic of Chile*, p. 653.

24. Clemente Palma, *La cuestión de Tacna y Arica y la conferencia de Washington*, Lima, Appendix, pp. 89, 90.

25. Note: The decision of President Coolidge is printed as a government document under the full title of *Opinion and Award of the Arbitrator in the Matter of the Arbitration between the Republic of Chile and the Republic of Peru, with Respect to the Unfulfilled Provisions of the Treaty of Peace of October 20, 1883, under the Protocol and Supplementary Act Signed at Washington July 20, 1922*. In this work it is referred to under the abbreviated title *Opinion and Award*. Essential extracts are found in the Appendix, *infra*, pp. 310–315.

CHAPTER XI

OPINION AND AWARD OF PRESIDENT COOLIDGE

THE Opinion and Award was favorable to Chile in that the plebiscite was ordered held. The contentions of Peru regarding the Chileanization of Tacna-Arica were partly sustained, but not sufficiently to invalidate the plebiscite clause. The manner of holding the plebiscite was favorable to Peru and the districts of Tarata were awarded outright to her.[1] Chile won the main contention, that the plebiscite clause should be executed. The arbiter would not go back of that clause and reopen the main question. In this he followed the precedent of President Harding who early in the negotiations refused the request of Bolivia to sit in the conferences, on the ground that the mediation contemplated only the unfulfilled clause of the treaty between Chile and Peru. Historical considerations were ruled out, a legalistic interpretation of the plebiscite clause was given for the Award, and a hypothetical basis was taken for the opinion. Mr. Lansing gave to the press a statement in which he said, "From the beginning to the end the award is a complete vindication of the course pursued by Chile during the past thirty years and an indorsement of Chile's position in the case and countercase which she has submitted to the arbitrator."[2] Apart from the lack of diplomatic taste and the historical and factual inaccuracy of the statement,[3] the connection with the case of a former Secretary of State, and particularly one of so recent incumbency, might well be termed questionable diplomatic ethics.

In Chile the Award came as an agreeable surprise. It was also coincident with the return of President Alessandri from Italy where he had been exiled by a military *junta*. Since the Tacna-Arica settlement was one of his important policies he arrived home with increased prestige.[4] It would not be too much to say that the favorable Award made safe his reassuming the presidency.

In Peru the disappointment was extreme. Popular manifestations occurred in Lima and Callao which required all the tact of the Government to handle. Strangely enough a remarkable natural phenomenon aided in limiting the political disturbances to minor outbreaks. There occurred in Lima and along the desert coast an all-night rain. Since such a rain had not fallen in the history of the coast, buildings had not been roofed for turning water other than heavy dews and mists. Consequently the attention of the population was directed to the exigencies of the calamity which accompanied their diplomatic defeat. It was a hard blow. Added to the expense of restoring buildings, bridges, and power stations, would be the expense of holding the plebiscite. It would be easy to get ten million pesos to pay for a won territory, but hard to get a million to hold an election which they had so much wanted thirty years ago, but so hated under existing conditions.

Serious violence was avoided, however, although the parades and other demonstrations were enormous. The most impressive protest against the Award was a procession of thousands of women who marched in silence past the United States embassy each carrying a flower to the monument to veterans of the War of the Pacific. At the close of the speeches by women, a man prominent in public affairs was called upon to speak for the aged widow of Admiral Miguel Grau. He closed his remarks with the conclusion that Peru's only hope was in her own might for, "there is no international justice."

It was thought at first that Peru might not accept the Award. March 11 President Leguía sent the following telegram of thanks to President Coolidge:

Although in my opinion your excellency's award has undeservedly improved the moral position of the Republic of Chile, guilty without any doubt, for more than forty years, of indescribable persecutions and crimes against Peruvian citizens of Tacna and Arica, I express to your excellency without reserve my sincere thanks for the high responsibility which you have so disinterestedly assumed to reëstablish peace and tranquillity finally, under the dominance of justice, in this part of the western hemisphere which owing to the culpability of Chile has lived during almost a half century on the brink of war.

But the Award was not all in favor of Chile. Provisions for the qualification of voters were favorable to Peruvians, and Peru was awarded the three disputed districts of Tarata.* An error in the treaty had described the river Sama as rising on the Bolivian frontier, but it is formed farther down by the rivers Tala and Chaspaya and so it could not mark the northern boundary of Tacna. Following the war Chile retained three districts of Tarata assuming that one of the affluents of the Sama was the boundary. The Award returned them to Peru.

The Award provided thorough machinery for the execution of the plebiscite. A plebiscitary commission

* See *supra*, pp. 191, 203.

with registration and election boards was created as well as a special boundary commission to mark out the disputed courses of the rivers Sama and Camarones. The main commission consisted of three members, one named by each contending nation and a third, who was to be the chairman, named by the arbitrator. President Coolidge named Gen. John J. Pershing as chairman. Chile named Agustín Edwards and Peru, Manuel de Freyre Santander, while Col. J. J. Morrow, Governor of the Canal Zone, was named chairman of the special boundary commission. Judging from the high standing of the commissioners and the thoroughness of the provisions of the Award for appeals and other emergencies, it seemed as though the long overdue plebiscite was soon to be held and the famous Tacna-Arica question settled.

In analyzing the Opinion and Award of the arbitrator it may be said at the outset that the decision of an arbitrator should be little criticized and less questioned. The submission of a question to an umpire implies acceptance of the award. However, any opinion that may accompany a decision is open to analysis and criticism. In this respect President Coolidge, who usually was very fortunate politically, was very unfortunate as developments in Tacna-Arica soon showed. In the summer of 1923 when the first dispatches of the illness of President Harding were received a group of townsmen, friends of the Vice-President, were discussing the dispatches in the railway station at Northampton. One of the group jokingly remarked that he should not want to be in President Harding's place. When asked why, he remarked, "Cal's lucky; I wouldn't want to be in line ahead of him." In the Chile-Peru arbitration, however, the luck seemed to have abandoned him, for the plebiscite which he held to be not only legal, but practicable, was found to be impossible by the plebiscite commission which he created in his Award.

Under the Protocol of Submission the arbitrator defined his duties in the case to consist, first, in deciding whether a plebiscite should be held to determine the definite ownership of Tacna-Arica, second, if a plebiscite were decided upon he was to determine the qualifications of voters and voting regulations, third, if the arbitrator decided against the plebiscite to take no further action as an arbitrator, except that, fourth, in either case he was to decide the questions about the northern and southern boundaries of Tacna-Arica.

Regarding the question as to whether the plebiscite should be held or not the arbitrator defined it as depending on whether or not that article of the Treaty of Ancón had expired by lapse of time or had been rendered invalid by the conduct of the parties so that its fulfilment could no longer be demanded. Taking up the question of the lapse of time after the ten years provided in the treaty the arbitrator gave a remarkable grammatical opinion. He said:

At the outset, it should be observed that the second and third paragraphs of Article 3 do not provide for the termination of their obligations by lapse of time. The Article contains no provision for forfeiture. It fixed no period within which the plebiscite must be taken. The plebiscite was to be had "*after* the expiration of that term," that is, after the ten years but no limit was defined. It was to be taken pursuant to a special agreement which it was left to the Parties to make. But no time was fixed within which the special protocol for the plebiscite was to be negotiated. Whatever may have been the reasons for

leaving the matter thus at large, the fact remains that it
was left without prescribed limit of time and the obligations of the Parties under the treaty must be determined
accordingly.

If it be suggested that such an agreement—an agreement to agree with no time specified and no forfeiture
provided—is unsatisfactory or meaningless, a three-fold
answer presents itself, first, that the Arbitrator is not
empowered to alter the treaty or to insert provisions,
however salutary they might be in his judgment viewing
the matter retrospectively, which the High Contracting
Parties did not see fit to include; second, that the Treaty
of Ancon was a peace treaty—the parties were engaged
in a devastating war. Apparently the Parties in 1883–
1884 thought it better to agree that they would agree at
some unspecified time in the future than to agree to disagree in the present. They may well have taken into account the fact that failure to agree upon the terms of a
plebiscite when the matter came up again for adjustment would leave unsettled one of the great issues of the
War of the Pacific, and they may have believed that inasmuch as a reopening of hostilities on this account after
a lapse of at least ten years was improbable and an
amicable agreement would be in the interest of both
parties, it was at once unnecessary and inadvisable to
prescribe a time limit for the negotiations. Finally, the
present arbitration is the best evidence that the agreement, elastic as it was, was not without force, since these
great States, in response to its provisions, having failed
again and again during the course of years to make the
contemplated protocol, have now submitted to arbitration
the question of the plebiscite and its conditions.

The literal interpretation of the English "after the

expiration of that period" for the Spanish *expirado este plazo* and the hypothetical intention attributed to the makers of the treaty are especially open to criticism grammatically and historically. The word *expirado*,[5] "expired," used with *este plazo*, "this period," means, "this period having expired." *Expirado* is a past participle and could be translated loosely in several ways, such as "upon the expiration of this period," "this period being expired," and "after the expiration of this period (*after* being used in the sense of *immediately after*)." The Spanish uses a past participle as the English does and in addition uses it adjectively more than the English. If the English word "after" in its indefinite sense had been intended the Spanish *después* would have been employed. It is true that a better expression could have been used in the treaty to convey the meaning of the framers. In preliminary correspondence and texts they had used *al fin de los diez años*,[6] "at the end of the ten years," and *al terminarse este plazo* which would amount to "on finishing itself this period." Since five, ten, and fifteen years had been discussed as the period of occupation there was not the least idea of indefiniteness in the framing of the treaty.*

Of the various possible translations employed by the ministers of the United States who reported the negotiations, "after" was used a few times. Nor would such a translation be wrong; it is merely ambiguous. Peru used the word in the Appendix to her case,[7] but in the main body had clearly explained the language of the text both as to the status of sovereignty in Tacna-Arica at the end of the period and in connection with the Chilean allegation of disguised cession. The resorting

* *Supra*, pp. 187, 188, and 217.

by the arbitrator to such grammatical and historical disingenuousness with wordplay was, by the most charitable judgment, a remarkable expedient.

As to the special protocol the Opinion is also open to criticism. It reads:

> But no time limit was fixed within which the special protocol for the plebiscite was to be negotiated. Whatever may have been the reasons for leaving the matter thus at large the fact remains that it was left without prescribed limit of time and the obligations of the Parties under the treaty must be determined accordingly.

It seems strange that the arbitrator did not take judicial notice of the fact that the third clause of Article III of the treaty stated that the special protocol was to "be considered an integral part of the present treaty." Since it was the usage in such cases to have supplementary protocols included before ratification and since the word "integral" indicates that it was intended to form a component part of the treaty, and as this was not done—Chile being responsible for the omission[8]—was not the validity of the whole treaty seriously impaired?

Besides holding that the plebiscite clause was not invalidated by lapse of time the arbitrator held that there was no physical reason why it could not be held. He said:

> It is apparent that there are no physical obstacles to the holding of a plebiscite at the present time. So far as the necessary arrangements for a plebiscite are concerned, it cannot be said that it must be abandoned because it has become in the nature of things impracticable to hold it.

This statement is especially unfortunate in view of the

actual conditions encountered by the Plebiscite Commissioners when they reached Arica—they had to abandon the attempt.

In her case before the arbitrator Peru had asked to have the plebiscite clause declared invalid on other counts besides the lapse of time. She charged Chile with having rejected all protocols for a plebiscite, wanting more time for the Chileanization of the provinces, and with aiding the Chileanization of them by persecuting and expelling loyal Peruvians and subsidizing Chilean colonies.

The arbitrator held that had either party wilfully refused to hold the plebiscite under prescribed conditions that refusal would have invalidated the plebiscite article of the treaty. It would be necessary to establish bad faith on the part of Chile to invalidate the plebiscite provision on this score. The burden of proof was held to lie with Peru, and after reviewing superficially the history of the principal attempts to secure a plebiscite protocol as related in the cases and countercases of both litigants the arbiter failed to find "that Chile has ever arbitrarily refused to negotiate with Peru the terms of the plebiscitary protocol."[9]

The principal ground on which Peru hoped to have the plebiscite held invalid was the Chileanization of Tacna-Arica. In this she was again unfortunate. If there is anything plain, but hard to prove, it is propaganda extending over a long period of time where because of its obviousness little evidence is collected. Regarding such administrative acts as the closing of Peruvian schools, expulsion of Peruvian priests, and the subsidizing of colonization and newspapers for propaganda, the arbitrator held that according to the treaty Chile had a right to perform any acts of sovereignty.

This was based on the clause which stated that during the ten years the provinces of Tacna and Arica should "continue in the possession of Chile subject to Chilean laws and authority." Holding that the same status with respect to sovereignty existed after the failure to hold the plebiscite, that is, the territory continued "under Chilean law and authority," the arbitrator decided that none of the administrative acts which Chileanized Tacna-Arica could be ground for invalidating the election. In other words he held that an election provided for in 1884 to be held under conditions existing or expecting to exist in 1894 would be valid under conditions obtaining in 1926.

Regarding charges of mob violence the arbitrator made a distinction between responsible acts of the Government and acts of mere mobs and found that there was insufficient evidence. He accepted the statement on behalf of Chile that only fifty-two persons had been formally expelled, and the expulsions recorded in the archives of the Ministry of Foreign Relations. He recognized that expulsions could be brought about informally, but found that "Peru's charges of wholesale expulsions and depopulation are not supported by the record."[10] The situation was similar to the persecution of slaves in our southern states. The official acts and documents that could have been laid before an arbitrator were comparatively few. The analogy regarding the collection of evidence also holds. When negroes filtered northward to Canada few northern persons thought of taking evidence.

The Peruvian case was ably presented, but it was a difficult one virtually asking the conviction of a nation. Peru relied much on the moral certainty that she was right and on what was manifest and well known in

South America, namely, that Chile had not consented to a plebiscite until Tacna-Arica was sufficiently nationalized to make the election sure. Peru might have strengthened her case by submitting the entire proceedings of the Chilean nationalization committee instead of portions of it. These reports including statement of sums of money raised for the purpose, the settling of old soldiers in Tacna-Arica, and other nationalization methods were very convincing. Her case needed to have been much stronger than that of Chile because the burden of proof rested with her. However, the Award was apparently not based on the arguments but, in order to avoid historical responsibility, it was based on the general idea that plebiscites are fair and that this was a question for the people to decide.

The arbitrator held that many of the contentions of Peru were true, but that they were of insufficient consequence to invalidate the plebiscite clause of the treaty. The trend of the Opinion is as follows:

Little need be said with respect to the question of mob violence which occupies a considerable place in the record. Unfortunately mob violence is not unknown in any country. It occurred in Chile at Iquique both in 1911 and in 1918 and Peruvians suffered. Iquique is some seventy-five miles south of the southern border of Tacna and Arica and what happened at Iquique has no direct bearing upon the matters with which this arbitration is concerned. Unfortunately again a little later on, both in 1911 and in 1918–1919, mob violence occurred in Tacna and Arica and again Peruvians were the sufferers. The responsibility for the mob violence in Tacna and Arica in 1911 and in 1918–1919 on the part of the Chilean Government is not established on this record. Again, the record is full of miscellaneous charges of official persecution of Peruvian citizens in Tacna and Arica. These charges in so far as they are serious, and some of them are very serious, are not sustained by credible and specific evidence. They rest on general declarations, and the Arbitrator is constrained to hold that these charges of general persecution are not adequately supported. There are also numerous charges of petty persecution, some of which if taken individually might be sustained, but all of which put together are not sufficiently serious to affect the decision of the weighty question under consideration.

Conclusion. The Arbitrator is far from approving the course of Chilean administration and condoning the acts committed against Peruvians to which reference has been made, but finds no reason to conclude that a fair plebiscite in the present circumstances cannot be held under proper conditions or that a plebiscite should not be had. The agreement which the Parties made that the ultimate disposition of the territory of Tacna and Arica should be determined by popular vote is in accord with democratic postulates. It furnished when it was made a desirable alternative to a continuance of strife and it affords today a method of avoiding the recurrence of a not improbably disastrous clash of opposing sentiments and interests which enter into the very fiber of the respective nations. In agreeing upon a determination of the embittered controversy by popular vote, the Parties had recourse to a solution which the present circumstances not only do not render impracticable but rather the more imperative as a means of amicable disposition. The Parties in the Treaty of Ancon provided no alternative mode of settlement and made no provision for limitation of time or for forfeiture. It is manifest that if abuses of administration could have the effect of terminating such an agreement, it would be necessary to establish such serious conditions as the consequence of administrative wrongs as would operate to frustrate the purpose of the agreement, and, in the opinion of the Arbitrator, a situation of such gravity has not been shown.

The Arbitrator holds that the provisions of the second and third paragraphs of Article 3 of the Treaty of Ancon are still in effect; that the plebiscite should be held; and that the interests of both Parties can be properly safeguarded by establishing suitable conditions therefor.[11]

Within less than a year, as will be seen in the following chapter, the entire structure of this Opinion and Award was to be rudely demolished; historical methods were to vanquish mere legalism and a whole new procedure in settling the dispute adopted. In justice to President Coolidge it must be remembered that he did not initiate the mediation but rather inherited it somewhat suddenly from President Harding. Further consideration later of the Opinion and Award as a necessary legalistic step in the final settlement of the larger question also relieves very much the criticism that history would have pronounced on that document had the action of the United States ceased with the attempted plebiscite.

REFERENCES

1. *Opinion and Award,* pp. 53–60. [Also *supra,* pp. 191, 203, 205.]
2. *Daily Iowan,* Iowa City, for March 10, 1925.
3. José María Barreto, *El problema peruano-chileno (1883–1911),* 3d ed., p. 51 ff. See also reference 9.
4. Ernesto Montenegro, "Award's Influence on Chilean Policy," *Current History Magazine,* May, 1925, p. 219.
5. In this discussion the Castilian spelling *expirado* is used instead of the Chilean *espirado.*

6. Gonzalo Búlnes, *Guerra del Pacífico*, III, 414, 417. See *supra,* pp. 169, 176, 186, 187, 189, 192, 196, and 200, for evolution of "after ten years."

7. *Arbitration between Peru and Chile, The Memorial of Peru and the Ruling and Observations of the Arbitrator,* pp. 12–20.

8. Búlnes, *op. cit.,* III, 526–529. Note: This contains the correspondence in which the Chilean peace commissioner Novoa asked instructions from President Santa María regarding the terms of the plebiscite protocol. Santa María said they should be deferred until after the treaty was approved. Novoa said that both he and Aldunate as well as the Peruvian commissioners understood that the protocol should be included in the treaty for ratification, but since President Santa María said not there was no more to be said. For legal aspect, see Edwin M. Borchard, *Opinion on the Controversy between Peru and Chile,* 1920.

9. Búlnes, Article in *El Ferrocarril,* May, 1914. [For extracts from this see *supra,* pp. 197, 200.]

10. Compare with statement of General Lassiter on adjourning the Plebiscitary Commission, full text *United States Daily,* June 18 and 19, 1926. For extracts see *infra,* p. 258.

11. *Opinion and Award,* pp. 35, 36. Note: Another discussion of the Coolidge Award may be found in Graham H. Stuart, *The Tacna-Arica Dispute,* World Peace Foundation Pamphlets, Vol. X, No. 1, 1927. Also Hans Steffen, "Der Streit um das Gebiet Tacna-Arica in Südamerika," *Zeitschrift für Politik,* XV, 72 ff.

CHAPTER XII

THE ATTEMPTED TACNA-ARICA PLEBI-SCITE OF 1925–26

IN the forty years that had elapsed between the ratifying of the Treaty of Ancón and the belated attempt to carry out its plebiscite provisions a reversal of domestic conditions had occurred in Chile and Peru. Whereas following the War of the Pacific, Peru was rent with divided leadership and confusion while Chile with the exception of the Balmaceda Revolution had peace and stable government, now following the Coolidge Award Chile was torn with political turmoil and division while Peru enjoyed stable government. This fact had an important bearing on the career of the attempted plebiscite.

While not attempting to analyze extensively political conditions in 1925, a brief summary of the drama will be given because many of the men included in the *dramatis personae* of the political arena were also prominent actors in the plebiscite. In September, 1924, President Arturo Alessandri of Chile, a liberal civilist, was replaced by a military *junta* of high officials including naval and army heads. The following January this *junta* was overthrown by another. In both *juntas* there was friction between navy and army officers and a clash was narrowly averted. Prominent civilians including Agustín Edwards, former minister to England and president of the League of Nations, succeeded in averting civil war and Alessandri's friends recalled him from exile in Europe to reinaugurate a constitutional *régime*. The announcement at this time of the favorable Coolidge Award helped restore Alessandri to favor and power in Chile, and he set about to meet the dilemma facing the nation. This dilemma in brief was a complication of militarism in politics, too advanced social legislation, and a tincture of sovietism on one hand with a proud aristocracy on the other. Added to this the whole nation was in a bad economic state. At the time the Award was issued several places were in a state of siege and certain newspapers were under censorship. So it is evident that Chile was not in a domestic condition favorable to the maintenance of a fixed and proper policy in the plebiscite area far to the north. Another reason why the best Chilean statesmanship was not employed in Tacna-Arica was that the apparently victorious Award led many to think the provinces already won. It was known that not many male Peruvians remained and it was not believed that they would vote for reincorporation into Peru. When confronted with the provisions of the Award so favorable to Peruvian voters and the news that Peru was bringing back "thousands" of exiles to vote, surprise and panicky methods were added to political confusion at home.

The Award had been received gladly and Chile did not delay in appointing her commissioner. Perhaps in recognition of his efforts in conciliating clashing elements at home, and owing to his international prestige, Agustín Edwards was appointed to serve at Tacna-Arica, and Chile was soon ready to proceed with the election in spite of the political storms which continued for over a year to beset the Government.

In Peru, Augusto Leguía was still president. Although ruling with a rigid hand he ruled so well that his popularity combined with his stern measures enabled Peru to present a united front in the battle for votes.

President Leguía had accomplished such prodigies of economic and social management that the country was enjoying a comparative state of prosperity in a season of post-World War depression when economic conditions were generally bad. The spirit of the nation was sorely tried by the Award and especially by the accompanying Opinion, and it is much to the credit of its leaders, the President, Minister Salomón, and Congress, that Peru was able to accept the bad situation with considerable dignity. In fact some observers had believed that the Award would not be accepted in spite of the message of President Leguía on March 11 thanking President Coolidge for his efforts and promising to accept the decision of the Arbitrator.

News of President Coolidge's decision to have the plebiscite held was scarcely received before complaints were heard that Peruvians were being persecuted in Tacna-Arica for the purpose of expelling them before the date of voting. On April 2 the Peruvian Defense Commission filed a memorial to the Arbitrator protesting the translation of the *expirado* clause, and requesting that the United States or some other neutral power immediately assume the police power in the plebiscite area, saying that no fair election could be held under Chilean control.[1] President Coolidge answered firmly, almost harshly, that the rendition of *expirado* was based on a Peruvian translation and the translation was merely incidental, that it was rather a question of interpretation, and that the Plebiscitary Commission could do nothing to protect voters in Tacna-Arica until Peru should appoint her member which at that date she had not done.

These observations were received by Peru April 9, and it was not until June 16 that notice was given of the appointment of her member of the Plebiscitary Commission, Sr. Manuel de Freyre Santander. In sending the notice of the appointment to Washington the Peruvian Government took occasion to have a final word regarding the Coolidge note of April 9. It insisted that several hundred Peruvians had been sent south from Tacna-Arica following the Award, denied the Chilean explanation that they had gone south to work, and called upon the Plebiscitary Commission to afford rigorous guaranties.

Four days after the appointment was made public the President of Peru issued a manifesto explaining his handling of the case and calling upon his people not to fear. There was something heroic in the call he made to a people so disappointed and discouraged. He said: ". . . why doubt? To doubt is to declare ourselves beaten beforehand." In another place he said, "Battles are not gained when fear has taken possession of the spirit." Assuming full responsibility for the outcome he called upon the people to take part in the plebiscite without fear or wavering. He stated that if the plebiscite favored Peru a great injustice of forty years would be wiped out. And in his remarks about the event of its going against Peru may be seen some of the responsibility weighing on the Arbitrator and his representative, General Pershing. President Leguía said:

If the plebiscite should go against us, the verdict will justify one of the bloodiest and most ferocious wars in all history. The series of crimes committed by Chile in annexing the provinces of Tacna and Arica will be condoned. And at the same time it will have been shown how distant is yet the hour of realizing the ideals of justice and peace for which those two great protagonists strove—Lincoln, the humble woodcutter and Liberator of slaves, and Wilson the Apostle of a Universal Brotherhood undreamed of before by the peoples of the world.[2]

The people of Peru responded to the appeal of the President and not only gave demonstrations of agreement but made heavy subscriptions to a voluntary fund to defray Peru's share of the great expenses of the Plebiscitary Commission and staffs of election experts which were preparing to assemble at Arica.

The assembling of the Commission and staffs was not long in taking place. The Chilean Commissioner, Sr. Agustín Edwards, arrived July 26. Among his staff were many experts and authorities on the Tacna-Arica case, including Srs. Ernesto Barros Jarpa, Victor Robles, José Luis Santa María, Samuel Claro Lastarria, and Jorge Aldunate. On July 31 the Peruvian Commissioner Sr. Manuel de Freyre Santander sailed for Arica. Accompanying him were Dr. Alberto Salomón, who had been minister of foreign relations, Dr. Anselmo Barreto, Dr. María Forero, Dr. Emilio Valverde, and other experts on the subject of Tacna-Arica. The delegation was carried by a transport which was to serve as headquarters at Arica.

On July 19 General Pershing and his personnel sailed from Key West stopping in Panama for some members who were to aid in carrying out the Award. General Pershing had as legal and expert advisers, Dr. Harold W. Dodd, Mr. William C. Dennis,[3] and Col. Edward A. Kreger, besides secretaries and other staff members. The North American delegation arrived August 2 on the cruiser *Rochester*. This ship is an old and historic one having been the *New York* of the days of Admiral Sampson. The Pershing staff, however, was lodged on shore in an office building. Here then in August, 1925, in the historic Bay of Arica a correspondent from the heights of the Morro could have seen the Chilean warship *O'Higgins*, the Peruvian transport *Ucayali*, and the old North American cruiser *Rochester* anchored below, while busy launches carried back and forth emissaries of peace. There also came over a dozen correspondents and journalists, fifteen at one time, looking for copy in that historic setting, but most of the North American press representatives knew little of Latin American history in general and Tacna-Arica in particular. They ran the whole gamut from *guapa* "flapper" reporters to grizzled war correspondents.

The first formal meeting of the Plebiscitary Commission took place August 5, and this session as well as those of the first few weeks was taken up largely with organization matters and the question of free transit about the territory.

On July 31 the Chilean local police authorities had put into effect a system of permits for those who would go ashore, to Tacna or the interior. Certain roads only were designated for travel to interior towns and a complicated traffic surveillance established. The Chilean authorities explained that this system was to insure safety for travelers and to prevent the assembling of groups who might start riots. The members of the Peruvian delegation and their nationals saw in it a restriction and an annoyance calculated to hinder a free plebiscite. One of the first to be stopped was Colonel Ordóñez of the Special Boundary Commission who was on his way August 7 to meet with the Commission at Tacna. Although the act was disavowed by Sr. Edwards and a general permit issued to members of the

THE FAMOUS MORRO OF ARICA, MADE A PEACE MONUMENT BY THE TREATY
OF SANTIAGO, 1929

Peruvian staff on board the *Ucayali* to come ashore, the system of passes and identification cards required by the Chilean police were considered by Dr. Salomón, who gave out an interview a few days later, as a restriction of freedom of movement violating one of the fundamental conditions of the Award.

There was no lack of petty annoyances and supersensitive complaints. In fact there was a fundamental difference of opinion between the delegations as to the nature of the plebiscite to be held. Chile and Peru had agreed in letter to an election, but in spirit neither wanted it. At the outset President Alessandri indulged in an intemperate speech which partly annulled the dignified utterances of Sr. Edwards, the Chilean Commissioner at Arica.

In Chile the impression seemed to be that they had won the provinces merely by the Award, that there were few or no pro-Peruvians left and that the election should take place in a few weeks. In Peru a campaign was being made to return to Tacna-Arica expatriated voters on whom it counted to win the election. A large encampment was to be constructed at Arica to house the pilgrims, commissions were sent to Bolivia and other regions where exiled nationals lived, and elaborate machinery set in motion to prepare the campaign for votes. However, beneath all this was an undercurrent of discontent with an election held under Chilean occupation, fear and distrust of Chilean police control, and a secret hope that the plebiscite would be called off. They never ceased to believe that it would be a failure. They did not doubt the integrity of General Pershing and his delegation, but they doubted his ability to establish protection for their nationals as long as Tacna-

Arica were under close police surveillance by a large body of Chilean police, soldiers, and *carabineros*.

Of the seven plebiscites growing out of the political chaos which followed the World War the Schleswig election was probably the fairest and best conducted.[4] In this case both Danes and Germans carried on their campaigns for votes through a long period of preparation with meetings, periodicals, placards, free meals, and other means of propaganda. Naturally the North American delegation had in mind something similar in Tacna-Arica.

If that was the purpose of the delegation its members overlooked several great differences. In Schleswig while the Allied police may have been favorable to Denmark they were neither Danes nor Germans and moreover there were two neutral countries represented on the commission, viz., Norway and Sweden. Again there was no such great or recent enmity between the Danes and Germans as between the Chileans and Peruvians. The Schleswig occupation was from a more remote time and there did not rankle in the memories of the people a bitter war and a bitter attempt at nationalization. Of course Germany had carried on active Germanization in Schleswig but with less animosity and actual violence. With conditions so very different it is surprising that a successful plebiscite, if even the Schleswig Plebiscite can be called such, could have been expected in Tacna-Arica.

Tense feeling was evident from the outset although the speeches of the commissioners and high officials seemed optimistic. A Peruvian paper, *La Prensa* of Lima, published a Tacna-Arica edition on board the transport *Ucayali* and gave it the name, *La Voz del Sur*, the name of the last Peruvian paper permitted by the Chileans to be published in the lost provinces. It was a part of the Peruvian campaign for votes to have this paper sold on shore. At first no great amount of propaganda was started, most of it being confined to visiting known pro-Peruvians in Arica and Tacna while the machinery for the plebiscite was being erected. In these visits ashore it was soon charged by the Peruvian paper that Peruvians were always under close surveillance by Chilean *carabineros* and plain clothes men. The local Chilean papers answered in kind the propaganda articles of *La Voz del Sur* and published the names of persons who received visits from Peruvians. Within a few weeks the vendors of the Peruvian paper were having difficulties with angry Chileans. Besides the existing local papers the Chileans later established a special organ called *El Plebiscito* to maintain their cause and offset the work of *La Voz del Sur*.

There was attached to the Peruvian staff a North American plebiscite authority, Miss Sarah Wambaugh, whose experience illustrates the tension existing in the area. Desiring to let in a little light of publicity Miss Wambaugh attempted to send a cable message to the United States for publication, but it was refused by the company, which was under censorship by Chilean police. Returning to the *Ucayali* she sent a radiogram as follows:

Tell newspapers spies follow us everywhere. Peruvian inhabitants terrorised dare not speak to us. Two women jailed for speaking. Military control absolute. Chilean governor today decrees no inhabitants can go from town to country or contrariwise without special police permit which must be shown at every picketpost and they can travel only by designated roads controlled by carabineers.

If Chilean troops not evacuate Arica be grave of Monroe
Doctrine. Note Chilean censor refuses to pass this so am
relaying *via* Lima.[5]

The idea of neutral police control during the election
period was frequently urged by Peru and her friends,
but of course the terms of the Protocol and also President Coolidge's statement of April 9 prevented such an
arrangement.

Another annoyance objected to by the Peruvian delegation was that the *fleteros* or boatmen of Arica would
not take them or their cargoes out to the *Ucayali*. Later
better launch service from their own ship was secured,
but a long wait was required for the ship was anchored
more than a mile out. They also complained that their
movements ashore were not only followed, but their
coming ashore announced by blasts of the whistles of
hoisting engines. On the other hand when a Chilean
boat, the *Aconcagua*, stopped at the Peruvian port of
Mollendo there was difficulty in getting longshoremen
to work. These incidents will show how charged was the
atmosphere and what a difficult task was ahead of General Pershing and his staff.

On August 21 a vendor of *La Voz del Sur* was pursued by a mob and took refuge at General Pershing's
headquarters. The latter, being called out, told the
vendor to go on selling his papers. He said: "I want
you to go on selling your papers. You have as much
right as any one else to do so, and you have an equal
right to move freely about the city." Accompanied by
members of the North American delegation the vendor
continued selling although not without incidents. The
following day policemen were detailed by the Chilean
authorities to accompany the paper vendors. The

Chilean authorities also announced on this day the withdrawal of the traffic surveillance of which the Peruvians had complained, saying that this was done to avoid the suspicion of partiality. A few days earlier Sr. Edwards had called a meeting of the *fleteros* urging them not to discriminate against Peruvians, while on the twenty-third President Alessandri sent a telegram urging calm and restraint and asking that the free exercise of legitimate electoral activities of none be interfered with. This was in great contrast to his speech of a fortnight before. The same day the Chileans staged a meeting of some five thousand people and optimistic reports came from those who believed the atmosphere could be cleared for an election.

That the winning of the election seemed a foregone conclusion in Chile was shown by the announcement on August 15 of the arrival of the silver with which Peru was to be paid. The Treaty of Ancón provided that payment by the winner should be made in silver coin equivalent in value to the money in circulation at that time. Santiago papers described at some length the arrival and storage of the bars of bullion.[6] It must be remembered that the political situation in Chile proper was still unsettled, an election was in progress there on the adoption of a new constitution, so the matter of Tacna-Arica was not always the chief topic of political interest as it was in Peru.

As the first month of the functioning of the Plebiscitary Commission drew to a close it seemed that some progress was being made. On August 29 an adjournment was made until September 15, to allow Sr. Edwards to return to Chile to help receive the Prince of Wales who was visiting there and to allow time for a special committee on registration of voters to prepare the election rules.

This registration committee consisted of six members: Manuel Antonio María and Galvarino Gallardo-Nieto were the Chilean members; Alberto Salomón and Anselmo Barreto served for Peru; and William C. Dennis and Col. E. A. Kreger were the North American members. The *modus operandi* adopted for this committee by the Plebiscitary Commission was that the Chilean and Peruvian members should each prepare and submit a draft of a law to the North American members of the committee, who in secret session would compare these with a draft which they had made, and report the final form of the law. It is anticipating somewhat, but the work of these six men was very remarkable. It contained twelve chapters or 133 articles and required until January 27 for completion.[7] But so thorough was the work that only one article, Article 5, was appealed to the Arbitrator and he approved it.[8] This was what was being done when a certain section of the Chilean press was clamoring for an immediate voting and accusing the North American delegation of obstructive and pro-Peruvian tactics. Some of these same men were also members of a special investigating or grievance committee, so that considering everything the completion of the election rules by January 27 was a good piece of work.

The Plebiscitary Commission had hardly taken its recess beginning August 29 when more trouble started. A Chilean *carabinero*, Manuel Aguavo, was found dead near the Tarata boundary and the body was brought to Tacna for burial. His death was laid to Peruvians and an indignation meeting was held in Arica.

On September 1 Tarata was the scene of historic interest. In the town of Tarata, which is the capital of the district by that name, the Chilean flag was lowered and the formal transfer of the three districts, Tarata, Tarucachi, and Estique, took place. This event was celebrated in Lima with great rejoicing as the first step in the revindication of their lost cause.* The transfer of these districts, though, was marred by the death of the Chilean *carabinero* and recriminations incident to the affair.

At this juncture Sr. Agustín Edwards, the Chilean Commissioner, left for Chile. His pacific influence was missed. Barros Jarpa also was in Chile at this time. This, coupled with the chaotic political state of Chile, left Tacna-Arica at the discretion of the *intendente* and military officials who as a restraining influence to violence were not effective. On September 3 three Peruvian soldiers with a mule train of supplies for the Special Boundary Commission were seized on the road near Tacna and after being relieved of certain papers were, by order of the *intendente*, released. The Peruvian member of the Commission, Colonel Ordóñez, notified General Morrow that he would withdraw from the commission until satisfaction was given. A military court found the Chilean officer who made the arrest guilty of conduct unbecoming an officer, the explanations were accepted, and the Special Boundary Commission resumed its sittings after a delay of two weeks. On the fourth, fifth, and sixth there were a series of assaults on members of the Peruvian delegation: a chauffeur was seriously injured, Dr. Manuel Belaúnde was badly injured, and a man, claimed both as a Chilean and a Peruvian, Miguel Herrera Salas, was killed.

* *Supra,* pp. 191, 203, 215.

The difficulty of holding plebiscites is illustrated in the Herrera Salas case and similar ones that took place shortly afterward. A companion of Herrera Salas, Vilca by name, took refuge at the North American headquarters where he got first aid and was taken to the *Ucayali*. There he stated that he and his companion were the victims of Chilean espionage and mob violence. The next day the Chilean papers carried news of the brutal killing of Herrera Salas, a Chilean, by a Peruvian named Vilca who, after the crime, was given asylum on board the *Ucayali*. So the people on both sides were claiming the victim and blaming the other side for his death. Similarly the three brothers Corbacho from Azapa were brought before the North American delegation, or the committee on complaints which was headed by a North American, and they told how they were intimidated by Chilean officers. When confronted with the fact that their names were on the Chilean register as voters they said they were obliged to register and had at first worked to intimidate Peruvian and North American investigators who had gone to Azapa, but had repented and come to seek refuge in Arica. In another case, that of Pedro Quina Castañon, Peruvian papers alleged that he died as a result of an attack by a Chileanizing band, while a Chilean version declared it was calumny, that the man died of acute alcoholism. It would take a Solomon to know the truth concerning the real allegiances and loyalties of many people living in a territory under doubtful or disputed sovereignty.

The rest of September passed without any unusual incidents and the two principal preoccupations of those in charge were the preparation of the election rules and the question of guaranties for voters and those making propaganda. By the twenty-third the Peruvian members of the committee of election rules were said to have their draft ready, but would not submit it until the Plebiscitary Commission passed on the question of guaranties. Sr. Edwards returned the middle of the month and expressed disappointment at the slowness of proceedings. On the twenty-fifth Lieutenant Rodríguez, connected with the Special Boundary Commission, was forcibly relieved of some papers by five men in the station at Arica. The papers were returned, at least in part, but Colonel Ordóñez again refused on the part of Peru to take part in the proceedings of the commission until satisfaction was received. This again delayed the work of the commission for a few weeks. There were also some minor cases of assault before the second month of the attempted plebiscite closed.

Although it was known that political conditions in Chile all this time were uncertain there was general surprise when on October 1 President Alessandri resigned, turning over his duties to the Minister of Interior, Sr. Barros Borgoña. This did not tend to stabilize plebiscitary conditions in Tacna-Arica, of course, and caused some changes in the personnel. Sr. Barros Jarpa, who was attached to the Chilean staff of experts at Arica, resigned to become a member of the cabinet under the new *régime*. Later Sr. Alessandri came to Arica.

The month of October was relatively uneventful in the plebiscite area. On the twenty-seventh and twenty-eighth about a thousand recruits of the Chilean army who had been in training in Tacna embarked for the south. Because of the efforts of Messrs. Kreger and Dennis to investigate allegations of assaults on Peruvians, local Chilean papers began to talk of the partiality of the American delegation. Later more was heard in that tenor. But November was a more critical month.

At the session of the Plebiscitary Commission held October 8 the matter of guaranties came to a head in a resolution of eleven points, sometimes referred to as Pershing's eleven points. These included the reduction of the number of Chilean soldiers and *carabineros* in the territory, the reduction of the number of secret police to the number existing in July, 1922, the suspension during the plebiscite period of all soldiers, police, and *carabineros* from civil and executive positions and their replacement by civilians, the suspension from service of every public functionary who, in the judgment of the Commission, had used his official position to prevent free expression of opinion, the transfer beyond the plebiscitary area of all such suspended officers who were not natives of the territory, the suppression of restrictions on travel, the establishment of equal facilities for meetings and all propaganda including the use of the flag, the suppression of the censorship over cables and other communications, and the return at Chilean expense of persons who had been banished from the plebiscitary area. Of course there were provisos and limitations, but the above is a summary of the guaranties asked for by the resolution.[9]

The Chilean Government not only agreed to the rigid and rather incriminating resolution of the Commission but also agreed later to remove eleven officials from the plebiscitary area whose resignations were asked for. The Chilean Commissioner, Sr. Edwards, though, made a formal reservation in the name of his Government. He objected to any construction of the resolutions which might be considered as impairing

Chilean sovereign rights under the Treaty of Ancón and the Protocol of Submission. He held that none of those rights could be annulled or restricted by resolutions of the Plebiscitary Commission. The Peruvian Commissioner, Sr. de Freyre Santander, made the reservation that while he voted for the removal of the eleven Chilean officials he reserved the right to ask for fuller measures. Both the Chilean Commissioner and the Minister of Foreign Affairs soon made it clear that they expected proceedings to be speeded up and the election to be held soon.

On November 8 former President Alessandri arrived from Chile and while he came in no official capacity he was given a splendid reception and his words were expected to have much weight. Unfortunately he chose to make very intemperate speeches. In one he said that come what may Tacna-Arica would remain Chilean, and again that Chile never would allow the loss of a bit of the territory.

On the thirteenth there were a number of incidents, two of which were serious. In Arica a man attached to the Peruvian delegation was attacked and rendered unconscious and in Tacna five Peruvians were attacked with the result that one, Luis Basadre, was seriously wounded by a gunshot. On the nineteenth a post of Chilean *carabineros* was attacked at Challavientos, near the Tarata border, and one *carabinero* was killed and two wounded. At the funeral of the slain man in Tacna, Sr. Alessandri again gave vent to extreme utterances. He said:

> But it is to be noted that if in the final hour we are not given the justice to which we are entitled you may be certain that our patience may become exhausted, and we

will arise to demonstrate to the world how the sons of this country defend their honour, justice and right.[10]

The Peruvian version was that the *carabinero* had assaulted the wife of a Peruvian sympathizer.

The Chilean Commissioner was absent from a meeting on the twenty-first, and the following day it was announced officially that Chile would take no further part in the proceedings of the Plebiscitary Commission until it set a date for the election. The *communiqué*[11] of the Foreign Office stated that the delays in holding the election contravened the spirit of the Award and created such great antagonism that Chile would take no further part until rules were drawn and a date set for the election. In communicating this to General Pershing, Sr. Edwards attached a sort of eleven-pointed ultimatum of agenda that should occupy the commission. He said that the committee on election rules should report not later than December 10, that the rules be adopted by December 15, that registration of voters begin December 20 and end January 10, and the election be held February 1, 1926. In the preamble to his communication Sr. Edwards implied that the commission, which in effect would be General Pershing who cast the deciding vote, was frustrating the spirit of the Award, and was causing discord by dilatory proceedings. But General Pershing held that the date of the plebiscite could not be fixed "as long as the state of terror reigning in the mind of one of the parties was not changed into confidence and security." He also objected to the inflammatory speeches of Sr. Alessandri.

On November 24 Colonel Marchant of the Chilean army published a report in *El Pacífico* to the effect that the recent attack made on the Chilean *carabinero* post at Challavientos was organized by Peruvian soldiers connected with the Special Boundary Commission working in that region. Colonel Ordóñez, the Peruvian member, protested to General Morrow against the report and asked that the commission investigate in order to clear his soldiers of the charge.* The Chilean member, Sr. Greve, denied the jurisdiction of the commission, and when Mr. Morrow voted with Colonel Ordóñez affirming the right to investigate since the report held up the work of the commission, Sr. Greve announced his withdrawal until the commission should confine its work to boundary surveying. So once again the Special Boundary Commission found its work suspended.

The following day Sr. Edwards addressed a note reiterating his previous reasons for an immediate election. The next day Barros Jarpa issued a statement from Santiago stating that General Pershing was being influenced by the "tearful policy" practiced by Peru and was induced to adopt measures and express opinions which were unjust and inaccurate. He insisted that great calm reigned in Tacna-Arica, and that in the four months of the work of the Commission but ten Peruvians had been injured while four Chileans had been assassinated.

The climax was reached at the next meeting of the Plebiscitary Commission in a remarkable speech by the Chilean Commissioner, Sr. Agustín Edwards, whose calmness and poise had previously been noteworthy. On November 15 at a banquet to Sr. Alessandri in proposing a toast he had said:

It has been repeated over and over again that General Pershing was asking too much of us. A duty to loyalty

* *Infra*, p. 276.

compels me to say that the representative of the Arbitrator on the Commission has never held any other idea than to give Chile a clear title without stain.

But scarcely a week later on November 28 Sr. Edwards' speech was full of sharp and intemperate accusations. He said in part: "The time has come to ascertain who are the members of the Commission who are frustrating the Plebiscite." Again, "It is necessary to fix the responsibility of each one of the members of the Commission for the result of its labors." In another place, "The Commission is leading to shipwreck the principle of arbitration and the execution of arbitral decrees by pursuing a myth, a thing intangible." He accused Peru of delaying the election on the pretext of a reign of terror and continued, "It is the tactics of Peruvian sobs, which failed at Washington but which unfortunately have received a favorable reception from the president of the Commission, and particularly from his two assessors." The committee in charge of investigation of assaults came in for special mention. He said:

I am bound to declare that these men are wholly unfitted for the task which was assigned to them; they form moreover an organization created by the President himself since there is no mention made of it in the Award. They are men who knowing nothing of the language have fallen into the hands of the Peruvians. They have never requested the assistance of Chileans in making these investigations. The conduct in particular of Messrs. Kreger and Dennis is abominable, and the honor of my country cannot be delivered into their hands. Recruited from the Canal Zone among vulgar people, they cannot judge or destroy the reputation of the carabineros who are carefully selected men.

After sending out this speech the United Press cabled to suppress the reference to Kreger and Dennis. Regarding these two men it might be worth noting that they were not recruited from among very ordinary people. Colonel Kreger was a college graduate, a graduate of the Infantry and Cavalry School and the Staff College, had been Professor of Military Law at West Point, Assistant Provost Marshal General, later Assistant and Acting Judge Advocate General, American Expeditionary Forces, and had received the D.S.C. and D.S.M. for distinguished service in the Philippines and the World War. Mr. Dennis had been a professor of international law, assistant solicitor of the State Department, served in United States and Venezuelan arbitration at The Hague, represented the United States before the Mexican Boundary Commission, was secretary to Justice White in the Costa Rica–Panama Boundary Case, legal adviser to the Chinese Government, represented the United States at The Hague in the Norway Arbitration, and at London on the British-American Claims Commission, etc. It is very probable that much of the Coolidge Opinion and Award originated under his advice, and if that be true the remarks of Sr. Edwards constituted a swift and severe punishment for the many shortcomings of that Opinion and Award.

Sr. Edwards directly charged General Pershing with partiality.* Referring to a session of November 12 he said:

The President, in his desire to support the Peruvians,

* *Infra*, p. 262.

went so far as to accuse Barceló of criminal acts. I protested, and I asked the President to present proofs of this grave accusation. [Continuing he said:] At the meeting on November 21 at which I was not present, the President made fresh observations, launching a violent attack against Sr. Alessandri. I deny the right of the President to censure the speeches of Alessandri; Leguía has made others still more violent.

Of course Sr. Edwards had stayed away from the meeting of the twenty-first of his own choosing. The reference to Leguía must have been to a speech similar to those of Alessandri, but it was made on the twentieth and in Lima so that it is improbable that General Pershing knew of it on the twenty-first. Just what General Pershing said about the Alessandri speech was not made public at the time, in fact it was understood that none of the members of the Commission would give out controversial statements to the press, but what later was given out of his statement at this critical meeting was calm and dignified. Sr. Edwards in his speech also reiterated his statement that he would not take part in the proceedings of the Commission unless and until it dealt with the matter of the election itself.

Simultaneously Sr. Greve, the Chilean member of the Special Boundary Commission, made public a letter which he had sent to General Morrow reprimanding him for the Commission's "busying itself with matters which are outside its jurisdiction." In the desire to investigate the Marchand charges he saw "the hand of a lawyer alien" to the technical commission. He withdrew from meetings of the Commission that did not confine themselves to technical matters. So again the work of the boundary commission was interrupted.

At about the same time the Chilean Chargé of Berne gave an unofficial memorandum of Chile's position in the plebiscite argument to the secretary of the League of Nations. So it seemed that Chile was going to carry her case beyond the president of the Plebiscitary Commission to the bar of public opinion as well as to appeal to the Arbitrator.

In a meeting of December 9 General Pershing presented a motion providing that the committee on rules should present a report as soon as possible so that the rules might be approved and promulgated not later than January 15. In a preamble to the motion he discussed the accusations of Sr. Edwards in a fair and dignified manner yet made his position perfectly clear.[12] At least the text of the speech was dignified and in fact a good state paper. He said he could not take part in a plebiscite which did not represent the free and unobstructed will of the electorate, that there had been expulsions and deportations after the arbitration had been accepted, that a state of terror and subjection existed incompatible with the free exercise of electoral rights. He said that in announcing that its member would not attend the meetings of the Commission, and that the Chilean authorities on Tacna-Arica had orders to ignore requests of the Commission, before appealing to the Arbitrator, the Chilean Government had not complied with the prescriptions of the Award. He stated that in giving out his address to the press Sr. Edwards had undermined and delayed the work of the Commission and that he had attempted to dictate to the Commission conditions under which its decisions would be accepted. General Pershing stated it would be impossible to set the dates as early as demanded by

Sr. Edwards and fixed in his motion January 15 as the day for announcing the rules.

At the same meeting Sr. de Freyre Santander made a long statement of Peru's position, answering allegations of Sr. Edwards and making forty-seven charges against the Chilean authorities in Tacna-Arica. These ranged from coercion and intimidation to assault and assassinations.

At the next meeting, December 14 and 15, the Chilean Commissioner duly presented for certification an appeal to the Arbitrator, President Coolidge. These events were overshadowed in Chile by the change of administration, a new cabinet being completed on the twenty-first and the new President, Sr. Figueroa Larrain, inaugurated on the twenty-third of December. A statement of the Minister of Finance indicated a deficit of some three hundred million pesos, so that the diplomatic crisis in the Tacna-Arica case was accompanied by an economic crisis at home. The new *régime* being of a different political complexion it was expected that the direction of policy if not the personnel at Tacna-Arica would undergo a change. Barros Jarpa was succeeded as Minister of Foreign Relations by Beltrán Mathieu, former Ambassador to the United States; and Sr. Agustín Edwards, who departed from Arica December 19, soon announced his resignation from the Commission, but it was not accepted. On the twenty-ninth General Pershing announced that he was going to take a leave of absence soon in order to secure dental treatment. The Special Boundary Commission then suspended operations for the rainy season. The committee on election rules had frequent sessions during the last week of December, and the eventful year of 1925 closed with the plebiscite question still an enigma.

However, in acknowledging the receipt of the appeal made by Chile, President Coolidge intimated that a prompt decision would be made and stated that in the meantime the Plebiscitary Commission would continue functioning. Peruvian press reports claimed a virtual state of siege for their nationals in Tacna-Arica and that was denied by the Chilean press.

The new year, 1926, started off with an eventful month for the plebiscite. A group of returned Peruvian voters and election workers who had come to Arica on the transport *Rimac*, which relieved the *Ucayali*, went to Tacna on January 6 and were met at the station by a mob and in the clash some thirty were injured. Later the same day, Commander Rotalde of the *Rimac* with two companions came to Tacna on a track car which was derailed on the outskirts of the city and the Commander with his companions roughly handled. He was rescued by Chilean officials but one of his companions was beaten insensible. Chilean reports claimed that General Pizarro in charge of Peruvian headquarters in Tacna, at whose house the Peruvians took refuge, fired a pistol at the Chilean crowd from his balcony. A special Chilean court which sat on the case a few weeks later sentenced four Chileans to four years, and one to one year imprisonment. The charges against General Pizarro, which he denied, were dropped. At a meeting of the Plebiscitary Commission, January 12, Sr. Edwards, who had returned from Santiago, expressed deep regret for the attack of January 6 and called upon all Chileans in the area to discourage such conduct which reacted on the good name of Chile.

On January 9 the Chilean appeal to the Arbitrator as well as allegations on the subject by Peruvian representatives was presented. Chile withdrew a part of the appeal, that dealing with the demand for an advancing of the definite date for voting and certain other matters concerning electors. In the Peruvian allegations were statements including the report of a committee of neutral observers tending to show that conditions suitable for a just plebiscite did not yet exist in Tacna-Arica. On the fifteenth President Coolidge handed down a decision sustaining the Plebiscitary Commission. While giving complete approval of the holdings of the Commission the note was extremely conciliatory and fair, and explained the legal rights of the Commission under the Protocol of Submission.

In view of the fact that the Tacna-Arica question in its larger aspect included more than a settlement of Article III of the Treaty of Ancón, attention should be called to a visit to Lima by former President Saavedra of Bolivia. He was received in state although *en route* to Europe as a minister there. In proposing a toast of welcome President Leguía made significant remarks on the historical question. He said the spiritual and material union of Bolivia and Peru were more necessary than ever, that danger from the south was not over and that such union rested on the historic and geographic necessity of undoing deeds of the past. He then held out to Bolivia in the following language hopes of a port:

Peru at the moment is liquidating her dispute with Chile. When she has recovered her provinces and freed them from the terror to which they are daily submitted by the *mazorqueros* who enjoy full freedom to elevate murder to the category of an official function, we shall offer Bolivia an outlet to the sea, with the understanding that this provisional solution will be the prelude to that

final solution when their lawful owners will receive back
the territory which today the conqueror holds in an ill-
omened captivity.

Of course this was uttered during the bitterest period
of the attempted plebiscite but there are ideas in it
which will not be completely eradicated even by the recent Solomonic settlement of the Tacna-Arica question
between Chile and Peru.

Two days before the Coolidge ruling on the Appeal
was given out, it was announced that General William
Lassiter had been named to relieve General Pershing
on the Plebiscitary Commission. On the twenty-seventh,
the committee on electoral rules having finished its
work, those rules and regulations were adopted at a
session of the Commission and General Pershing sailed
for the United States. Before leaving, General Pershing issued a farewell statement to the people of the
plebiscitary area couched in amiable and conciliatory
terms. The press both in Chile proper and in the
plebiscite area paid high tribute to the departing Commissioner, especially to his good intentions. One paper
in Arica which had been particularly denunciatory
stated on January 22 that it had never been responsible
for "the slightest insinuation of evil intention against
the illustrious General."[13] Likewise the Santiago and
Valparaiso press generally since late December had
been calmer in their attitude. In Peru, especially after
Pershing's reply to the statement of Sr. Edwards, the
greatest satisfaction and praise were expressed. In this
connection the ruling of President Coolidge of January
15 was highly satisfactory, and helped to offset the general resentment of his April 9 answer to the Peruvian
memorial protesting the Award. Nevertheless President

Coolidge and General Pershing could not have believed
that the beatitude regarding peacemakers applied to
this world, or at least to Tacna-Arica.

Early in February after six months' work on the
plebiscite two currents set in beneath the surface but
were kept secret for several weeks. Even before General Pershing returned to Washington and reported to
President Coolidge, it was seen that a fair election
could not be held in spite of the dismissal of several objectionable Chilean officials and a marked improvement
in police conditions. One current sought a solution of
the Tacna-Arica case by direct negotiations instead of
a vote. The other continued the preparation for registration. Both parties on February 8 appealed to the
Arbitrator from the decision of the Commission on one
clause of the electoral rules. At about the same time Sr.
Agustín Edwards resigned again and was replaced by
Sr. Claro Lastarria.

The announcement of the rules and dates for registration and voting was on the whole well received in
both countries, although there remained a bone of contention regarding the rights of government employees
to vote and who constituted government employees.
This announcement, the coming of a large staff of election officials from the United States together with the
arrival of more Peruvians caused February to take on
the appearance of a plebiscite month, rumors of direct
negotiations being still scouted by the press in both
countries. Except for some disturbances on the second,
conditions were rather quiet, at least on the surface.
Several Chilean officials and semiofficials were sent
south, their expulsion having been asked for by the
Commission. The farewell address of Sr. Edwards was
very earnest and pacific, and withal, had it not been for

the rumors of direct negotiations arising in Washington, an election would have seemed imminent.

There were always Peruvian charges that terrorism and intimidation were still going on among the voters of Tacna-Arica, most of which were denied by Chile. On March 5, however, a serious clash occurred in Tacna. On that date a contingent of Peruvians just arrived from a transport attempted for the first time to form a procession and parade with a band. This was too much for Chilean patriotism to stand and soon clubs and stones were flying with the result that some ninety Peruvians and a few Chileans were wounded. There were reports of other clashes in interior villages, and at a session of the Plebiscitary Commission on March 14, at the insistence of the Peruvian Commissioner, in which General Lassiter concurred, the date of registering was postponed until March 27. At a meeting on March 25 the Chilean Commissioner, Claro Lastarria, proposed that no further postponements be allowed and the Peruvian Commissioner, Sr. de Freyre Santander, proposed two motions, one that registration be indefinitely postponed, and the other that the territory be neutrally policed. General Lassiter refrained from voting on the motion to neutralize and voted against the other two motions. Although he did not deem that the previous requisites and guaranties had been satisfactorily realized yet he voted against postponing the registration evidently with the hope that conditions would improve as registration proceeded.

The agreement of the two governments to negotiate directly under the good offices of the United States was announced publicly in Peru and Chile by the twenty-seventh, the date on which registration was to begin. A misunderstanding now arose as to whether registration would continue or be suspended during these negotiations. Owing to this and to the lack of guaranties which Peru insisted on, her Government instructed its representatives and voters to remain away from the registration booths. So registration began on the twenty-seventh, with the North American and Chilean officials only in charge. Only Chileans registered except in some remote districts where the orders of Peru were not received.

If General Pershing had a difficult position, his successor on the Commission, General Lassiter, had an equally hard task. Not only did General Lassiter have local troubles but he found that with direct negotiations pending in Washington the very policies of the three state departments were badly defined. To maintain the *status quo*, keep the registration machinery intact, secure guaranties for Peruvian voters who never ceased reporting assaults, and all the while make no false step for the United States, formed a part of his task. He succeeded in postponing the date of closing registration which pleased neither side and the Chilean press saw in it a move favoring Peru. The Peruvian Commissioner voted with him in the motion, but stated that he did it with the reservation that he recognized none of the registrations since they began as valid; he held that for Peru registration had not yet begun while Chile insisted that it was over and demanded the vote. The press in each country vied in its desire for a plebiscite and in accusing the other of obstructionistic tactics. But by the middle of May important principals in the case including Salomón, Claro Lastarria, and William C. Dennis were either in Washington or on the way, and it seemed certain that the Tacna-Arica contest was to be decided by diplomacy. The cancellation of the sailing of another group of election experts from the United States, the departure from Arica of groups of voters, and other straws indicated the wind was blowing away from the ill-starred plebiscite.

Finally at a meeting of the Plebiscitary Commission on June 14, General Lassiter, acting evidently under instructions from Washington, brought the attempt to hold an election to a close. In a long speech with all the directness of General Hurlbut himself and with specific statements he explained the failure of the attempted plebiscite. While from all of the foregoing chapter it can be seen why the election was impossible yet it will be well to note General Lassiter's resolution. And lest his statements might seem to exaggerate the temper of the plebiscite area, a quotation is cited here from a resident of the area who, by his calling and opportunities for observation, would be expected to speak temperately and advisedly. Luis Fermandois, a priest from Tacna-Arica, being interviewed in Santiago opposed the cession even of Tacna as a compromise in direct negotiations saying:

When the hour arrives to deliver Tacna, neither the Peruvians nor the Americans will find anything except the ashes of the city, destroyed from its four sides by fire, to illuminate in a suitable manner the most grotesque diplomatic maneuver of all times.

In fairness to those who attempted to hold the plebiscite, especially to the North American delegation, who were not only accused by some of the foreign press with partiality, but by the press of their own country with lack of tact, the entire text of General Lassiter's speech should be read.[14] The motion which was sustained by the Peruvian Commissioner is as follows:

The Plebiscitary Commission of Tacna-Arica, in the exercise of its duties and functions under the Award, hereby formulates and declares its findings and conclusions as follows:

1. Pursuant to the terms of the Treaty of Ancón, the plebiscitary territory has been and still remains subject to the authorities and laws of Chile. Under these circumstances, the creation and maintenance of the conditions necessary for the celebration of a free and correct plebiscite, as required by the Treaty and Award, constituted an obligation resting upon Chile. This obligation has not been discharged and the Commission finds, as a fact, that the failure of Chile in this regard has frustrated the efforts of the Commission to hold the Plebiscite as contemplated by the Award, and rendered its task impracticable of accomplishment:

2. As a result of its experience and observations throughout the course of the plebiscitary proceedings, the Commission has the settled conviction that further prosecution of the plebiscitary proceedings in an effort to hold the plebiscite as contemplated by the Award, would be futile. The Commission cannot ignore its paramount duty under the Award, of holding only a free and fair plebiscite as contemplated by the Treaty and Award, and not to hold a plebiscite which would not be in accord with the intent of the Treaty and Award. The Plebiscitary Commission accordingly decides upon the grounds above stated:

(a) That a free and fair plebiscite as required by the Award is impracticable of accomplishment.

(b) That the plebiscitary proceedings be, and are hereby, terminated, subject, however, to the formulation and execution of such measures as may be required for the proper liquidation of the affairs of the Commission and the transfer of its records and final report to the Arbitrator.

On June 21 a final liquidating session was held suspending indefinitely the sessions of the Commission but providing that it might be reconvened by call of the chairman. General Lassiter and his delegation left the same day. Two days later the Chilean and Peruvian commissioners left, the plebiscitary camp was rapidly dismantled and embarked along with the remaining personnel, and soon Tacna-Arica took on a deserted air, while the repercussion of General Lassiter's speech reverberated through foreign chancelleries in circulars issued pro and con by Peru and Chile.

REFERENCES

1. *Arbitration between Peru and Chile, The Memorial of Peru and the Ruling and Observations of the Arbitrator*, pp. 12–20.
2. *West Coast Leader*, June 23, 1925, Supplement 1.
3. Note: Not William J. Dennis, the author of this work; they are not related and are acquainted only by reputation.
4. Sarah Wambaugh, *A Monograph on Plebiscites*, pp. 147–155, 864–944; also *La pratique des plebiscites internationaux*, chapitre v, Académie de droit international, 1927, III.
5. *West Coast Leader*, August 11, 1925.
6. *El Mercurio*, August 15, 1925.
7. *United States Daily*, March 17, 1926. Note: This is the text of the plebiscite law or rules for voters.
8. Ministerio de Relaciones Exteriores del Peru; *Documentos relativos al plebiscito de Tacna y Arica*, VI, 72–78.
9. Cesar A. Elguera, *Memoria que el Ministro de Relaciones Exteriores presenta al Congreso Ordinario de 1926*, pp. lxvii–lxx.
10. *West Coast Leader*, November 24, 1925, Supplement.
11. Circular of the Chilean Foreign Office.
12. Ministerio de Relaciones Exteriores del Peru, *Documentos relativos al plebiscito de Tacna y Arica*, III, 136–162.
13. *El Pacífico*, January 22, 1926.
14. *United States Daily*, June 19, 1926. [Text of Lassiter speech.]

CHAPTER XIII

FINAL SETTLEMENT BY DIRECT NEGOTIATIONS

IT has been the custom to speak of the Tacna-Arica plebiscite as a failure. In some Latin American journals it was called a *farsa* and *fracaso*. As a method of self-determination it was a failure, complete and ungraceful. Sufficient mention has been made of the lack of a historical point of view in the Opinion accompanying the Award that designated this method of settlement; in fact the whole train of events recorded in the previous chapter sets at naught the Opinion of the Arbitrator. However, it was a step, awkward but necessary, which complied with a legalism, and in that step the moral claims of Peru were justified while the diplomatic status of Chile was so compromised that a definitive settlement was now made imperative.

It is difficult to arrive at a proper statement of the estimation of the attempted plebiscite by any informed group, or even by the governments of the interested nations, because direct negotiations under the good offices of the United States had begun before the plebiscite ended. Any opinion at the time regarding the plebiscite was always confounded with its status as compared with the new offer of good offices of February 16, 1926. Did the ending of the plebiscite effort end the attempted mediation? What would the Arbitrator hold? In Peru the adjournment of the Plebiscitary Commission, with the bold statement of General Lassiter placing the blame on Chile for the failure and confirming the claims of Chileanization made by Peru, was a great moral victory. President Leguía in his annual message July 29 called it "a triumph tantamount to the recovery of the lost provinces of Tacna and Arica." A Chilean circular protested the Lassiter action as illegal, and Sr. Alessandri held that since the efforts at holding the election had ended the provinces would remain definitively with Chile. Yet even in Chile it was realized that the plebiscite attempt was diplomatically, if not legally, more than a farce. There was no doubt that Peru's case had gained immensely in the estimation of the world. A Chilean paper called attention to this fact and attributed it to inferior Chilean diplomacy.[1] There was some point in the observation perhaps because Chile, owing to its depressed financial state, had made cuts in appropriations for government affairs, but the observation was suggestive in view of the traditionally high state of Chilean foreign service.*

As to the work of General Pershing and his assistants, criticism would be expected from one or the other of the disputants when their interests were affected. There was some opinion even in the United States that the naming of any soldier, however well qualified, was ill advised because it would smack of military pressure. Theoretically, a staff of statesmen and civilians would have been better and might have pleased Latin American sentiments more, but in practice the civilian members of the staff came in for as much criticism as the men of the army. And then it should be remembered that while General Pershing and the officers who assisted him were soldiers, they were more than soldiers. They all had had special experience and training which fitted them for the task.† Also it should be pointed out that conditions in Arica were exceptional. Men ac-

* *Supra*, pp. 166 and 208. † *Supra*, p. 247.

customed to the legations and embassies of capital cities
would have encountered considerable hardship at the
bare port of Arica and among the sandy interior districts.

Practically all of the small amount of adverse criticism that was made of the president of the Plebiscitary
Commission and his assistants was groundless. The
worst was made by the Chilean Commissioner, Sr.
Agustín Edwards, and unfortunately, as has been related, he chose to make it public, against the wishes of
the other commissioners. These accusations, consisting
of charges of prejudice and lack of qualifications of
General Pershing's advisers and observers, together
with personal criticisms, were well answered, after considerable forbearance on the General's part, in the
session of December 9, 1925. The answer was brief compared to the extended attack of Sr. Edwards, but it
met categorically the charges, defending especially his
North American assistants from the accusations of
being prejudiced or unqualified. The personal criticisms which Sr. Edwards made of Pershing were veiled
with platitudes and his acts insinuatingly excused
as "unintentional," "involuntary," "against his desires," and the like. The General frankly defended his
actions and rulings, unmasking the phraseology of his
critic. He said: "With full understanding of the real
value of the extenuating phrases employed by my distinguished colleague, and with due respect, I refuse to
take advantage of them and save my reputation at the
expense of my intelligence."[2]

The attack of Edwards, who up to that time had
been calm and judicial, took place in the session of
November 28, in statements to the press, and in a letter
to the president of the Commission on December 7. It

could not have been left unanswered longer, and it is difficult to see how it could have been better answered than it was by General Pershing. In the opinion of a North American member of the Peruvian staff of experts who, as an authority on plebiscites, had had the opportunity of much observation in similar cases, General Pershing was "a diplomat of the first rank."[3] His position was most difficult, and since he knew from previous visits to South America the nature of the case, his accepting of the task was as meritorious as any other duty he ever performed in his long and distinguished career as an officer.

Although the impossibility of holding a plebiscite without neutral police was a foregone conclusion among those well acquainted with the history of the case, it should be said that there were two things most instrumental in causing the failure. Owing to the long lapse of time and the work tending toward nationalization that even in its normal state brought many Chileans into the territory, it is probable that a fair plebiscite would have given the territory in dispute to Chile. It is doubtful, although possible, that Peru could have returned enough voters to have won the election. The failure of Chile to win then by means of the plebiscite Award was due mostly to the overzealous unrestrained Chilean element in Tacna-Arica. Those superpatriots and *carabineros* who failed to heed the calm admonitions which Sr. Edwards usually uttered, are the ones mostly responsible for her loss of Tacna in the final settlement. Next in line of responsibility is Sr. Edwards himself, who failed to restrain these zealous elements, and finally attempted to impugn the motives of the Commission for not overlooking and condoning their violent activities. The extenuating circumstances of there being a chaotic political condition in Chile proper at the time has been mentioned several times.

In the last analysis the failure of the plebiscite is due to the fact that neither Chile nor Peru could afford to have the other win absolute title to the territory. Peru could not escape the call for revindication of at least Tacna, and Chile could not risk her northern frontier's being dislodged by a nation which might logically decide to revindicate the Department of Tarapacá, so rich in nitrates. A fixed and safe northern line was essential and that fact was important in the direct negotiations which began formally April 6, 1926.

From the high feeling existing at the time of adjourning the Plebiscitary Commission, June 14, 1926, to the final friendly settlement by the treaty of July 29, 1929, was an arduous diplomatic interval.

About the time that General Pershing reached Washington, Secretary Kellogg instructed Ambassador Collier at Santiago to inquire "if the government of Chile would be disposed to avail itself of the good offices of the United States in an endeavor to arrive at a friendly adjustment" of the Tacna-Arica dispute. The note was presented February 17, 1926, and two days later Chile replied in the affirmative. Similar inquiry was made of Peru, the Government of which required some clarifying of the invitation. On March 11 Secretary Kellogg issued another note explaining the scope of the good offices tendered in the previous note. In the meantime Peru had accepted and the question had arisen as to the bearing such negotiations would have on the plebiscite then in effect. On March 25 Secretary Kellogg elucidated further the intent of his invitation and explained his attitude toward the plebiscite as follows:

. . . Pursuant to the terms of the offer, appropriate steps should be at once taken by the Plebiscitary Commission looking to a suspension of the plebiscitary proceedings, without prejudice to their resumption if it should later appear that the differences between the two countries are not susceptible of adjustment other than by the celebration of a plebiscite.[4]

It was also provided that pending the negotiations the arrangements for holding the plebiscite should "be maintained unimpaired."

The negotiations regarding the tender of good offices were not made public until March 26 and interest in the plebiscite up to that time was centered at Arica. Now it was to alternate between Arica and Washington. The first meeting under the good offices was held April 6. Chile was represented by Ambassador Miguel Cruchaga Torconal and Peru by Ambassador Hernán Velarde. Not since the sending of the Trescot mission by Secretary Blaine in 1881 had the United States so seriously essayed to settle this famous question. The earnestness of Secretary Kellogg and some of his purpose were set forth in his speech opening the conferences. He said:

I am very greatly pleased to welcome to this conference the plenipotentiaries of Peru and Chile, who, I am sure, are imbued with an earnest desire to settle this long-standing difficulty; and I am confident that they share with me the feeling that it can be settled. In offering the good offices of the United States you will appreciate that I have no desire other than to bring the representatives of your great countries together in the sincere hope that a common basis of adjustment may be found. In this age it is vitally important that two of the great nations of

the Western Hemisphere should set an example to the
world of a willingness to make concessions and adjust their
difficulties and again restore their diplomatic and commercial relations. I earnestly urge upon the distinguished
representatives of both countries the greatest forbearance
and conciliatory spirit. If we all determine that this difficulty shall be settled it can be done, maintaining the
honor and dignity of both countries. I suggest that in
taking this matter up we have the most informal discussion, which shall be treated as confidential unless we agree
upon a statement to be given out. I should like to have
you feel perfectly free to make any suggestions and to
speak your minds openly, because in this way we can
best reach a basis of mutual understanding.[5]

A few days later President Coolidge, on opening the
Pan-American Congress of Journalists, emphasized the
ideas of American conciliation in the following phrases:

We of the Western Hemisphere are one people, striving
for a common purpose, animated by common ideals and
bound together in a common destiny. Unto us has been
bequeathed the precious heritage and the high obligation
of developing and consecrating a New World to the great
cause of Humanity.

How similar is this statement of Pan-American solidarity to that of Secretary Blaine in his instructions to
Trescot, but how much more of a fact than a wish is
the statement of that unity today!* When Osborn,
Christiancy, and Adams were trying to mediate on
board the old *Lackawanna* in the harbor of Arica, if
they could have received direct cables from Washington, or if Trescot could have been in cable connection

* *Supra,* pp. 145, 158, 162.

with home as were the visiting journalists listening to Coolidge's address, the history of this controversy would have been different.

For two years little actual progress was made with negotiations; feeling was still high and at times a settlement seemed hopeless. Naturally, there could be but three or four possible solutions. The territory could continue all in the hands of Chile and breed a South American war in the near future; it could be divided, with or without a corridor for Bolivia; it could be neutralized either as an independent state or under the protection of another power or powers; and, finally, it could be ceded to another nation not a party to the negotiations. Secretary Kellogg explored these various possibilities and devised some formulas. On April 17 it was given out that he had suggested either a transfer to Bolivia or neutralization of the territory. Although the sessions were secret, rumors of the proposed transfer to Bolivia had reached South America. Hopes were raised in Bolivia, of course, but a wave of criticism swept both Peru and Chile, especially the latter.

The mediation of the United States had already been harshly criticized in Chile and adverse comment was intensified on receipt of the rumored proposals. General Harms, who had been expatriated during the military uprising in Santiago a few months before, returned at this time and gave out an interview in which the whole neutralization idea was described as merely another scheme for the advancement of North American imperialism. Capitalists from the north, he said, who already had their tentacles on Bolivia, would loan the money needed for the purchase, thereby securing for themselves a strangle hold on Bolivian resources. Furthermore, he reasoned, the North American navy needed a base at Arica. With Arica either a port of Bolivia or neutralized under a more direct Yankee aegis, he warned that there would be a Yankee peril of the first magnitude.

Yet while this old cry of dollar diplomacy and economic imperialism with the aid of the government at Washington was being raised in the Chilean press, and echoed by some papers in the United States who like to see sinister motives in the State Department, what did North American business men really think of it? A fair summary of the view of most of them is contained in the following statements taken from an article by a trade investigator for a print paper corporation. He said:

Neither Mr. Harding nor Mr. Hughes knew a great deal of Latin American temperament, habit or instinct. Yet it was Mr. Hughes, with the approval of Mr. Harding, who injected the United States of America into the most tangled diplomatic web Latin America ever knew, as arbitrator between nations whose annual business with us—business for which we have to fight every inch— amounted in 1926 to the grand total of $186,450,000. . . . Irrespective of right or wrong, a decision one way gains us nothing, a decision the other way verges on a boycott of American goods. . . . I am free to confess that the Tacna-Arica problem cannot be solved.[6]

While not a prophet as to the solution of the case, this trade investigator knew the effects of political intervention on business, and if this old dispute illustrates anything it is the fallacy of business expansion in Latin America through the State Department. If anybody disagrees with this conclusion he might invest money in some claims—at a great discount—now pending.

One of the leading Chilean papers, *El Mercurio,* took a view equally critical of Mr. Kellogg's suggestion for dividing the territory. After recounting how Tacna and Arica were dependent on each other for supplies, the editorial almost made a historical repetition. It said:

Neither Peru, nor Chile, nor the United States has the right to dispose of these populations like flocks of sheep which are handed over together with rural property when property is sold. . . . We ask, by what right the United States proposes that this population, these fifteen or twenty thousand white men, with clear notions of right and duties within a democratic society, be given like human cattle to this or that nationality? What has happened to the principles established by Woodrow Wilson in his famous fourteen points?

Comparing this obviously humane plea of *El Mercurio* with one made by José Lavalle for the same people, March 22, 1883, at the Conference of Chorrillos, one could almost say that history does repeat itself.* The only difference was that the tables were reversed. While discussing terms of peace before the Treaty of Ancón, where it had been proposed to cede Tarapacá unconditionally and to sell Tacna-Arica for ten million pesos, Lavalle, the Peruvian envoy, said:

With respect to the second point I stated that the sacrifice of Tarapacá and Iquique which did not represent more than riches, although immense, did not matter to me, but that of Tacna-Arica horrified me; a man can sell his house or his lands or give them away, but a man cannot sell nor cede his brothers. . . .

* *Supra,* p. 185.

And this was said at a time when there were no other Chileans in Tacna-Arica than an invading army.

Placed in this perspective it is worth while recalling the statement of Secretary James G. Blaine, made in instructions to Minister Trescot, June 15, 1881. Opposing the large territorial indemnities which Chile then demanded as a *sine qua non* of peace discussions, he said:

At this day, when the right of the people to govern themselves, the fundamental basis of republican institutions, is so universally recognized, there is nothing more difficult or more dangerous than the forced transfer of territory, carrying with it an indignant and hostile population, and nothing but a necessity proven before the world can justify it.*

The great Maine statesman never saw more clearly into the future than he did in the Tacna-Arica case. In fact we have hardly yet caught up to the far-seeing policy of joint American mediations which he suggested.†

From the opening of the direct negotiations, April 6, 1926, to the adjournment of the Plebiscitary Commission's sittings, June 21, was the most active period of the entire Harding-Coolidge-Hoover mediation. In plenary session of April 15, Secretary Kellogg's proposal which aroused such criticism was made, and April 17 he had issued his public statement. This was forced by attacks in the Chilean press. One paper concluded an attack by saying:

The evident interest of that great power which did not shrink from foreign complications in the Antilles and Panama, in order to secure positions for the consolida-

* *Supra*, p. 144.   † *Supra*, p. 162.

tion of its empire on this side of the world, would evidently be favorably inclined to the idea of the neutralization of the territory.[7]

In the Kellogg statement the Secretary said his only purpose was to examine every possible road that might lead to a settlement.

It frequently happens that an ambassador to a country is more concerned with the prestige which his country enjoys at the capital where he is accredited, than he is with the correctness of its position in the case at hand. But this was not true at this time in Chile and Peru. Ambassador Poindexter, during all the critical period following the unpopular Coolidge Award, had maintained an impressive attitude and while probably sympathizing with Peru in her disappointment he did not belittle his Government. In Chile when the criticism in April, 1926, became so virulent, Ambassador Collier protested, setting forth the disinterestedness of the United States in its efforts to mediate, and he pointed out the fact that Secretary Kellogg was not the author of the idea of neutralizing Tacna-Arica, that when General Pershing first came to Arica, Sr. Edwards had made the suggestion.* On April 15 in reply to the Collier note the Chilean Minister of Foreign Relations deplored the press attacks which had been made on the United States and recognized the disinterestedness of its mediation. He stated, however, that Sr. Edwards had no authority to make the suggestion of neutralization.

While Secretary Kellogg did not mention a name in proposing the sale of the territory to "a South American State not a party" to the negotiations, Bolivia was

* *Supra*, p. 267.

obviously that state. On April 19 President Siles cabled to President Coolidge expressing satisfaction at the suggestion of the Secretary of State; he presented Bolivia's interests and claims and wished to send a representative to sit in on the negotiations. President Coolidge replied that under the Protocol of Submission that was not contemplated, and the Secretary of State considered an invitation by Chile and Peru necessary for Bolivian participation. Naturally, this was not forthcoming. One of the fundamental facts regarding the Tacna-Arica case is the unnatural position of Bolivia geographically and politically. Her geographical handicap has been shown in earlier chapters; politically, while she was an ally of Peru in the War of the Pacific, she was not an effective ally and so did not cement the nominal relationship. Contrary to a current belief she is not so close to Peru as her racial similarity would indicate. Her Spanish and Aymará population should be very similar to the Spanish and Quechuan composition of Peru.

It is interesting to note that during 1924 there was a recrudescence of the idea of a Peru-Bolivia confederation. In the prologue to a history of Gen. Andrés de Santa Cruz, former Protector of the Peru-Bolivian Confederation of 1837, two writers, one a Bolivian and the other a Peruvian, advanced a forceful argument in favor of the consolidation of the two peoples in one strong nation, a move that would at once solve the port problem for Bolivia.[8] However, while the idea is good politically it is poor sociologically. The isolation and localism of Bolivia on one hand, and the equally formidable barriers presented by Peru and Chile for her outlet to the sea on the other hand, have rendered Bolivia aloof and vacillating. It is difficult to say which opposed more heartily the proposed transfer of Tacna-Arica to Bolivia, Chile, or Peru, and mobs in La Paz were as quick to demonstrate against Peru as against Chile, all depending on how it was felt that Bolivian interests were affected.

So strong was the reaction against the proposals of April that it was thought that negotiations had ended. On May 26, Sr. Alessandri arrived in the United States with a petition signed by four thousand members of the Sons of Tacna and Arica asking that the territory not be divided or ceded and that the plebiscite continue in effect. There was little progress made during the summer, and on November 30 Secretary Kellogg sent a lengthy statement to Peru and Chile reviewing his efforts and proposing that some one of his formulas be accepted. There was little new except that he urged the acceptance of the proposal to transfer Tacna-Arica to Bolivia, and that the Morro which would be disarmed be made an international monument.

While both nations rejected the proposal it served to place in exhibit the whole problem and to see where the parties in the negotiations stood. There were intimations in each reply that certain parts of certain proposals would be considered favorably. The Chilean reply in fact offered to consider all the proposals, but, of course, Chile was still in possession of the territory and would have no objection to lengthy discussions. Her reply stressed a point that was the crux of the whole matter for her, viz., the necessity of demilitarizing Tacna-Arica. It was now finally coming out in the mediation that the Tacna-Arica question for Chile was a question of a safe and fixed northern frontier.

Peru first sent a preliminary note of inquiry before answering the Kellogg proposals. Would the people be consulted in the proposed transfer, and, if so, what form of consultation would be used, and who would discharge that task? The making of this reference to the recent dramatically inadequate plebiscitary proceedings was too much of a temptation for the Peruvian ministry to resist. The Peruvian main reply, which was dated January 11, 1927, reminded Secretary Kellogg that Peru had rejected the transfer formula in April, that if Peru had not consented to cede the territory under pressure of arms she would not now cede for compensation. It stated that Peru would consider the matter of a corridor for Bolivia, but would want Tacna province and the town and Morro of Arica. In the Kellogg note of November 30, he had referred to the national honor involved as a very tangible thing, and he had suggested that nothing would elevate the honor and dignity of Chile and Peru so much as to be able to arrange definitely their case, and to present themselves before the world as friends. In the Peruvian note Minister Rada y Gamio said:

This statement is of importance, and it is a matter for congratulation that it has been introduced into the document with which we are dealing. The controversy over Tacna-Arica is intimately bound up with the honor and dignity of Peru. Tacna and Arica were since the Colonial days up to the present time an integral part of our territory.

He then said that it would be an outrage to this feeling to cede the territory for a pecuniary consideration. The position of Peru, he pointed out, was that since the Lassiter pronouncement of June 21 placed the blame for not carrying out the plebiscitary award on Chile, the provinces legally belonged to Peru. He reiterated his belief in the justice of Peru's position and her final revindication of the lost provinces. The same idea was expressed by President Leguía, who reviewed the case at a banquet on November 1, 1926. He defended the submission of the case to Washington and said much had been accomplished in "discovering who is the criminal and who the victim."

Naturally, this attitude of Peru was a damper to Bolivian hopes, but it settled some premature strife over Bolivia's future moves. When Congress convened at La Paz, August 6, Felipe Guzmán, President of the Senate, discoursed on the hope of securing a seaport. Chile asked the Bolivian Government for a repudiation of the remarks. The Congress rebuked Chile and approved the remarks of Senator Guzmán. Soon the Chilean Minister was recalled. It was stated that the recall was due to ill health, but on the twenty-sixth a mob assembled to make demonstrations, and was kept away from the Chilean legation by details of soldiers. Somewhat later a Bolivian note to the American Minister in La Paz, conveying the impression that it was taken for granted that Secretary Kellogg was about to have Tacna-Arica transferred to Bolivia, called forth a sharp reply from Senator Curletti of Peru. Now the definite refusal of Peru in her note of January 11 ended the diplomatic side play in Bolivia.

The next year, 1927, was a quiet but critical one for the Tacna-Arica question. There were important changes in all of the governments. February 9 Gen. Carlos Ibáñez took over the government in Chile, claiming that radicalism was such as to require a dictatorship. On May 1 President Figueroa Larrain resigned, and on the twenty-second General Ibáñez was elected. During the year Ambassador William M. Collier was succeeded by Ambassador William S. Culbertson at Santiago. In Lima, Ambassador Miles Poindexter was followed by Ambassador Alexander Moore. In 1928 the Congress of Peru amended the constitution so as to allow another term and President Leguía was reëlected the following year.

General Ibáñez was not long in office in Chile when he announced a policy of nationalization in Tacna-Arica. This included teaching patriotism in the schools, the celebration of special days, public flag exercises, and the like. The Peruvian Minister, Rada y Gamio, on April 28 instructed Ambassador Velarde in Washington to call to the attention of Secretary Kellogg this Chileanizing order. The Lassiter motion left the plebiscitary area "subject to the authorities and laws of Chile." Rada y Gamio called attention to the difference between "administering" and "nationalizing" the territory in dispute.

Meanwhile the Special Boundary Commission had been in recess since August 2, 1926. On May 3 of the following year it met in New York and concluded the trouble over the Challaviento incident by exonerating the Peruvian delegation from all accusations.* There was some difficulty over the attendance of the Chilean member and since an article in the regulations had required three for a quorum little progress was possible. A motion was now made making two a quorum and in June the Chilean member resigned. While the operations of this commission which was created to demark the limits of Tacna, especially in the environs of Tarata, received very little notice, it did remarkable work. The rugged nature of the Andean slopes, canyons, and plateaus made accessibility very difficult.

* *Supra*, p. 245.

The documents, drawn largely from the ecclesiastical archives of Arequipa and Puno, were voluminous and ancient, so that in all there was a great amount of work to do.

As late as July, 1927, there was every indication of the continuance of the deadlock. President Ibáñez stood for the *status quo* in Tacna-Arica and his Minister of Foreign Affairs, Sr. Ríos Gallardo, spoke of "the obstinacy of the adversary honorably conquered in '79, in seeking to prolong her hostility for nearly fifty years by means of diplomacy." However, the Kellogg tentative had revealed that some concessions were possible. Then, there was something more than obstinacy on the part of the "adversary" and persistency on the part of the mediator. The question could not remain open indefinitely. In this decade war is not easily resorted to; moreover, with the decline of "king nitrates" in Chile, and the great economic development of modern Peru, a race for armaments might be favorable to the latter country, which is potentially vastly the stronger. Then, above all, Peru and Chile needed each other economically and socially.

Not the least consideration was the legal status of Tacna-Arica after the adjournment of the Plebiscitary Commission. The blame for the failure to carry out Article III of the Treaty of Ancón was placed by General Lassiter and the Peruvian Commissioner, Sr. Freyre Santander, upon Chile. As far back as October 7, 1927, Pershing's legal aids, Messrs. Kreger and Dennis, gave the following opinion on that phase of the question:

. . . Chile's right to retain possession of the territory in dispute is conditioned upon her agreement for the plebiscite, which necessarily implies the use of her authority properly to safeguard it. Any failure on her part to do this, particularly when requested by the Plebiscitary Commission, might not only justify the setting aside of any plebiscite vitiated thereby, as provided in the award, but might turn the whole logic of the award against Chile and, if persisted in sufficiently, might amount to a violation of the Treaty of Ancon, and a forfeiture of Chile's rights in the provinces thereunder.[9]

Circulars might in a measure discredit the plebiscite attempt, but the legal logic of Chile's responsibility and the mass of evidence, much of which still has not been made public, showing that she failed to discharge that responsibility could not be gainsaid. In this legal sense the Coolidge Award and its attendant plebiscite was not a failure. A definitive settlement now became imperative.

In the latter part of 1927 there were many indications of a better spirit, of some conciliatory tendencies, and an earnest desire to settle finally the old question. Senator Curletti of Peru, *en route* to a Congress of Journalists at Rio de Janeiro, expressed himself in an interview in Chile as favoring a direct settlement. On November 26 the boundary commission resumed sittings and the Chilean press talked of formulas as possibilities. However, progress was slow; as late as January, 1928, President Ibáñez asserted that the *status quo* was necessary for Tacna-Arica. All of the foregoing, it must be admitted, makes the peace arrangement soon to follow the more remarkable diplomatic accomplishment.

In May, 1928, in the remote capital of Paraguay occurred the last public situation that was a result of the high feeling that had prevented the settlement of the question. Gonzalo Montt, the Chilean Minister at Asunción, gave a dinner celebrating the anniversary of the Battle of Iquique. The Peruvian *attaché*, Col. Federico Recavarren, wrote a letter which was published in a paper in which he criticized the giving of the dinner in a friendly capital as an offense against good taste and diplomatic usage. He was challenged to a duel by Sr. Montt. Fortunately, it resulted in but slight saber wounds and the principals were reconciled.

The following July came the surprising announcement that Peru and Chile were to resume diplomatic and commercial relations. This was accomplished through the efforts of Secretary Kellogg whose note explains the purpose of the important move. He said:

> After long and careful deliberations I have now come to the conclusion that an accommodation of mutual interests would be promoted should the Governments of Chile and Peru re-establish diplomatic relations through the appointment of diplomatic representatives at Lima and at Santiago.
>
> I feel confident that such re-establishment of diplomatic relations is consistent with the highest interests of the two great nations and presents an opportunity for their respective representatives to interpret not only the high ideals which I have been happy to find animating both Governments, but also the basic good-will which I am convinced exists in each country toward the other, and that it would also afford a favorable means for facilitating the definite removal of all existing misunderstandings and hence lead to permanent readjustment of the relations between the two countries mutually satisfactory to both.[10]

In September Dr. Cesar Elguera was received as Peruvian ambassador at *La Moneda* in Santiago, and on October 3 Ambassador Figueroa Larrain was received by President Leguía at the *Palacio de Pizarro*, and so was diplomatic friendship resumed after a lapse of nearly twenty years.

In the reapproachment of these two nations, much credit should be given to commercial contacts and means of intercommunication. It has been the custom for writers to point out only the ill effects of economic determination, and to make unfavorable comparisons of the so-called materialistic motives of men with so-called spiritual or academic ones. Historically it was the benefits of British free commerce that broke down the abominable Spanish system of *repartimientos* and political monopolies and gave all Latin America independence of government. Most of the revolutions that have beset those republics have been due to economic backwardness and abuse rather than economic usage. Now the economic affinity of Chile and Peru had much to do with the renewal of their relations. In acknowledging the Kellogg note the Chilean Minister, Ríos Gallardo, mentions, rather more than incidentally, that the two countries had lost five hundred million pesos during the previous ten years by having no diplomatic and commercial relations. And there had been no interdict of trade and Chilean ships did some business at Peruvian ports. These contacts helped somewhat and the possibilities of a full commercial and friendly relationship were a great factor in the final settlement.

The visit of President-elect Hoover stimulated progress in the settlement. His statement that he had come to "better prepare myself for the task . . . of serving in some way to promote friendship and unity" was a happily worded one. Although riding on a battleship he had no panaceas to ram down Latin American chancelleries. Closely connected with this visit was the opening of Pan-American aerial communication. President Leguía had sent greetings of welcome to Mr. Hoover at Guayaquil, on the plane that made the first northbound flight of the service. A reporter for *El Comercio* of Lima had flown north and met the Hoover party and returned with a "scoop" for his paper. In the same speech referred to above, Mr. Hoover made other significant observations. He said:

. . . It is impossible to estimate the important consequences that will be derived from this evolution in the means of transport and communication between our peoples. It is a benevolent paradox to say that to destroy the distance between two peoples is to build up friendship between them.

While this was said apparently as applying to Peru and the United States it applied with equal force to Peru and Chile. The Hoover tour and the coincidental opening of aerial communication between all the countries of the Americas helped cement the relations resumed diplomatically between Peru and Chile, and it was a pleasant sequel that as a result of direct negotiations a final arrangement of their ancient dispute was brought about, the announcement of which was later made by President Hoover.

So much time had elapsed since the beginning of direct negotiations April 6, 1926, and even since the resumption of diplomatic relations July 13, 1928, that it had begun to appear as though the Tacna-Arica question were going to lapse indefinitely. As President Coolidge's term expired with no announcement from the

Arbitrator, or a public report from the chairman of the Plebiscite Commission, the prospect for a settlement was not very hopeful. There were no announcements or press reports on the subject and it looked as though the Harding-Coolidge-Hoover mediation were going the way of the Evarts-Blaine-Frelinghuysen attempts.

However, in early May there was a rumor that a group of engineers were examining harbors along the coast of Tacna and Arica, and then on May 17 President Hoover announced a final settlement of the dispute. Peru was to receive Tacna, and Chile, Arica. It must have been with peculiar pleasure that President Hoover and Secretary Stimson announced the solution of the dispute. A complete text of the treaty and supplement is given in Appendix X. The following are the salient points of the famous document:

In giving Tacna to Peru, and Arica to Chile, the dividing line is to run parallel to the Arica La Paz railroad, at approximately ten kilometers distance from the railroad; Chile grants to Peru on Arica Bay a wharf, customhouse, and railroad station; Chile pays Peru six million pesos; the children of Peruvians born in Arica shall be considered Peruvians until they attain the age of twenty-one when they shall have the right to elect their definitive nationality, and Chileans born in Tacna shall have the same right; a monument will be erected on the Morro of Arica to commemorate the consolidation of friendly relations; and Chile and Peru reciprocally will release any obligation of indebtedness between the two countries.[11] Final ratifications were exchanged at Santiago, July 28.

The settlement was well received by the majority of the people both in the nations involved and in foreign countries. Naturally, the political enemies of President

MAP OF FINAL SETTLEMENT, 1929

*The territory occupied by Chile was divided at
the black line paralleling the railroad.*

Leguía and President Ibáñez were opposed to the treaty, but in each country the Congress ratified it with large majorities. In Peru there was a small demonstration of students in the capital when the announcement was made; there, as in some other Latin American universities, there has always been a tendency on the part of *universitarios* to take their opinions on politics and international affairs very seriously. In the Amazon departments there was some criticism of the policy of a government that would lose an immense tract in its settlement with Colombia and gain a small one in Tacna. In Chile critics of the settlement said the relinquishment of Tacna just for the friendship of Peru was weak and unnecessary, but on the whole in both countries there was apparent satisfaction at the termination of the famous old quarrel.

The press in foreign countries, with the exception of Bolivia, applauded the settlement. When on May 3 it was reported that an agreement had been reached and transmitted to Washington for public announcement, the press of La Paz warned that no settlement would be lasting that did not include Bolivia. Before the complete text* was announced it was rumored in Bolivia that there was a secret supplementary protocol between Chile and Peru which was not given out in President Hoover's summary, and that this secret treaty was an agreement not to allow Bolivia an outlet to the sea. When it was later found that the proviso in question merely prevented the cession to a third power, by either party, of any portion of Tacna or Arica without the previous consent of the other party to the treaty, feeling in Bolivia was somewhat improved, but

* Appendix X.

there was still conviction that the settlement had not completely liquidated the shortcomings of the ill-omened Treaty of Ancón.

Legally and obviously Bolivia's claims may be passed over. The settlement between Chile and Peru is very good; it is, indeed, a commendable piece of work. Peru has recovered Tacna which contained the major portion of her former citizens. Chile has Arica where the population brought there for government and railroad work is largely Chilean. Peru has discharged her duty toward her lost citizens, and Chile by this treaty is relieved of anxiety over her northern frontier. The old Gordian knot has been cut and friendly and commercial relations resumed. South America has been purged of the need for balances of powers and other menacing specters.

A few confirmed critics in the United States and of the United States have hinted at economic pressure being used to bring about the settlement; that old term which may mean everything and nothing, "dollar diplomacy," has been applied to it. While of course no North American financiers have demanded the settlement of a quarrel the existence of which has benefited them in keeping Chilean shipping and commerce out of Peru and Bolivia, economics were no small factor in the settlement, as has been pointed out. It would take a much less able economist than President Leguía or any of the several Chilean statesmen who have directed efforts toward peace not to see that the investments which they so assiduously seek would come faster, and rates of interest would be less in their countries were a disruption of commerce not momentarily expected. The new and progressing Chile and Peru have great commercial interests depending much on stable conditions and if this be dollar diplomacy it certainly cannot be condemned.

It is a matter of congratulation to note the spirit of friendliness animating the men connected with framing the agreement. In transmitting the Hoover summary on May 15, Conrado Ríos Gallardo accepted the settlement for Chile as wholly and finally deciding the question. He added that

the people of Chile, placing confidence in their destiny and concentrating their energies on work, note the utmost importance of this action which guarantees their safety and promotes their progress.

Pedro José Rada y Gamio for Peru said:

. . . The government of Peru accepts each and every one of the bases proposed by the President of the United States of America for a final settlement of the question of Tacna-Arica, and that, with the acceptance of them by both parties, it considers the question absolutely and finally settled.

Former President Figueroa Larrain, who was Ambassador of Chile in Lima when the treaty was made, said:

. . . Viewing on one side the past with its memories, and on the other the future with its promises, I have fully exercised my constitutional powers as the chief magistrate of a great people, assuming an historical responsibility in order to assure the future of the Republic and the peace of the continent.

The only shortcoming of all this amity and of the settlement is with regard to Bolivia. As has been said, Bolivia has no legal rights in the matter, but she does have some strong extralegal claims to consideration owing to having been involved historically in the Tacna-Arica case. Being historically unfortunate is not the same as being dismissed from historical consideration. As recently as 1928 a book on South America appeared in which was found the following statement concerning Bolivia:*

. . . So we can be silent on ninety years of Bolivian history without withholding from our readers anything that they would be interested in or profit by knowing. To throw light upon the existing situation we do not need to go far back of the revolution of 1920.[12]

It was true in 1880, as so prophetically stated by Santa María,† that peace with Bolivia was a necessity in securing peace with Peru. While legal conditions are now different, geographical, social, and moral requisites are just as important today to a satisfactory arrangement with Bolivia as they were then. Bolivia has had some unworthy leaders and the best part of her history may be in the future, but even on the grounds of futurity she should be given an outlet to the Pacific.

Bolivia is a potentially great nation and on merely economic grounds should not be driven to the Atlantic by way of the Pilcomayo and Madeira rivers for international commercial and social relations. Fortunately, the supplementary protocol to the treaty permits a possible arrangement, if it does restrict it to one in which Chile and Peru must be in accord, and it is to be hoped that their statesmen will soon see the advisability of arranging a corridor to the sea for their neighbor and thus completely liquidate the old Tacna-Arica case.

The Bolivian difficulty should not detract from the

* By permission of The Century Company.   † *Supra,* pp. 99, 109.

appreciation of what has been accomplished by the Treaty of Santiago in its present form and the settlement of the dispute between Peru and Chile. The importance of this settlement cannot be overstated in this critical era of attempted and frustrated peace moves. While Europe has talked of peace and world conciliation, the New World has stopped talking and has acted for peace. In an address at a banquet in Lima, June 18, 1929, Ambassador Moore pointed out this accomplishment succinctly and much of what he said can apply as well to Chile. He said:

You, Mr. President, were the first to sign the multilateral treaty outlawing war and you, Mr. President, were the first to carry out its principles. You have led the whole world to the pathway of peace, and as you so well said to President Hoover on the occasion of his inauguration to the presidency, "To have peace there must be sacrifice and Peru is willing to make a sacrifice for the happiness and contentment of the world."

From the standpoint of United States mediations the Treaty of Santiago is very gratifying. The other mediations under Evarts, Blaine, and Frelinghuysen had been so barren of results and so misunderstood, that successful and constructive aid in this famous case was almost imperative since mediation had been attempted at all; and there is no gainsaying that the United States had a duty to perform in the case. It is not too much to hope that the Tacna-Arica settlement will form a turning point in our Latin American diplomacy. The only case at all similar, still on the docket, is the Falkland Islands dispute with Argentina. While that may be technically a case first for Great

Britain and Argentina, it might be possible to clear up the part of the United States in the matter in either dual or tripartite negotiations. Friendliness with other South American nations is now well established, and with an Argentine settlement criticism from that continent would be about removed. Nicaragua, Haiti, and the Dominican Republic should have prompt attention also. They are not nations in the sense that are the South American countries with which we have had mediation experience, but they are geographical divisions with nominal statehood and since their subnormal condition requires special relationships it is not easy to understand why the United States should assume all the responsibility and criticism. This responsibility should be either shared by the other republics or their advice should be secured. It would be prostituting the splendid general service of the Pan-American Union to make it a political organization, but a council of American ambassadors similar to the one that functioned in Europe following the World War should participate, at least in an advisory capacity, in the interventions which the most casual observer knows are necessary and will be necessary for a decade in those subnormal states.

That the steps above indicated are possible and that a happy and rational solution may be found for all Pan-American relations, is as much to be hoped for as was the settlement of the complex Tacna-Arica case. If one should doubt this assertion, it would suffice to read the preceding chapter on the Attempted Plebiscite of 1925–26 and then read the following casual news item from a paper in one of the former contending states:

EVENTS OF AUGUST 28 [1929]

The wind-up of a half century of controversy over the Tacna-Arica question came to a quiet and peaceful end on August 28th.

In the town of Tacna, a Chilean delegation delivered the civil and military administration of the province over to a delegation headed by Sr. Pedro José Rada y Gamio, Peruvian Minister of Foreign Affairs. Peruvian civil servants, judges and police took over the administrative archives and business of the town and province.

In Lima, the 28th was the occasion of a national holiday [Declaration of Independence from Spain], with a military review at the Santa Beatriz race track.

In Tacna, Lima and Santiago, and elsewhere in the two republics, the day passed without untoward incident.

REFERENCES

1. *El Diario Ilustrado*, July 5, 1926.
2. *Documentos relativos al plebiscito*, III, 140.
3. Note: Opinion of Sarah Wambaugh, author of *A Monograph on Plebiscites*, etc., in an interview after returning from Arica. The only criticism adverse to the Chairman of the Plebiscitary Commission that was at all open was by John R. Robertson, "What Tacna-Arica Means to American Business," *Printers Ink*, March, 1927, p. 108. He was a trade investigator for a corporation and feared for the effect of United States mediation on trade with Latin America. See *supra*, p. 268.
4. *United States Daily*, March 29, 1926.
5. *Current History Magazine*, June, 1926, p. 450.
6. Robertson, *op. cit.*, pp. 32, 107.
7. *El Mercurio*, April 14, 1926.
8. Victor Muñoz Reyer and Victor J. Guevara, in Introduction to Oscar de Santa-Cruz, *El General Andrés de Santa-Cruz*.
9. *Current History Magazine*, August, 1926, p. 703.
10. *Ibid.*, October, 1928, p. 142.
11. *Ibid.*, July, 1929.
12. Herbert Adams Gibbons, *The New Map of South America*, p. 77.

APPENDIX I

TABLE OF GUANO SHIPMENTS

Extracts from a table of the guano shipments and operation for the Government of Peru in 1870. There were some shipments to other countries, but those to Europe were the most important. From *Oficio Dirigido al Sr. Ministro de Hacienda y Comercio por el Inspector Fiscal sobre la Administración de las Consignaciones del Guano en Europa y en Mauricio, durante el año de 1870.*

	Tons in storage	No. of ships	Cargoes in tons	Tons sold	Value in soles	Soles per ton	Expense per ton	Total expense	Net returns	Jan. 1, 1871 tons in storage
England	136,709	170	254,442	171,206	10,977,648	64.12	22.72	5,606,056	5,371,612	217,472
France	53,993	150	130,160	69,379	4,486,458	64.66	22.76	2,805,654	1,680,784	115,204
Mauritius	13,116	28	21,013	22,668	1,485,061	65.51	24.66	527,446	957,614	12,481
Germany	48,804	18	29,190	62,792	4,064,496	64.75	26.31	863,582	3,200,915	15,339
Belgium	54,318	72	95,092	69,857	4,923,670	70.50	22.41	2,077,010	2,846,660	79,669
Spain	36,880	21	23,313	33,064	2,237,014	67.65	26.57	651,967	1,585,047	26,353
Holland	7,056	5	6,872	6,523	411,167	63.02	24.15	165,047	246,120	7,469
Italy	6,274	14	11,682	5,305	348,782	65.74	25.56	281,912	66,869	12,650
TOTAL	357,153	478	571,768	440,778	28,934,278			12,978,656	15,955,621	486,641

[Round numbers only are given, fractions of tons and soles being omitted, which will account for apparent error in totals.]

APPENDIX II

TEXT OF THE TREATY OF MUTUAL
BENEFITS OF 1866

[*The material included in this and the following appendixes
is not inserted primarily as documentary proof of this history, but mainly for the purpose of furnishing to those de-
sirous of making a legal or diplomatic study of the famous
international case the texts of all the treaties involved. The
following treaty made between Chile and Bolivia was the
first international agreement pertaining to the question. In
this and the treaties following some omissions of routine
clauses occur in the text, but nothing is omitted that is
necessary to convey the purpose and spirit of the treaties.
Translated from Prescott,* El problema continental, *pp.
253–264.*]

ARTICLE 1. The line of demarcation of the boundaries
between Bolivia and Chile in the desert of Atacama,
shall, hereafter, be parallel 24° south latitude from
the littoral of the Pacific to the eastern limits of Chile, so that
Chile on the south and Bolivia on the north will have possession and dominion of the territories extending from the mentioned parallel 24°, exercising in them all acts of jurisdiction
and sovereignty corresponding to owners of the land.

The exact survey of the line of demarcation between the
two countries shall be undertaken by a commission of properly qualified experts, half of whose members shall be appointed by each one of the high contracting parties.

Once the dividing line is determined it shall be marked by
visible and permanent landmarks, the expense of which shall
be borne equally by the governments of Bolivia and Chile.

Article 2. Notwithstanding the territorial division specified
in the foregoing article, the republics of Bolivia and Chile

shall share equally the proceeds of the exploitation of the guano deposits discovered in Mejillones, and in all such further deposits of this same fertilizer which may be discovered in the territory comprised between 23° and 25° south latitude, as well as the export duties which shall be collected upon the minerals mined within the same territorial extension herein previously specified.

Article 3. The republic of Bolivia undertakes to establish a customs house and open up the port at Mejillones, with the number of officers which the development and commerce may require. This customs house shall be the only revenue office which shall be empowered to receive the proceeds of the guano and the export duties on metals to which the preceding article refers.

The Government of Chile may appoint one or more revenue officers, duly authorized to exercise the right of supervision and inspection of the receipts of the referred-to customs of Mejillones, and to receive directly from the same office quarterly, or in such manner as may be mutually decided upon by both States, the portion of the profit due to Chile to which Article 2 refers.

. . . . . .

Article 4. Exemption from all export duties is granted on the products of the territories comprised between 24° and 25° south latitude, which may be exported through the port of Mejillones. The natural products of Chile introduced through the port of Mejillones shall likewise be exempt from all import duties.

Article 5. The method of exportation or sale of guano, and the export duties assessed upon minerals, to which Article 2 of the treaty refers, shall be mutually agreed upon by the high contracting parties, either by means of special agreements or according as both may consider more convenient or appropriate.

Article 6. The contracting republics bind themselves not to transfer their rights to the possession or dominion of the territory which is divided between them by the present treaty, in favor of any other State, association or private individual. In case either of them may wish to effect such a transfer, the purchaser may only be the other contracting party.

Article 7. With respect to the losses which the question of limits between Chile and Bolivia has caused, as is well-known, to those individuals who together were the first to exploit effectually the guano deposits of Mejillones and whose work was suspended by order of the authorities of Chile the 17th of February, 1863, the high contracting parties agree to pay equally to said individuals an indemnity of eighty thousand pesos, paid from ten per cent of the revenue of the customs house at Mejillones.

[There follows another article and an additional act dealing with ratifications.]

> SIGNED: JUAN R. MUÑOZ CABRERA (L.S.)
> ALVARO COVARRUBIAS (L.S.)

．　　．　　．　　．　　．　　．

[Between the time of this treaty and the War of the Pacific to which its entangling provisions led, there were two other modifying treaties intended to clarify certain clauses, viz., the Lindsay-Corral Agreement of 1872, and the Martínez-Baptista agreement, or Treaty of Sucre, of 1874. They did not change at all the joint participation in the benefits of the nitrate zone which was in effect until the territory was occupied by Chilean armies and the Pact of Truce of 1884, and was definitely ceded by the Treaty of Friendship, of 1904.]

APPENDIX III

TREATY OF DEFENSIVE ALLIANCE, OR "SECRET TREATY," OF 1873

[Translated from Gonzalo Búlnes, *Guerra del Pacífico*, I, 65.]

ARTICLE 1. The high contracting parties unite and join mutually to guarantee their independence, sovereignty, and the integrity of their respective territory, binding themselves by the terms of the present treaty to defend themselves against all foreign aggressions, whether proceeding from another or other independent state, or from a force without a flag, owing obedience to no recognized power.

Article 2. The alliance will become effective to protect the rights expressed in the preceding article and particularly in cases of offense consisting:

1st. In acts tending to deprive either of the contracting parties of a portion of their territory, in order to assume dominion over it; or to yield it to another power.

2nd. In acts tending to oblige either of the contracting parties to submit to a protectorate, sale or cession of territory, or to establish over it any superiority, right, or preeminence whatsoever, which may injure or offend the full and ample exercise of its sovereignty and independence.

3d. In acts tending to do away with or change the form of government, the political constitution or laws that the contracting parties have made, or may in future make, in the exercise of their sovereignty.

Article 3. As both the contracting parties recognize that every legitimate act of alliance is based upon justice, for each of them respectively, the right is established of deciding whether the offense inferred to the other is comprised amongst those mentioned in the preceding article.

Article 4. The *casus foederis* once declared, the contracting parties bind themselves to cease immediately their relations with the offending state; to hand their passports to its diplomatic ministers; to cancel the appointments of the consular agents; to forbid the importation of its natural and industrial products; and to close their ports against its ships.

Article 5. The same parties shall also appoint plenipotentiaries to adjust by protocol the arrangements necessary to determine upon the subsidies, the contingents of either sea or land forces, or the aid of whatever kind that must be lent to the offended republic, and whatever else may be convenient for the success of the defense. The meeting of the plenipotentiaries will be held in the place assigned by the offended party for that purpose.

Article 6. The contracting parties bind themselves to provide the one offended with means of defense which each may consider it can furnish, though the arrangements pointed out in the preceding article may not have taken place, provided that they consider the case urgent.

Article 7. The *casus foederis* once declared, the offended party will not be able to make arrangements for peace, truce or armistice without the concurrence of the ally who may have taken part in the war.

Article 8. The contracting parties bind themselves in addition:

1st. To employ with preference, whenever it is possible, every conciliatory measure in order to avoid a rupture or to put an end to the war, holding as the most effective the arbitration of a third power.

2nd. Not to admit or accept from any nation or government protectorate or superiority that which may injure and lessen their independence or sovereignty, and not to yield or transfer in favor of any nation or government any part whatsoever of their territories, excepting in the cases of better demarcation of limits.

3d. Not to celebrate treaties of limits, or of other territorial arrangements, without the other contracting party first knowing of them.

Article 9. The stipulations of the present treaty do not extend to acts performed by political parties or to the result of internal disturbance independent of the intervention of foreign governments; inasmuch as the principal object of the present alliance being the mutual guarantee of the sovereign rights of both nations, none of its clauses must be interpreted in opposition to its primary end.

Article 10. The contracting parties will, separately or collectively, when by subsequent agreement they may consider it convenient, solicit the adherence of another or other American states to the present treaty of defensive alliance.

Article 11. The present treaty will be exchanged in Lima or in La Paz, as soon as it is legally perfected, and will be in full force from the twentieth day after the said exchange takes place. Its duration shall be for an indefinite period, each party reserving to itself the right of terminating it when that shall be thought convenient.

In such a case the party desiring to annul the treaty must notify the other party, and the treaty will no longer have effect on the expiration of four months from such notification.

In testimony whereof the respective plenipotentiaries signed it in duplicate and sealed it with their private seals.

Done in Lima on the sixth day of the month of February, one thousand eight hundred and seventy-three.

JUAN DE LA CRUZ BENAVENTE
J. DE LA RIVA-AGÜERO

Additional Article. The present treaty of defensive alliance between Bolivia and Peru shall be kept secret so long as the high contracting parties shall mutually agree that its publication is unnecessary.

·　　·　　·　　·　　·　　·

APPENDIX IV

TEXT OF THE TREATY OF ANCÓN

[Note: Owing to the failure to fulfil Article 3 of this treaty and the fact that its interpretation was the point to be determined in the Harding-Coolidge mediation, this article, commonly called the "Plebiscite Clause," will be given in both English and Spanish. For reference to disputes over the wording and interpretation of this clause see chapter ix, supra, pp. 174–189, and corresponding reference notes. The text is translated from Spanish and compared with texts in the Cases and Countercases of Chile and Peru.]

ARTICLE 1. The relations of peace and friendship between the Republics of Chile and Peru to be reestablished.

Article 2. The Republic of Peru cedes to the Republic of Chile in perpetuity and unconditionally the territory of the littoral province of Tarapacá, the boundaries of which are, on the north the ravine and river Camarones, on the south the ravine and river Loa, on the east the Republic of Bolivia, and on the west the Pacific Ocean.

Article 3. The territory of the provinces of Tacna and Arica, bounded on the north by the river Sama from its source in the Cordilleras on the frontier of Bolivia to its mouth at the sea, on the south by the ravine and river Camarones, on the east by the Republic of Bolivia, and on the west by the Pacific Ocean, shall continue in the possession of Chile subject to Chilean laws and authority during a period of ten years, to be reckoned from the date of the ratification of the present treaty of peace.

That term expired, a plebiscite will decide by popular vote whether the territory of the above-mentioned provinces is to remain definitely under the dominion and sovereignty of Chile or is to continue to constitute a part of Peru. That country of the two, to which the provinces of Tacna and Arica remain annexed, shall pay to the other ten million pesos of Chilean silver or of Peruvian soles of equal weight and fineness.

A special protocol, which shall be considered an integral part of the present treaty, will prescribe the manner in which the plebiscite is to be carried out, and the terms and time for the payment of the ten millions by the nation which remains the owner of the provinces of Tacna and Arica.

[Spanish text of the article]

El territorio de las provincias de Tacna y Arica, que limita, por el Norte, con el río Sama, desde su nacimiento en las cordilleras limítrofes con Bolivia hasta su desembocadura en el mar; por el Sur con la quebrada y río de Camarones; por el Oriente, con la República de Bolivia; y, por el Poniente, con el mar Pacífico, continuará poseído por Chile y sujeto a la legislación y autoridades chilenas durante el término de diez años contados desde que se ratifique el presente Tratado de Paz.

Espirado este plazo, un plebiscito decidirá en votación popular, si el territorio de las provincias referidas queda definitivamente del dominio y soberanía de Chile, o si continúa siendo parte del territorio peruano. Aquél de los dos países a cuyo favor queden anexadas las provincias de Tacna y Arica, pagará al otro diez millones de pesos moneda chilena de plata, o soles peruanos de igual ley y peso que aquella.

Un protocolo especial que se considerará como parte integrante del presente Tratado, establecerá la forma en que el plebiscito deba tener lugar y los términos y plazos en que hayan de pagarse los diez millones por el país que quede dueño de las provincias de Tacna y Arica.

Article 4. In compliance with the stipulations of the supreme decree of February 9, 1882, by which the Government of Chile ordered the sale of one million tons of guano, the net proceeds of which, after deducting the expenses and other disbursements, as referred to in Article 13 of said decree, will be divided in equal parts between the Government of Chile and those creditors of Peru whose claims appear to be guaranteed by lien on the guano. After the sale of the million tons of guano has been effected, referred to in the previous paragraph, the Government of Chile will continue paying over to the Peruvian creditors fifty per cent of the net proceeds of guano, as stipulated in the above-mentioned Article 13, until the extinction of the debt or the exhaustion of the deposits now being worked.

The proceeds of deposits or beds that may be hereafter discovered in the territories that have been ceded will belong exclusively to Chile.

Article 5. If, in the territories that remain in possession of Peru, there should be discovered deposits or beds of guano, in order to avoid competition in the sale of the article by the Governments of Chile and Peru, the two Governments, by mutual agreement, will first determine the proportion and conditions to which each of them binds itself in the disposal of the said fertilizer.

The stipulations in the preceding paragraph will also be binding in regard to the existing guano now known and which may remain over in the Lobos Islands when the time comes for delivering these to the Government of Peru, in conformity with the terms of the ninth article of the present treaty.

Article 6. The Peruvian creditors, to whom may be awarded the proceeds stipulated in Article 4, must submit themselves, in proving their titles and in other procedures, to the regulations stated in the supreme decree of February 9, 1882.

Article 7. The obligation which the Government of Chile accepts, in accordance with the fourth article, to deliver over fifty per cent of the net proceeds of guano from the deposits now actually being worked, will be carried out whether the work be done by virtue of the existing contract for the sale of one million tons or through any other contract, or on account of the Government of Chile.

Article 8. Beyond the stipulations contained in the preceding articles, and the obligations that the Chilean Government has voluntarily accepted in the supreme decree of March 28, 1882, which relates to the saltpeter works in Tarapacá, the said Government of Chile will recognize no debts, whatever their nature or source, that will affect the new territories acquired by virtue of this treaty.

Article 9. The Lobos Islands will remain under the administration of the Government of Chile until the completion of the excavation from existing deposits of the million tons of guano, in conformity with Articles 4 and 7. After this they will be returned to Peru.

Article 10. The Government of Chile declares that it will cede to Peru, to commence from the date of the constitutional ratification and exchange of the present treaty, the fifty per cent pertaining to Chile from the proceeds of the guano of the Lobos Islands.

Article 11. Pending a special treaty to be entered upon, mercantile relations shall be maintained on the same footing as before April 5, 1879.

Article 12. Indemnities due by Peru to Chileans, who may have suffered damages on account of the war, will be adjudged by a tribunal of arbitration or mixed international commission, to be appointed immediately after the ratification of the present treaty, in the manner established by conventions recently adjusted between Chile and the Governments of England, France and Italy.

Article 13. The contracting Governments recognize and accept the validity of all administrative and judicial acts during the occupation of Peru arising from the martial jurisdiction exercised by the Government of Chile.

Article 14. The present treaty to be ratified and the ratifications exchanged in the city of Lima as soon as possible during a period not exceeding one hundred and sixty days to be reckoned from this date.

In testimony whereof the several Plenipotentiaries have signed this in duplicate and affixed their private seals.

APPENDIX V

THE PACT OF TRUCE, OF 1884

[Translated from Prescott, *El problema continental*, pp. 308–313.]

I

THE Republics of Chile and Bolivia celebrate an indefinite truce, and in consequence, they declare the state of war terminated, and that it cannot be again carried on unless one of the contracting parties notifies the other, with at least one year of anticipation, of its determination to resume hostilities. In this case the notification shall be made directly, or through the diplomatic representative of a friendly nation.

II

The Republic of Chile, during the period that this treaty is in force, shall continue to govern according to Chilean law, the territories situated between the parallel 23° S. and the mouth of the River Loa . . . [Here follows the description of the boundary line of Bolivia's former littoral.]

In case difficulties may arise, both parties shall appoint a commission of engineers, which shall fix the limits as indicated, subject to the landmarks here determined.

III

The property and goods confiscated from Chilean citizens, by Government edict, or by order of civil and military authorities, shall be immediately returned to their owners or to their representatives.

There shall also be returned the products that the Government of Bolivia may have received from these properties and that appear to be proved by the documents in the case.

The damages that in these cases have been suffered by Chilean citizens shall be indemnified by reason of the actions that the interested parties may bring before the Government of Bolivia.

IV

If no agreement can be arrived at between the Government of Bolivia and the parties interested, with respect to the amount of indemnity for the loss and damage suffered, the points in dispute shall be submitted to a commission of arbitration composed of three members, one named by Chile, one by Bolivia and the third to be named, in Chile, by mutual accord, from among the representatives of neutral nations, resident in Chile. This commission shall be appointed as soon as possible.

V

Commercial relations are reëstablished between Chile and Bolivia.

.　　.　　.　　.　　.　　.

Until an agreement to the contrary is made, Chile and Bolivia shall enjoy the commercial advantages and freedom that either nation accords to the most favored nation.

VI

At the port of Arica foreign merchandise, entering for consumption in Bolivia, shall pay the customs dues in force by the Chilean tariff; this merchandise shall not pay, in the interior, any further duty. The sums received in payment of duty shall be divided in this way: 25 per cent shall be applied as dues received for merchandise to be consumed in the territories of Tacna and Arica, and as working expenses, and 75 per cent shall be for Bolivia. . . .

.　　.　　.　　.　　.　　.

VII

Any acts of the subaltern authorities of either nation that tend to alter the situation formed by the present treaty of truce, especially in what may refer to the limits that Chile continues to occupy, shall be repressed and punished by the respective governments, upon official notice or request.

VIII

As the object of the contracting parties, in celebrating this pact of truce, is to prepare and facilitate a solid and stable treaty of peace between the two republics, they reciprocally promise to carry on negotiations conducive to this object.

This pact shall be ratified by the Government of Bolivia in the term of forty days, and the ratifications exchanged at Santiago during the next month of June.

In proof of which, the Minister for Foreign Affairs of Chile and the Plenipotentiaries of Bolivia who showed their respective authorization and powers signed, in duplicate, the present treaty of truce, at Valparaiso, on the fourth of April of the year one thousand eight hundred and eighty-four.

(SIGNED) A. VERGARA ALBANO,
BELISARIO SALINAS,
BELISARIO BOETO.

APPENDIX VI

TREATY OF FRIENDSHIP, OF 1904

[Translated from Prescott, *El problema continental*, pp. 366–376.]

ARTICLE 1. Relations of peace and amity are established between the Republic of Bolivia and the Republic of Chile, thereby ending the regimen established by the Pact of Truce.

Article 2. By the present treaty the absolute and perpetual dominion of Chile over the territories occupied by her in virtue of Article 2 of the Pact of Truce of April 4th, 1884, is recognized.

The dividing line from north to south between Bolivia and Chile shall be as follows:

[Here follows a geographical delineation of limits corresponding closely to those of the former Bolivian littoral, the present Chilean Antofagasta.]

.　.　.　.　.　.

Article 3. For the purpose of cementing the political and commercial relations of both republics the High Contracting Parties agree to unite the port of Arica with La Paz by a railroad, the cost of which is to be paid by Chile, within one year from the date of the ratification of the present treaty.

The ownership of the Bolivian section of this railroad will pass to Bolivia at the end of fifteen years counting from the date that it is completed.

.　.　.　.　.　.

[Here follow some provisions for the subsidizing by Chile of guaranties which Bolivia might make for the funds with which to build certain other roads connecting the territory of the two republics.]

Article 4. The Government of Chile agrees to give to the

Government of Bolivia the sum of three hundred thousand pounds sterling in two payments of one hundred fifty thousand pounds each, the first payment six months after the ratification of this treaty and the second one year after the first payment.

.   .   .   .   .   .

[Article 5 provides that Chile shall pay several millions of pesos of debts or claims against Bolivia which grew out of nitrate and guano contracts in the captured littoral. Articles 6, 7, 8, 9, 10, and 11 provide for port and customs privileges for Bolivia.]

Article 12. All questions that might arise regarding the understanding or execution of this treaty shall be submitted to the Emperor of Germany for arbitration.

The ratification of this treaty shall take place within six months and the exchanges be made in La Paz.

In faith of which, &c., Santiago, October 20, 1904.

EMILIO BELLO C.
A. GUTIÉRREZ

APPENDIX VII

THE MEDIATION INVITATION OF PRESIDENT HARDING

[Text from *The Case of the Republic of Chile*, p. 2.]

THE Government of the United States, through the courtesy of the Ambassadors of Peru and Chile in Washington, has been kept informed of the progress of their negotiations carried on directly by telegraph between the two Governments of Peru and Chile looking toward a settlement of the long standing controversy with respect to the unfulfilled provisions of the Treaty of Ancon. It has noted with the greatest pleasure and satisfaction, the lofty spirit of conciliation which has animated the two Governments, and that as a result of these direct exchanges of views the idea of arbitration of the pending difficulties is acceptable in principle to both. It has also taken note of the suggestion that representatives of the two Governments be named to meet in Washington with a view to finding the means of settling the difficulties which have divided the two countries.

Desiring in the interest of American peace and concord to assist in a manner agreeable to both Governments concerned in finding a way to end this long standing controversy, the President of the United States would be pleased to welcome in Washington the representatives which the Government of Peru and Chile may see fit to appoint to the end that such representatives may settle, if happily it may be, the existing difficulties or may arrange for the settlement of them by arbitration.

APPENDIX VIII

PROTOCOL OF SUBMISSION TO ARBITRA-
TION AND SUPPLEMENTARY
AGREEMENT
JULY 20, 1922

[Text from *The Case of the Republic of Chile*, pp. 3–5.]

ASSEMBLED in Washington, D. C., pursuant to the invitation of the Government of the United States of America for the purpose of reaching a solution of the long standing controversy with respect to the unfulfilled provisions of the Treaty of Peace of October 20, 1883, the undersigned representatives of Peru and Chile to wit:

Don Carlos Aldunate and Don Luis Izquierdo, Envoys Extraordinary and Ministers Plenipotentiary of Chile on Special Mission; and

Don Meliton F. Porras and Don Hernan Velarde, Envoys Extraordinary and Ministers Plenipotentiary of Peru on Special Mission;

After exchanging their respective full powers, have agreed upon the following:

Article 1. It is hereby recorded that the only difficulties arising out of the Treaty of Peace, regarding which the two countries have not been able to reach an agreement, are the questions arising out of the unfulfilled stipulations of Article III of said Treaty.

Article 2. The difficulties referred to in the preceding article will be submitted to the arbitration of the President of the United States of America who shall decide them without appeal after hearing the parties and taking into consideration the arguments and evidence which they may present. The times and the procedure shall be determined by the arbitrator.

Article 3. The present Protocol shall be submitted for approval to the respective Governments and the ratifications shall be exchanged in Washington through the diplomatic representatives of Chile and Peru within the maximum period of three months.

Signed and sealed in duplicate in Washington, D. C., the twentieth of July, one thousand nine hundred twenty-two.

[The Supplementary Agreement reads as follows:]

In order to determine with precision the scope of the arbitration provided for in Article 2 of the Protocol signed on this date, the undersigned agree to place on record hereby the following points:

First. The following question, raised by Peru at the session of the Conference held on May 27th last, is included in the arbitration:

"For the purpose of determining the manner in which the stipulations of Article III of the Treaty of Ancon shall be fulfilled there shall be submitted to arbitration the question whether, in the present circumstances, the plebiscite shall or shall not be held."

The Government of Chile, on its part, may present to the arbitrator all the arguments that it may deem necessary to its case.

Second. In case that it is decided that the plebiscite shall be held, the arbitrator is empowered to determine the conditions under which it shall be held.

Third. If the arbitrator should decide that the plebiscite shall not be held, both parties, at the request of either of them, shall discuss the situation created by this decision.

It is understood, in the interest of peace and good order, that, in this event, and pending an agreement as to the disposition of the territory, the administrative organization of the provinces shall not be disturbed.

Fourth. The two Governments shall solicit, in case that they should not reach an agreement, the good offices of the Government of the United States of America, in order that an agreement may be reached.

Fifth. The pending claims regarding Tarata and Chilcaya likewise are included in the arbitration, subject to the determination of the final fate of the territory to which Article III of the said Treaty refers.

This Act is an integral part of the Protocol to which it refers.

Signed and sealed in duplicate in Washington, D. C., the twentieth of July, one thousand nine hundred twenty-two.

ARBITRATION OPINION AND AWARD OF PRESIDENT COOLIDGE
1925

[The full title of this document, which may be secured from the Superintendent of Documents, Government Printing Office, Washington, D.C., is, Opinion and Award of the Arbitrator in the Matter of the Arbitration between the Republic of Chile and the Republic of Peru, with Respect to the Unfulfilled Provisions of the Treaty of Peace of October 20, 1883, under the Protocol and Supplementary Act Signed at Washington July 20, 1922. *It comprises sixty-four pages, but only the important decisional parts are given here.]*

.　　.　　.　　.　　.　　.

THE question whether a plebiscite shall or shall not be held depends upon the question whether the second and third paragraphs of Article 3 of the Treaty of Ancon are still in effect. If these provisions have not expired by lapse of time, if they have not been abrogated or discharged by the conduct of the Parties so that performance can no longer be demanded, the plebiscite should be held because that is the agreement. If that agreement for any reason is no longer binding, then the plebiscite should not be held unless a new agreement for that purpose is made.

As the question thus relates to the construction, operation and obligation of this part of the treaty, the province of the Arbitrator is more narrow than the range of the arguments which have been presented. It is neither the duty nor the privilege of the Arbitrator to pass upon the causes or the conduct of the War of the Pacific, or upon the justice of the terms of peace, or upon the relations of either Party to the

Republic of Bolivia, or upon the wisdom of the provisions of Article 3 of the Treaty of Ancon, or upon the economic effects of the treaty, or upon alleged general equities of the present situation, or upon any questions whatever which are aside from the meaning and efficacy of the agreement itself.

.   .   .   .   .   .

At the outset, it should be observed that the second and third paragraphs of Article 3 do not provide for the termination of their obligations by lapse of time. The Article contains no provision for forfeiture. It fixed no period within which the plebiscite must be taken. The plebiscite was to be had *"after the expiration of that term,"* that is, after the ten years but no limit was defined. It was to be taken pursuant to a special agreement which it was left to the Parties to make. But no time was fixed within which the special protocol for the plebiscite was to be negotiated. Whatever may have been the reasons for leaving the matter thus at large, the fact remains that it was left without prescribed limit of time and the obligations of the Parties under the treaty must be determined accordingly.

If it be suggested that such an agreement—an agreement to agree with no time specified and no forfeiture provided—is unsatisfactory or meaningless, a three-fold answer presents itself, first, that the Arbitrator is not empowered to alter the treaty or to insert provisions, however salutary they might be in his judgment viewing the matter retrospectively, which the High Contracting Parties did not see fit to include; second, that the Treaty of Ancon was a peace treaty—the parties were engaged in a devastating war. Apparently the Parties in 1883–1884 thought it better to agree that they would agree at some unspecified time in the future than to agree to disagree in the present. They may well have taken into account the fact that failure to agree upon the terms of a plebiscite when the matter came up again for adjustment would leave unsettled one of the great issues of the War of the Pacific, and they may have believed that inasmuch as a reopening of hostilities on this account after a lapse of at least ten years was improbable and an amicable agreement would be in the interest of both parties, it was at once unnecessary and inadvisable to prescribe a time limit for the negotiations. Finally, the present arbitration is the best evidence that the agreement, elastic as it was, was not without force. . . .

.   .   .   .   .   .

It is the contention of Peru, maintained with earnestness and eloquence, that Chile wilfully prevented the timely holding of a plebiscite and that her action in the course of her administration of the territory constituted a perversion of the conditions essential to the plebiscite as contemplated by the treaty; in short, that Chile by preventing the performance of Article 3 has discharged Peru from her obligations thereunder, and hence that a plebiscite should not now be held and that Chile should be regarded as a trespasser in the territory in question since the year 1894.

This contention raises two principal questions: *first*, with respect to the conduct of Chile in relation to the efforts to reach an agreement for a plebiscite; and, *second* with respect to her Administration of the territory of the provinces of Tacna and Arica.

.   .   .   .   .   .

From an examination of the history of the negotiations the Arbitrator is unable to find any proper basis for the conclusion that Chile acted in bad faith. The record fails to show that Chile has ever arbitrarily refused to negotiate with Peru the terms of the plebiscitary protocol.

.   .   .   .   .   .

The Arbitrator is of the opinion that so far as the negotiations for the special protocol are concerned neither Party can be charged with bad faith and that there is no ground for the conclusion that Chile's action in respect to these negotiations has resulted in the abrogation of the second and third paragraphs of Article 3 of the Treaty of Ancon or absolved Peru from the obligation to proceed to their fulfillment.

Chilean Administration in Tacna and Arica

It follows from what has been said that the provisions in question of the Treaty of Ancon must be regarded as still in effect unless the course of Chile in the administration of Tacna and Arica has been of such a character as to frustrate the purposes of these provisions and hence to deprive them of force.

.   .   .   .   .   .

The Arbitrator finds the conclusion inescapable that the territory continued "subject to Chilean laws and authority" pending the negotiations for the special protocol. The question then is whether this authority has been used in such a way as to frustrate the purpose of the agreement for the plebiscite.

.   .   .   .   .   .

The Arbitrator therefore holds that, with respect to the specific acts adduced by Peru as tending to show the subsidized introduction of Chilean citizens, either as a matter of law these acts were within Chile's right under the treaty during the period in which the territory is "subject to Chilean laws and authority" or there is no sufficient evidence to show that they were in fact committed.

.   .   .   .   .   .

While there is no sufficient evidence in the record to show that Chile has either suppressed or censored the Peruvian press of Tacna and Arica by operation of law or by action of the Chilean Government, there is satisfactory evidence to show that Peruvian newspapers were destroyed by mob violence in 1911. Although it is not possible on the evidence to charge this action to the Government of Chile, it does appear that the Peruvian newspapers have not been reëstablished and the situation thus existing demands consideration in fixing the conditions of a possible plebiscite.

.   .   .   .   .   .

. . . While the affidavits indicate that the enforcement of the law [conscription law] has been intermittent as to time and sporadic as to places and persons, and that many young Peruvians have not been molested even in places and at times when the law was being enforced against other Peruvians, they also indicate that in a considerable number of cases, particularly in the year 1923, the Chilean conscription laws have been used not so much for the obtaining of recruits (for so far the policy of leniency appears to have been reasonably well carried out) but with the result, if not the purpose, of driving young Peruvians from the provinces. So far as this has been done, the Arbitrator holds it to be an abuse of Chilean authority. . . .

. . . . . .

. . . These charges [general persecution] in so far as they are serious, and some of them are very serious, are not sustained by credible and specific evidence. They rest on general declarations, and the Arbitrator is constrained to hold that these charges of general persecution are not adequately supported. There are also numerous charges of petty persecution, some of which if taken individually might be sustained, but all of which put together are not sufficiently serious to affect the decision of the weighty question under consideration.

Conclusion: The Arbitrator is far from approving the course of Chilean administration and condoning the acts committed against Peruvians to which reference has been made, but finds no reason to conclude that a fair plebiscite in the present circumstances cannot be held under proper conditions or that a plebiscite should not be had. The agreement which the Parties made that the ultimate disposition of the territory of Tacna and Arica should be determined by popular vote is in accord with democratic postulates.

It furnished when it was made a desirable alternative to a continuance of strife and it affords to-day a method of avoiding the recurrence of a not improbably disastrous clash of opposing sentiments and interests which enter into the very fiber of the respective nations. In agreeing upon a determination of the embittered controversy by popular vote, the Parties had recourse to a solution which the present circumstances not only do not render impracticable but rather the more imperative as a means of amicable disposition. The Parties in the Treaty of Ancon provided no alternative mode of settlement and made no provision for limitation of time or for forfeiture. It is manifest that if abuses of administration could have the effect of terminating such an agreement, it would be necessary to establish such serious conditions as the consequence of administrative wrongs as would operate to frustrate the purpose of the agreement, and, in the opinion of the Arbitrator, a situation of such gravity has not been shown.

The Arbitrator holds that the provisions of the second and third paragraphs of Article 3 of the Treaty of Ancon are still in effect; that the plebiscite should be held; and that the interests of both Parties can be properly safeguarded by establishing suitable conditions therefor.

.   .   .   .   .   .

[Here follows a delineation of conditions of the plebiscite and ample machinery for carrying them out.]

APPENDIX X

TEXT OF THE TREATY OF SANTIAGO

[Text from The West Coast Leader, *Special Tacna-Arica number, Lima, August, 1929.]*

THE Governments of the Republics of Peru and Chile, wishing to remove all difficulties between both countries and to thus insure their friendship and good intelligence; have decided to celebrate a Treaty in conformity with the bases which the President of the United States of America, in the exercise of the good offices requested by the Parties and guiding himself by the direct agreements concerted between them, has proposed as final bases to solve the problem of Tacna and Arica and, for this purpose, have appointed their plenipotentiaries, to wit: His Excellency the President of Peru, His Excellency Doctor Pedro José Rada y Gamio, his Minister of Foreign Affairs and His Excellency the President of the Republic of Chile, His Excellency Emiliano Figueroa Larrain, his Ambassador Extraordinary and plenipotentiary in Peru; who, after exchanging their full powers and finding same to be in good form, have agreed upon the following articles:

Article 1. The controversy originated by Article Three of the Treaty of Peace and Friendship of October twentieth, One Thousand Eight Hundred and Eighty-three, which was the only difficulty pending between the signatory governments is definitely solved.

Article 2. The territory of Tacna and Arica shall be divided in two portions, Tacna for Peru and Arica for Chile. The dividing line between the said two portions and, consequently, the boundary between the territories of Peru and Chile, shall start from a point on the Coast, which shall be denominated "Concordia," distant ten kilometers to the North of the bridge of the Lluta River, to follow towards the East parallel to the line of the Chilean section of the Arica to La Paz railway and distant ten kilometers therefrom, with the inflections necessary to use, in demarcation, neighboring geographical accidents, permitting the Tacora sulphur deposits and dependencies thereof to be left in Chilean territory, passing thereafter through the center of Laguna Blanca, in a way such that one portion thereof remains in Peru and the other in Chile. Chile cedes in perpetuity in favor of Peru all its rights on the Uchusuma and Mauri Canals, the latter being known also as Azucarero, without prejudice of the sovereignty which it will be entitled to exercise over the portion of the said aqueducts remaining in Chilean territory after drawing the dividing line to which the present article refers. With respect to both canals Chile constitutes on the portion crossing its territory the fullest right of way in perpetuity, in favor of Peru. Such right of way includes the right of enlarging the present Canals, modify the flow thereof and collecting all waters which may be gathered in the flow thereof through Chilean territory, except the waters now flowing into the Lluta River and those serving the Tacora sulphur deposits.

Article 3. The boundary line, referred to by paragraph one of Article Two, shall be determined and shown on the territory by monuments, by a mixed commission formed by a member designated by each of the signatory Governments, which shall pay, in equal proportions, the common expenses required by this operation. If any disagreement should arise within the Commission, it shall be decided with the deciding vote of a third member, appointed by the President of the United States of America, whose award shall not be subject to appeal.

Article 4. The Government of Chile shall deliver to the Government of Peru thirty days after exchange of ratifications of the present Treaty, the territories which, according to it, are to remain in the possession of Peru. There shall be signed by plenipotentiaries of the Contracting Parties mentioned an affidavit of delivery, containing the detailed account of the location and definitive characteristics of the boundary monuments.

Article 5. For the service of Peru, the Government of Chile shall build at its cost, within one thousand five hundred and seventy-five meters of the bay of Arica a landing pier for draught steamers, a building for the Peruvian Customs Agency and a Terminal Station for the Tacna railway, in which establishments and zones transit commerce of Peru will enjoy independence pertaining to a free port of the greatest amplitude.

Article 6. The Government of Chile shall deliver to that of Peru, simultaneously with the exchange of ratifications, six million dollars, and, also, without any cost whatsoever to the latter Government, all the public works already performed or under construction and real estate of fiscal ownership, located in the territories which, in accordance with the present Treaty, shall remain under Peruvian sovereignty.

Article 7. The Governments of Peru and Chile shall respect private rights legally acquired in the territories remaining under their respective sovereignties, among which appears the concession granted by the Government of Peru to the Arica to Tacna Railway Company, in one thousand eight hundred and fifty-two, according to which the said railway, at the expiration of Contract, shall become the property of Peru. Without detriment to the sovereignty it is entitled to exercise, Chile grants in perpetuity, in the portion of its territory crossed by the line, the most extensive right of way in favor of Peru.

Article 8. The Governments of Peru and Chile shall reciprocally condone any pecuniary obligation pending between themselves, whether derived from the Treaty of Ancon or not.

Article 9. The High Contracting Parties shall execute an agreement of boundary police for the public security of respective territories, adjacent to the dividing line. This agreement shall become effective as soon as the province of Tacna passes to the sovereignty of Peru.

Article 10. The sons of Peruvians born in Arica shall be considered as being Peruvian up to the age of twenty-one years, at which age they shall be able to elect their final nationality; and the sons of Chileans born in Tacna, shall have the same right.

Article 11. The Governments of Peru and Chile, to commemorate the consolidation of their friendly relations, decide to erect on the Morro of Arica a symbolical monument, upon which plan they will come to an agreement.

Article 12. For the case in which the Governments of Peru and Chile should not agree regarding the interpretation they may give to every one of the different stipulations of this Treaty and upon which, their willingness notwithstanding, they may not come to an agreement, the President of the United States of America shall decide the controversy.

Article 13. The present Treaty shall be ratified and its ratifications shall be exchanged in Santiago as soon as may be possible.

In Faith Whereof the undersigned plenipotentiaries sign and seal the present Treaty, in duplicate, in Lima, on the third day of the month of June, one thousand nine hundred and twenty-nine.

Signed: Pedro José Rada y Gamio.—E. Figueroa.

Complementary Protocol

The Governments of Peru and Chile have agreed to subscribe a Complementary Protocol of the Treaty which is signed at this same date, and their respective plenipotentiaries, duly authorized, have therefore agreed to the following:

First Article.—The Governments of Peru and Chile shall not, without previous accord between them, cede to a third power the whole or any part of the territories, which in conformity with the Treaty of this date, remain under their respective sovereignties, nor shall they, without this accord, construct, across them, new international railway lines.

Second Article.—The Port facilities, which the Treaty in

its Fifth Article extends to Peru, shall consist in the most absolute free transit to persons, merchandise and armaments to Peruvian territory and from this across Chilean territory. Operations of embarkation and disembarkation shall be effected, when the works indicated in the Fifth Article of the Treaty are under construction, within the section of the Arica-La Paz Railway Mole reserved for the Arica-Tacna Railway service.

Third Article.—The Morro of Arica shall be disarmed [*desartillado*], and the Government of Chile shall construct at its own cost the monument agreed upon in the Eleventh Article of the Treaty.

The present Protocol shall form an integral part of the Treaty of this date, and, in consequence, shall be ratified and the ratifications exchanged in Santiago as soon as possible.

In faith whereof, the undersigned plenipotentiaries sign and seal the present Complementary Protocol in duplicate, in Lima, the 3rd day of the month of June, 1929.

Signed.—Pedro José Rada y Gamio, Peruvian Minister of Foreign Affairs.—E. Figueroa, Ambassador of Chile.

INDEX